Praise for *Redefining Retail*

"In the intricate realm of fashion and luxury retail, where challenges encompass shifting consumer expectations, technological advancements, and evolving regulations, Giuseppe and Philip's book serves as a navigational compass for retailers. Their ten steadfast principles offer illuminating guidance amidst the ever-changing landscape of consumer behaviour, technology, competition, and societal influences. This book is not just about thriving; it's about adapting to shape the future of retail."

Andrea Baldo, CEO of Ganni

"*Redefining Retail* showcases the dynamic synergy achieved when a seasoned author and an industry visionary unite forces. This collaboration propels the discourse on a continuously evolving industry to new heights. The insights shared within highlight the need for fresh perspectives and innovative principles. I'm thrilled to have the opportunity to contribute to this book."

Penny Brook, Chief Marketing & Experience Officer

"At its core, retailing is about curating a selection of products and services, training your staff to highlight the value of your offer, crafting an exceptional customer experience, and optimizing the 4Ps. This book equips retailers and brand managers with essential tools for excelling in a post-digital world."

Hans Carpels, President & Co-Founder of Euronics

"In an ever-evolving business landscape, brands across all industries must constantly look at new ways of doing business to remain relevant and successful. *Redefining Retail* equips readers with invaluable guidance and a practical playbook to successfully navigate the complexities of today's world."

Stéphane de La Faverie, Executive Group President at The Estée Lauder Companies

"In today's post-digital world, customers interact with brands on their own terms, regardless of what decisions are made by the brand team in corporate offices. Retail plays a vital role in this scenario, providing both the personal touch of in-store experiences and the smooth operations of online shopping. This book stands as an invaluable repository of best practices and guiding principles."

Cristiano Fagnani, CEO of Off White and CEO of NGGH++ (Reebok Europe and Reebok luxury worldwide)

"One of the key challenges for organizations is how to combine the power of data intelligence and human creativity to deliver the most meaningful value to our customers. *Redefining Retail* offers very valuable insights and relevant answers to this essential aspect."

Greg Hoffman, Former CMO of Nike, author and speaker

"In a rapidly evolving and intensely competitive landscape, organizations have to balance the pressure to exploit existing sources of strength with the exploration of new business prospects. Phil and Beppe have effectively delineated 10 guiding principles that warrant serious consideration by all managers."

Michael G. Jacobides, Sir Donald Gordon Professor of Entrepreneurship & Innovation and Professor of Strategy, London Business School

"In this book, I encountered numerous concepts that align with my leadership philosophy and mirror the dynamics within organizations like the Coca-Cola Company. The approach of the authors impressed me, as they effectively combined their real-world business expertise with authoritative academic insights. Kotler and Stigliano's strategic framework is exceptionally well-crafted, and I will definitely recommend my teams to embrace it."

Nikos Koumettis, President of Europe
at The Coca-Cola company.

"*Redefining Retail* stands out as the most comprehensive and original retail book I've encountered in years. Its invaluable insights will leave you intrigued and informed."

Martin Lindstrom, Author,
Consultant and Keynote Speaker

"In a post-digital era, with customer journeys spanning numerous digital and physical touchpoints, the role each of these interactions must be distinctive and strategically planned. This book provides valuable perspectives for managers aiming to design a resilient retail marketing strategy for the future."

Lucia Marcuzzo, SVP Managing Director
North Europe at Levi Strauss & Co.

"Beauty brands, among others, face the challenge of finding the right balance between the influence of technology and the personal touch of human interaction. 'Redefining Retail' provides precious insights for managers on how to address this critical issue."

Vasiliki Petrou,
Group CEO of Unilever Prestige.

"In challenging times, companies often shift their focus to short-term financial outcomes in order to safeguard their market share. However, this approach can cause them to lose sight of a fundamental element—the human beings they are designed to serve. The guiding principles outlined by Philip and Giuseppe serve as an effective inspiration for leaders and managers, helping them strike a balance between financial results and the long-term sustainability of their business while maintaining a human-centred approach."

Mauro Porcini, SVP & Chief Design Officer at PepsiCo

"I had the pleasure of hosting Professor Stigliano in my class during the preparation phase of this book. My students and I had the opportunity to explore the first version of the 10 BEs strategic framework and were truly impressed by its capacity to address managerial priorities while upholding clarity, focus, and immediate applicability. I believe *Redefining Retail* is a significant and valuable addition to the marketing literature."

Thomaï Serdari, Clinical Associate Professor of Marketing, NYU Stern School of Business

"This world needs companies that focus on maximizing the longevity of the products they make while preserving the moral dignity of all the stakeholders involved in their operations. This book excels at motivating business leaders to adopt fresh guiding principles to harmonize ethics and profitability."

Riccardo Stefanelli, CEO at Brunello Cucinelli

"The modern consumer goes beyond the limitations of in-store, mobile, digital, and virtual experiences, surpassing the traditional boundaries of marketing. This book offers managers 10 insightful guiding principles to understand consumers with a more comprehensive and holistic perspective."

Giovanni Valentini, General Manager for *Lancôme* USA

"People all over the world require companies to seamlessly merge offline and online, to be personal, diverse and inclusive, to understand and respect the cultural nuances of different markets. In such a complex landscape, this book and its guiding principles represent a beacon for the business community."

Sandro Veronesi, Founder & President of Calzedonia Group (Calzedonia, Intimissimi, Tezenis, Falconeri, Signorvino).

"Luxury department stores have been part of the retail landscape for generations. The 10 guiding principles presented in this book offer invaluable insights that can empower these iconic establishments to sustain their relevance."

Michael Ward, General Manager, Harrods

REDEFINING RETAIL

REDEFINING RETAIL

10 Guiding Principles for a Post-Digital World

PHILIP KOTLER
GIUSEPPE STIGLIANO

WILEY

This edition first published 2024

Registered Offices
John Wiley & Sons, Inc., 111 River Street, Hoboken, NJ 07030, USA
John Wiley & Sons Ltd, The Atrium, Southern Gate, Chichester, West Sussex, PO19 8SQ, UK

For details of our global editorial offices, customer services, and more information about Wiley products visit us at www.wiley.com.

Wiley also publishes its books in a variety of electronic formats and by print-on-demand. Some content that appears in standard print versions of this book may not be available in other formats.

Library of Congress Cataloging-in-Publication Data is Available:

ISBN 9781394204700 (Hardback)
ISBN 9781394204717 (ePub)
ISBN 9781394204724 (ePDF)

Cover Design: Wiley
Cover Image: © Denys Koltovskyi/Shutterstock
Author Photos: © Phillip Kotler; Courtesy of Matt Holyoak

SKY10061353_113023

Contents

Introduction: Change Is the Only Constant

> When we thought we had all the answers, all of a sudden, all the questions changed.
>
> —Mario Benedetti, Uruguayan journalist, novelist, and poet (1920–2009)

It is not news that change is inevitable. Indeed, we know from the sixth-century BC Greek philosopher Heraclitus that "the only constant in life is change." However, the speed, depth, and breadth of the transformation triggered by digital technology, accelerated by the pandemic, and exacerbated by the volatility of the macroeconomic context qualifies as an undeniable paradigm shift. The business community has long used the acronym VUCA—volatile, uncertain, complex, and ambiguous—to describe the state of flux that has replaced the sense of certainty, stability, and familiarity that people had previously been used to.[1] However, another acronym more aptly captures the times we live in today—BANI: brittle, anxious, nonlinear, and incomprehensible—coined in 2016 by Jamais Cascio, an American anthropologist, futurist, and author. The term BANI emphasizes even more the folly of relying on the concept of stability. In the words of Cascio: "It is a framework to articulate the increasingly commonplace situations in which simple volatility or complexity are insufficient lenses through which to understand what's taking place. Situations in which conditions aren't simply unstable, they're chaotic. In which outcomes aren't simply hard to foresee, they're completely unpredictable. Or, to use the particular language of these frameworks, situations where what happens isn't simply ambiguous, it's incomprehensible."[2] De facto, the future is no longer a marginal optimization of the past; instead, it's a constantly changing scenario evolving at an unprecedented speed. Case in point: in 2022 the editors of the *Collins English Dictionary* chose as their word of the year *permacrisis*, defined as an "an extended period of instability and insecurity."[3]

This scenario poses a critical threat to private and public organizations and undermines their ability to plan their own future. Macroeconomic assumptions and geopolitical certainties that have held for decades have all been dramatically shaken. We can no longer maintain that borders should be inviolable, rough material will be available at reasonable cost, manufacturing can be delocalized in most convenient parts of the world, supply chains will be stable, energy supply is granted, inflation will be contained, and global GDP will be sustained by emerging economies. In *The Age of Discontinuity: Guidelines to Our Changing Society*, Peter F. Drucker—unanimously celebrated as the father of management—was among the first authors to call attention to the impossibility of predicting the future in a context where the forward projection of current trends risks taking us nowhere or, even worse, to the wrong place.[4]

In such an unpredictable scenario, how can managers share with shareholders an accurate forecast, deliver predictable results, and meet customers' needs better than the competition? The short answer is they can't. Or at least they can't if they use the same playbook they've always relied on. The problem is that no one currently at the helm of an organization or leading a team has been trained for instability. Actually, the opposite is true. Managers are trained to achieve economies of scale, scope, and learning in a relatively stable context that allows maximal profit margin and return on investment. Most training courses don't teach how to deal with extreme volatility. The only solution is to do what the new normal requires: develop a flexible approach, learn by doing, and follow new guiding principles that are natively designed for this world and thus are inherently adaptive. Paraphrasing Drucker, the only way to decode this complexity is to understand the profound nature of its underlining discontinuities.

Retail: A Different Perspective

Starting from when Mesopotamian tribes invented the practice of bartering in 6000 BC, the logic at the basis of commerce has been a value exchange between two counterparts. The buyer can be either the end-user of the product or an intermediary that will resell to a third party. We typically refer to these two scenarios as B2C (Business to Customer) and B2B (Business to Business), and retailing is unequivocally associated to the former. In fact, the term "retail" refers to the sale of goods, services, or experiences from individuals or businesses to end users. Retailers are in the business of acquiring goods from wholesalers, manufacturers, or other retailers and then selling them to final consumers for a profit. As a consequence, B2C and B2B companies have historically adopted very different operating models and organizational structures. B2B players didn't directly interact with consumers and didn't need to have stores—so, rather than having to maintain large sales and marketing budgets, they were able to focus on sourcing, production, and logistics. B2C players, on the other hand, needed to excel in crafting customer experience, since the ability to increase the perceived quality of what people buy determines success—so they focused on branding, customer service, marketing communications, and promotions. Consumer companies like Coca-Cola, Estée Lauder, Procter & Gamble, or Unilever have traditionally operated as a sort of hybrid—functioning in both the B2B realm by utilizing distributors and retailers to reach end consumers, and embracing a strong B2C orientation through their marketing efforts.

However, the digital transformation we experienced during the two consecutive waves that we refer to as Retail 3.0 and Retail 4.0 (more on both soon) challenged this dichotomy and role of all players involved in the process. For 8,000 years—with the exception of mail order—to be a retailer one needed to physically interact with a customer, whether in a traditional market, in the street, or in a brick-and-mortar location. But when Amazon and eBay were founded, in 1994 and 1995, respectively, the world of commerce changed. Presence and localization were unbundled for the first time—one doesn't need to go somewhere to effectively be there. From that moment onward, a retailer could be also a pure digital player or even a "consumer" who decides to trade with their peers. And in the following two decades, the exponential acceleration of technology amplified this opportunity for newcomers so much that it posed strategic challenges to the established companies. The ubiquity of commerce—combined with the unprecedented possibility for potentially the vast majority of the world's population accessing products and services, regardless of location—redefined the competitive landscape. For the first time it was possible for manufacturers and any B2B firms to explore the market on their own—bypassing all intermediaries and interacting directly with the final consumers. We refer to this shift as B2Cization. A process through which a business or organization that traditionally operates in a B2B context borrows strategies commonly associated with B2C interactions. This can involve incorporating customer-centric approaches, building or reinforcing a marketing department, investing in customer-relationship management, public relations, and other forms of direct engagement with end users, similar to how B2C companies interact with consumers.

An immediate application of this new possibility is a strategy called D2C (Direct to Consumer), a business model in which a company (e.g., a manufacturer) sells its output directly to consumers without intermediaries such as retailers or wholesalers. Although this approach allows companies to acquire first-party data and insights and have more control over their brand, customer experience, and distribution, it is a double-edged sword, as we will discuss later in the book. Though it has great potential, it also disrupts the existing dynamic of the market and poses critical threats to established business practices, calling for different operations, more structured marketing efforts—essentially, all the variables of a different business model. What is relevant at this juncture is the fact that a huge number of companies not engineered to manage relationships with end-users were forced to restructure their organization and develop new skills. How can you sell something to an empowered and connected customer if you don't improve your brand image, have at least an e-commerce website, customer service, and a social media presence? And even if you decide not to sell but only to nurture your brand and perhaps build a community on a social media platform, how can you manage the interactions with a broader audience (compared to the sole industry professionals) if you don't develop specific B2C capabilities?

Ultimately, businesses need to contend with the fact that in a connected world—where digital channels are pervasive, and customers are tech-savvy and empowered—the line between B2B and B2C is inexorably blurring.

This is a critical point, since it calls even more conservative B2B players to develop an entirely new skillset rather than counting on intermediaries to manage the interaction with the final user. Since the Internet enables any consumer to publicly call into question any company, we clearly need to rewrite the definitions of "retail" and "retailer." Established retailers must also reckon with the fact that it can be relatively easy for newcomers to set up a D2C model—leaving incumbents scrambling to compete. Depending on the degree of B2Cization, efforts include consolidating the value chain, reengineering their processes, hiring employees with different competencies, reinventing their operating model—even redefining their organizational culture. (We will discuss this topic in detail in Chapter 13, and offer multiple means to address this cogent problem.)

There are two essential points to be made here: (1) today, a retailer can be defined as any entity that deals with a final customer (or client)—in a certain sense, pure B2B companies no longer exist in a connected world; and

(2) the principles that guide B2C companies should be studied, absorbed, and applied by B2B companies as well. This book is designed to provide all companies—regardless of size, industry, or location—a flexible playbook with which to navigate the complexity of the post-digital world.

Post-Digital: When Hype Meets Reality

Despite the fact that various cataclysms—such as wars, natural disasters, and, indeed, pandemics—have shaped the human experience over time, more often than not we assisted to progressive transformations. In other words, the future is built *with* the past, not *on* the past. For example, although we use far less paper than we did before digitization, paper books, newspapers, and magazines are still widely used. Though streaming and cloud storage is the new normal, many still store files in physical devices, and record companies still release DVDs and even vinyl. Yes, e-commerce is growing steadily, but brick-and-mortar stores will always exist. In other words, as new products and formats find their footing, the once-dominant formats lose relevance, but they don't disappear overnight—or at all. Though when we say ours is a "post-digital" age, that doesn't mean we're entering an era where everything we know about digital will be surpassed by something different. We use this term to refer to the beginning of a maturity phase: where hype meets reality. One in which people, institutions, and companies develop a more mature relationship with what was previously seen (even just a couple of decades earlier) as a disruptive technological revolution. In the post-digital age, we take that disruption for granted—and focus on the creation of a new reality.

Needless to say, the COVID-19 pandemic globally accelerated this transition. Businesses and markets alike were forced to adapt to restricted mobility and hence relied (even) more heavily on digital. And many reluctant companies were forced to stop procrastinating and engage in drastic digitalization to avoid going out of business. At the beginning of 2020, concepts like social commerce, voice commerce, and virtual reality were considered futuristic by many consumers; today, they are an integral part of the commerce fabric.

Of course this phenomenon is not new. Every time markets get disrupted by new technologies and competitors, the vast majority of legacy companies struggle to keep up. They are simply not prepared to leverage the same transformative innovation that the new players natively embrace. Azeem Azhar in the book *The Exponential Age: How Accelerating Technology Is Leaving Us Behind and What to Do About It*, refers to the current version of this phenomenon as an "exponential gap," the chasm between new forms of technology—along with the fresh approaches to business, work, politics, and civil society the technology brings about—and the corporations, employees, politics, and wider social norms that get left behind.[5] The exponential pace at which technologies are being invented and scaled, all while they are decreasing in price and increasing in availability, exacerbates the gap and widens the gulf between tech and society. Our existing rules around market power, monopoly, competition, and tax became obsolete if not anachronistic vis-à-vis the gigantic size of ecosystem companies like Alphabet, Apple, Amazon, or Meta. Existing laws and employment practices don't align with the new expectations of workers. The current structure of the market in many sectors, including retail, is such that both regulators and managers feel more inadequate than ever.

But, again, that's nothing new; when a new paradigm arises, those prospering in the previous one have always needed to reinvent themselves to avoid extinction—whether we're talking about the entire supply chain built around salt from when the Egyptians first used it to preserve food in 2000 BC or the 22-century business of candlemaking being disrupted following the development of electricity. Information technology is a General Purpose Technology (GPT), which, as defined by economists Richard Lipsey and Kenneth Carlaw, can affect an entire economy and has the potential to drastically alter societies through its impact on pre-existing economic and social structures.[6] Other examples include steam engines, railways, cars, and, of course, computers.

Our assumption is that we are today at one of those crossroads that determines the beginning of a new era—one built *with* the previous one but also with the potential to lead to a very different scenario. The peculiarity is that contemporary GPTs are exponentially more powerful, hence their transformative impact might be astonishing. In their book *Marketing 5.0: Technology for Humanity,* authors Philip Kotler, Hermawan Kartajaya, and Iwan Setiawan argue that this new wave has been made possible by the maturity of six enablers: (1) the huge increase in computing power, (2) open-source software that constantly improves thanks to the collaboration of people and companies all over the world, (3) the widespread diffusion of the Internet, (4) cloud computing in the form of shared access to software and storage, (5) the ubiquity of mobile devices, and (6) ready access to big data.[7]

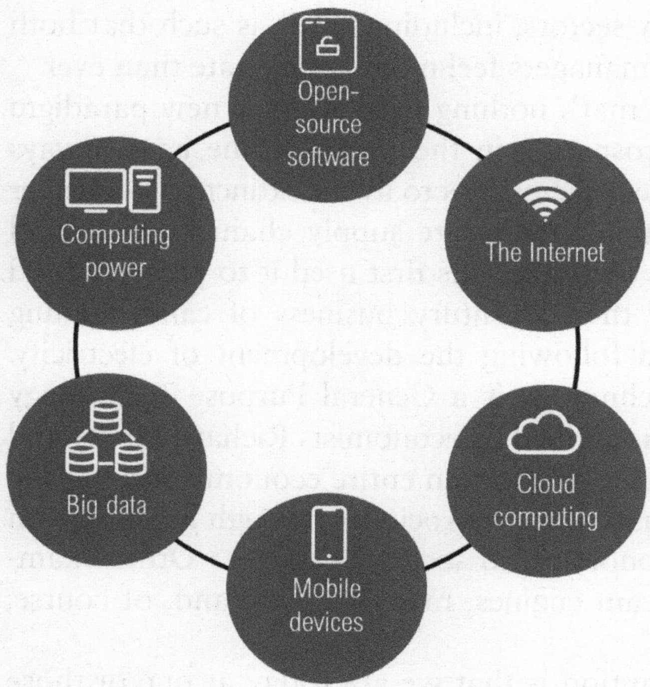

Fig. 0.1 The six enablers of next tech.
(Source: Kotler et al., Adapted from *Marketing 5.0*, 2021)

In addition, these technologies are more prone to combination than are those of the past, which creates a mutually reinforcing cycle that will redefine the world as we know it. This brings us to the essential question: Given that the transformation triggered by the mix of these technologies is at this point the connecting tissue of the new normal, how can established companies, retailers, and consumer brands survive and thrive in a post-digital world?

We argue that we are beyond the hyperbolic initial phase where positions tend to be polarized—we're entering the maturity stage. All the technological innovations described have been around for decades. It's time for markets and companies to face reality and take a full inventory of this new era. For example, consider the luxury electric-vehicle company Tesla. At the beginning of 2022 Tesla had reached yet another milestone: with a market value that exceeded $1.2 trillion, it left its competition in its wake. But just one year later, Tesla had dropped well behind, valued at less than one-third of what it had been previously. As noted in *The Economist,* "the main reason for the market's recalibration of Tesla's prospects is a dawning realization that the company is a new-generation carmaker . . . not a tech company."[8] Similarly, after the hype of the metaverse, Meta, the fiercest advocate of the new immersive virtual world, had to face reality and pivot after having lost $13.7 billion on Reality Labs in 2022. And even companies like Google, Microsoft, and Amazon, had to accept that, although their business models are inherently more in line with the new status quo, they are not exempt from the pressure exerted by inflation, recession, and a more generalized economic slowdown.

Maturity should also have led the business community to the full understanding that digital transformation is first and foremost a cultural shift.[9] If companies want to properly achieve it, it is not enough to simply "digitalize" (to use a word processor instead of pen and paper and send emails instead of letters); they need to holistically embrace a new modus operandi. Based on our analysis of the most successful digital transformations of the past decade, as well as our hundreds of conversations with top executives worldwide, we conclude that the majority of this effort cannot be achieved through technology. Digital transformation must be effected by people. This means coaching, training, and upskilling and reskilling the workforce as an indispensable prerequisite, combined with reorganizing the reporting lines, reviewing the incentive structure, updating KPIs, and developing new ways of working. These are all necessary conditions to unlocking the full potential of whatever technological innovation one hopes to bring to an organization. Technology is only as good as its weakest link, and its weakest link usually includes its users.

Finally, maturity means accepting that just because you *can,* that doesn't mean you *should.* In some cases a complete digital transformation may not be the most suitable option, as some companies may lack the necessary resources to undertake a sustainable transformation. Perhaps they're too small, or too siloed; perhaps their leadership isn't entirely on board or lack the right mindset.[10] In those cases, the solution simply sits somewhere else.

For example, a company might decide to transform their obsolete business and operating model into a specific value proposition, without any technological upgrade. Imagine a fishmonger forgoing e-commerce and embracing its brick-and-mortar location—offering customers the marine equivalent of a niche product range. Or, say a fashion house decides to invest in traditional ateliers to deliver very personalized human-to-human service to selected high-spending customers. As Marcello Pace—the chief executive officer (CEO) of Pittarosso, a leading Italian shoe retailer with more than 200 stores in Europe—told us: "Embracing digitalization is certainly important for our business, but we need to be careful when allocating our resources, as most of our clients still have a relatively linear and mainly analogue customer journey. It'd be a big mistake assuming that they would want to shift to online too rapidly. The challenge in our case is to keep the current business model while simultaneously testing new communication and sales channels, getting ready for the next generation of customers."[11]

For some the solution may reside in adopting a hybrid approach, leveraging digital in different ways depending on the service line or the product category. Simon Fox—CEO of the publishing and art fair group Frieze, and former CEO of the British newspaper publisher Reach—shared such a scenario with us:

> *It's important to understand the difference between product digitalization and leveraging digital channels to discover, learn about or buy physical products. Digitalization is when the product itself becomes digital—such as a music album moving from a CD to digital file. Whereas using a digital platform to discover a physical product requires a different set of supply chain skills, it's important to deeply understand customer needs. For example, in the books category Children, Cooking and Art books are still much preferred in their physical form whilst fiction is often preferred as a digital download to a Kindle or other device. So, it's all about understanding the customer journey, choosing the channel mix, and understanding the purpose of every purchase.*[12]

In summary, this new phase of maturity calls for accepting that we have evolved beyond the "digitalize or die" mentality that marked the beginning of the twenty-first century. In this phase, companies can avoid the mistakes born of either taking on too much transformation (from the fear of missing out) or of taking on too little (from sheer head-in-the-sand denial).

This scenario determines a new horizon for people and companies—one in which we should take for granted that advanced information technology is a *conditio sine qua non* for the new normal. The future of commerce is at the intersection of a plethora of critical technologies such as Artificial Intelligence (AI), the Internet of Things (IoT), Machine Learning (ML), Virtual Reality (VR), Augmented Reality (AR), Natural Language Processing (NLP), Vocal Interfaces (VI), Blockchain, Non-Fungible-Tokens (NFT), and the Metaverse. Before the COVID-19 pandemic, all these technologies were at least a dozen years away from becoming mainstream; now they constitute the fabric of the new normal. As such, the implications for retailers, manufacturers, and consumer brands are profound.

How We Got to Retail 5.0

Retail 5.0 will be enabled by the technological convergence described in the previous paragraph. But before we dig into the details of this new realm, let's retrace the evolution of the previous four phases. To do this, we benefit from the framework offered in McKinsey & Company's report "Retail 4.0: The Future of Retail Grocery in a Digital World," written by Parag Desai, Ali Potia, and Brian Salsberg.[13] And it's important to keep this in mind: although the different waves triggered a sequence of tectonic shifts in the world of retail, the new never replaced the old.

Retail 0.0: The Origins of Commerce

As noted earlier, we can argue that retail commerce was born in Mesopotamia in 6000 BC, when our ancestors started bartering or trading services or goods without using currency. Since then, many other civilizations all over the world adopted the practice, until it was replaced in most of the cases by money. The key elements of this phase are: (1) the fact that the transaction requires that the parties physically meet to negotiate the value exchange (no fixed prices); (2) there being a certain information asymmetry between buyer and seller; and (3) the role played by the skills of the sellers—the more they emphasized the virtues of their products and services, and the more they personalized the transaction and forged relationships with their customers, the greater their maximization of value. This dynamic was the dominant form of trade all over the world until the beginning of the twentieth century.

Retail 1.0: The Self-Service

You've no doubt seen shows or films where people acquired their goods not by milling through the aisles of a store but by naming the items they desired to the clerk behind the counter. With this setup the retailer is the centre of the transaction. But in 1916, in Memphis, Tennessee, a new model was born—and patented in 1917—the self-service approach, which others have named "Retail 1.0." According to the grocery retailer called Piggly Wiggly, "they were the first retailer to provide open shelves and checkout stands, and to price-mark every item in the store." In this scenario, the information asymmetry between seller and buyer started fading and the retailer ceded centre stage to the shopper. Components such as packaging and brand cachet increased their roles dramatically. Once the Piggly Wiggly Corporation franchised its model, the number of actual stores increased dramatically as well—from one to 2,500 nationwide by 1932. The format was since adopted all over the world in virtually every sector, although in some cases with some variants.

Retail 2.0: "Everything Under One Roof"

We can argue that the following shift in the world of retail has been represented by the concentration of different shops under the same roof, often located in suburban areas to accommodate the huge footprint. Although the first shopping malls were built in the United States in the 1920s and 1930s, they boomed globally in the second half of that century, in some regions more swiftly than others. The main factors that facilitated the success of this format were the profusion of cars, which allowed people to reach remote locations and transport goods; the adoption of electricity, and thus refrigerators and freezers in which products could be preserved for longer time; and last but not least the growing number of women with full-time jobs, who needed to shop more efficiently than they had before. The combined effect of these variables drastically reduced foot traffic and purchase frequency, forcing a reckoning upon traditional local stores.

Retail 3.0: The Birth of E-Commerce

The next portion of our tale begins its disruption in 1994. At that time the Internet could be considered primordial—connecting approximately 40 million people with a maximum transfer rate of 56 kilobits per second, compared to the 5.1 billion online users who today enjoy speeds between 100 and 6,000 *mega*bits per second.[14] Into this realm stepped Jeff Bezos: who began selling books but today sells everything from AAA batteries to zip ties. Two of the most innovative features of this new model were low-cost or no-cost shipping and the "now-famous recommendation engine," which McKinsey & Company see as being "as important to Amazon.com's success as anything." Fellow player eBay was founded in 1995; "by 1997 . . . 'e-commerce' had become a buzzword that ushered in a new era of retail"—one in which individuals could consider themselves "retailers" using a marketplace to sell goods to other individuals, and in which retailers' roles in recommending their wares took yet another step back, its voice muffled by the buzz of peer recommendation.[15]

Retail 4.0: Ubiquitous Commerce

We argue that Retail 4.0 starts approximately with the beginning of the new millennium and terminates with the COVID-19 global pandemic. This phase is marked by the progressive diffusion of feature phones before and smartphones later, combined with increasingly more powerful connections and technological infrastructure. In the first 20 years of this century, commerce has become ubiquitous, everyone can be a retailer, and every surface can be a store. Other characteristics of this phase are the consolidation of peer-to-peer commerce, the dematerialization of payments, the boom of e-commerce—including the adoption of D2C—and of course the hybridization between digital and physical stores in the so-called "phygital." This period culminated in the lockdowns, which, three months into 2020, applied to nearly 4 billion people—roughly half of the world's population.[16] This confinement required even the most reluctant consumers to develop a digital literacy, and forced all retailers, manufacturers, and consumer brands to rapidly upgrade their digital skills. In that phase you could either sell online or you couldn't sell at all. This caused an unforeseen acceleration that paved the way for a new era.

Retail 5.0: Post-Digital Commerce

We see several distinct angles regarding this next era.

ONE: In Retail 5.0, technology will be less visible but far more present. An array of minuscule sensors will collect and elaborate on real-time data about shoppers. Computers capable of seeing, hearing, and assessing the world around them will revolutionize the way brands and retailers communicate and sell, making every interaction contextually relevant and fully personalized to the single customer. To some extent, the relationship between supply and demand will resemble the tried-and-true model wherein sellers recognize and cater to individual customers. However, in this case the capacity of identifying customers and personalizing the experience will be powered by AI—and potentially scaled without limits. And, paradoxically, this mass personalization will be perceived as more rather than less human, since people will engage this technology using their bodies and voices rather than keyboards and screens. This aspect is part of a larger trend called "Zero UI" (Zero User Interface) whereby interactions with devices or systems happen more naturally and intuitively, often relying on voice commands, gestures, sensors, artificial intelligence, and other forms of ambient computing. The goal is to make technology fade into the background, enabling users to interact with devices or systems as effortlessly as possible.

TWO: In Retail 5.0, organizations will recognize the wisdom of concentrating on the most relevant channels and touchpoints, optimizing resources rather than being lured into a state of "ubiquity" that risks fragmenting resources and diminishing effectiveness. The notion of omnipresence will yield to "optipresence," allowing organizations to avoid the paradox of choice, where an excess of options ultimately reduces the overall ability to make savvy choices. Emerging technologies will streamline this process, prompting players across industries to explore new ways of interacting with customers while meticulously measuring the return on investment. This will unlock new opportunities for both B2B and B2C brands, providing a significant boost to the aforementioned direct-to-consumer strategy.

Three: Companies will need to redefine the role of human beings—employees, store managers, sales associates, cashiers—in light of technology. Finding the right balance between what we should delegate to machines and what we should leave to humans will determine strategic positioning, competitive advantage and shape the customer experience. In the United States, the retail chain Trader Joe's prefers its staff to stock stores *during* peak shopping hours so as to increase the chance they will interact with customers—and be on-hand to assist when needed. With this approach sales associates can humanize the shopping experience, optimize it, and potentially increase sales by making cross-selling suggestions.[17]

Four: Another critical aspect that characterizes this fifth wave is the stable presence of virtual, immersive worlds in increasingly larger segments of the world population. As a consequence, our digital selves—including avatars—will become more important. People will spend increasingly more money on digital products and virtual experiences. And the customer journey will become in many cases three-dimensional: physical, digital, and virtual. B2Cization is set to advance even more, propelled by the growing accessibility of these technologies. And the "C" in this scenario could represent a person, an avatar, or an AI, depending on the context (more on this in Chapters 14, 15, 16, and 17).

Five: Moreover, just because something is not physical, it doesn't mean it is less real. In Retail 5.0, digital is real, and virtual is real. Think about it: if we make a digital transaction, "real" money disappears from our "real" bank account. If we digitally sign a contract, or pass an exam during a video call, it has validity in the real world. What we write in an email we send into the digital sphere stands as a written agreement. If we play a video game online in the shape of an avatar with a friend located thousands of miles away, the way we behave has an impact on the relationship with that friend across all dimensions: real, digital, and virtual. If we buy an accessory for our virtual avatar paying crypto money from our digital wallet, that money is as much real as the digital product worn by the virtual avatar on the screen. And our analogue brains connect with this concept; as much as 60% of consumers declare they would buy the same products for their avatars as they'd buy for themselves.[18] We will further discuss the three-dimensional customer journey extensively in Part II.

In summary, thriving in such challenging conditions requires a different mindset, new skills, and new guiding principles in order to rethink entire business models. There's also no time to waste. Retailers with a "wait and see" approach will fall further behind.

The Journey to Come

In the first part of the book, we will analyze the driving forces that are keeping retailers, manufacturers, and consumer brands awake at night. The topics have been distilled out of 125 conversations with C-level executives located in 16 countries, in an effort to represent different perspectives and infer guiding principles that could be broadly relevant. In Part II, we present a comprehensive framework based on 10 guiding principles, carefully crafted to inspire retail and brand leaders as they embark on their transformational journey into the post-digital era.

The content of this book, particularly the framework presented in Part II, is applicable to a large audience—spanning from seasoned business professionals eager to update their strategic vision, to managers in search of a framework to filter their day-to-day endeavours, to entrepreneurs and small–medium enterprise managers, to management and marketing students who want to deepen their understanding of the driving forces of the markets they will soon be facing. In fact, the scenario we present as Retail 5.0 is not a futuristic horizon a decade down the line. It is the result of driving forces that are very much already in motion, and are set to deeply impact the way manufacturers, retailers, and consumer brands conduct their business.

Some questions we aim to answer in this book are:

- How can purpose, people, planet, and profit create a virtuous cycle that retailers, manufacturers, and consumer brands can all benefit from? (For more, see Chapters 2 and 12.)
- What are the opportunities and threats of "disintermediation"—cutting out the intermediary? How can we determine whether going D2C is a good idea? (For more, see Chapter 3.)
- What are the opportunities that small and medium brick-and-mortar retailers can unlock in the post-digital world? (Answers to this question begin in Chapter 4.)

- How can retailers nurture brand loyalty and increase customer lifetime value in a volatile and unpredictable world? (For more, see Chapters 5, 7, and 20.)
- Is Omnichannel—a business strategy aimed at providing a seamless shopping experience across all sales and communication channels—actually achievable and economically sustainable? Is there an alternative model? (Answers to this question begin in Chapter 6.)
- How can real-time data and insights lead to hyper-personalized interactions with customers, clients, suppliers, employees, and industrial partners? (For more, see Chapters 7, 8, 14, and 20.)
- Which role(s) will virtual spaces and other explorable, immersive digital worlds play in the customer journey and the larger retail ecosystem? (For more, see Chapters 7, 8, 14, and 19.)
- What is the role of sales associates in a world increasingly populated by computers, AI, and robots? (For more, see Chapters 8, 16, and 19.)
- How can established retailers, manufacturers, and consumer brands integrate next-generation innovations into their traditional business model? (Answers to this question begin in Part II.)

Welcome to the journey!

Part I

The Post-Digital Era

The future is already here, it's just not evenly distributed.
—William Gibson[1]

In this first part, we analyze the main challenges that retailers and consumer brands are facing in the post-digital world. We will focus on market trends, the customer journey, emerging demands from customers and the constantly evolving relationship between technology and people.

1

Running Backwards

The Ancient Greeks believed that, when approaching the future, we walk backwards—because, though we know where we come from, we don't know where we're going or what to expect along the way. Our risk is increased by the fact that, when we approach unexplored paths and uncertain conditions, we tend to base all our decisions on the only certainty we have: the experience of the past. The result is that no matter how cautiously we proceed, we are likely going to fail—or at least take the wrong way and get lost at some point.

This concept is still true today. Although we have much more visibility into the future compared to that of the Ancient Greeks, the current BANI scenario—again: brittle, anxious, nonlinear, and incomprehensible—is such that every prediction incorporates a considerable margin of error. In fact we could argue that, in a world that changes at the speed of an algorithm, the margin of error is exponentially higher. Therefore, it's not so much that we are walking backwards—we're *running* backwards. If we apply this metaphor to the way companies and other established organizations function today, we realize that this tendency to interpret information and make plans based on previous experiences is one of the main reasons why so many fail to catch what Steve Jobs called the next wave. In an unstable and fast-changing world, the more you rely on the past, the more you fail to read the present and foresee the future. The problem is that the majority of managers have been trained for more stable scenarios—where a competitive advantage would last for tens of years and companies could confidently alternate between exploration and exploitation and maintain a positive return on investment. Those managers who built a successful career applying principles that no longer apply find themselves ill-prepared today. Although from a biological standpoint this approach has significant precedence—our brain is engineered to cut corners, memorize patterns that proved to be true, minimize uncertainty, and save energy—it becomes very dangerous in the post-digital world, a brittle environment dominated by volatility.

The world changes faster than our companies and institutions can adapt, and humans are instinctively more prone to defend the status quo than to forge unexplored paths outside their comfort zone. Therefore, the majority of established companies struggle to cope with constant change and maintain their position vis-à-vis new-generation competitors and emerging technologies.

In 1975, Steve Sasson, an electrical engineer at Eastman Kodak, invented the first handheld digital camera. Though Kodak patented the concept, they opted against commercial production. Why? Kodak had told Sasson they "could sell the camera, but wouldn't—because it would eat away at the company's film sales." As Sasson told the *New York Times* in 2015: "Every digital camera that was sold took away from a film camera." "That was the argument. Of course, the problem is pretty soon you won't be able to sell film—and that was my position." Another dealbreaker was the anticipated time to market. Sasson shared: "When you're talking to a bunch of corporate guys about 18 to 20 years in the future, when none of those guys will still be in the company, they don't get too excited about it." Kodak's decision-makers had chosen the wrong lens through which to evaluate the potential of that opportunity. (Although they did benefit from their patent on the concept, they ultimately went bankrupt.)[1]

However, in many cases an innovation process can be slowed down, if not arrested, even when the top management of the company is aware of the market trend and the time to market is mature.

As Clayton M. Christensen and Michael Overdorf have pointed out: "It's not that managers in big companies can't see disruptive changes coming. Usually they can. Nor do they lack resources to confront them. Most big companies have talented managers and specialists, strong product portfolios, first-rate technological know-how, and deep pockets."[2] What managers often lack is the ability, possibility, intention, or courage to act. Perhaps because the company is private and the owners are not willing to pivot a business that is indescribably linked to the name of the family. Or maybe because the company is public, and the repercussions on the stock value until the move pays back would be hard to digest for the shareholders. Or because the high turnover of top managers in today's ultra-competitive market is such that most of those who are in charge today won't be working for the same company in five or six years, which is the typical time horizon for a strategic move to start paying dividends (similar to what happened to Kodak).

We could argue that another trait of the post-digital era is the need of a "digital maturity"—the ability to separate the voices from the echoes regarding if and how to leverage digital technology to disrupt a business. For example, though it would be terribly naive to pretend that digital transformation will have no impact on the way a company operates, it's also true that not every company, process, or business model requires a full digital transformation, as we noted in the Introduction. In fact, there are circumstances where it is better to not fully embrace an innovation—even when such seems to be the logical choice. As Freek Vermeulen writes in "What So Many Strategists Get Wrong About Digital Disruption": "In many businesses, digital technology will complement and alter the incumbents' existing resources and capabilities, but it certainly won't always entirely replace them altogether. Therefore, when making strategy, the focus should be on identifying complements, rather than assuming complete substitution."[3]

Speed of Change

The decision of how much, at which speed, and with what intensity your organization needs to adapt is what makes the difference between success and failure. In the case of Eastman Kodak, for example, while it makes sense they didn't suddenly U-turn toward the digital camera, they could have accepted the possibility of a disruption and started planning for the new scenario. Again quoting Vermeulen, "Business models and competitive advantages are complex systems . . . made of multiple elements [simultaneously interacting]."[4] There are situations where change will happen at the speed of an algorithm, and others where transformation will take time to produce visible results. Managers need to calibrate their actions according to all these variables.

A great way to understand this complex dynamic is the resources-processes-framework elaborated on by Christensen and Overdorf in 2000. Established organizations are the result of the interaction of their tangible resources (employees, real estate, stocks, vehicles, factories, technologies, money) and less tangible resources (brands, customer data, software, patents, contracts, clients, suppliers) following specific corporate *values*, which the authors define as "standards by which employees set priorities that enable them to judge whether an order is attractive or unattractive, whether a customer is more important or less important, whether an idea for a new product is attractive or marginal, and so on."[5]

In my experience [Giuseppe Stigliano speaking here] at the helm of international marketing communications companies, we've encountered this situation multiple times. On the one hand, the Internet had disrupted the business model of advertising, and new digitally native competitors were putting a lot of pressure on traditional agencies. But on the other hand, there was an intrinsic inability to react that derived from the organizations' culture—that intricate mix of consolidated processes perpetuated by the people in charge. In one particular instance, the opportunity arose to acquire a small supplier in order to internalize their skills and reinvigorate one of the service lines. However, once the due diligence was completed and both parties had reached a mutually satisfactory verbal agreement, the operation was vetoed by the agency's parent company since the supplier didn't meet all the necessary formal requirements. And, the business case didn't impress enough to justify making an exception: the potential of the additional market share just didn't seem big enough to bother with. Nine months later, that supplier was acquired by a competitor—and the merger was later celebrated by the business community as one of the most successful acquisitions in the realm of marketing technology of the last ten years. The acquired start-up flourished within the larger company and triggered a wave of growth on account of its ability to meet customers' needs. The opportunity for regret gets even worse: that established agency's time-tested criteria left it completely blind—for years—to all sorts of potential M&A (merger and acquisitions) opportunities. Those supposedly insufficient emerging players all had the potential to scale very fast if provided with the right infrastructure of capital and capabilities by a company with relevant awareness and flexibility of vision.

To conclude, the more ossified an organization's culture, the less likely that alternatives will be considered and exceptions made—sometimes to great detriment. Running backwards toward the future is an unwise approach in turbulent times.

Reflection Summary Questions

- If you are part of an organization, ask yourself: Does your organization's culture (resources, processes, values) allow you to thrive in the post-digital world?
- Does the management team have the power, the ability, the means, and the courage to challenge the status quo?
- Rather than sticking to what has worked in the past, and rather than expecting a clear plan before taking action, are you prepared to accept change, embrace uncertainty, experiment and fail, and learn by doing?
- How can you embrace the right mindset to identify and therefore avoid a Kodak moment in your personal and professional life?
- Which are the "values" that guide you and the organizations you are part of?

2

Purpose, People, Planet—*Therefore* Profit

In June 2023, we did a Google search of the word "purpose"—and got more than 10 billion hits—which is astonishing given that the word "sex" produces roughly half of that result. Consider the following from the *Harvard Business Review*: "[D]espite its sudden elevation in corporate life, *purpose* remains a confusing subject" in part because "'purpose' is used in three senses: competence ('the function that our product serves'); culture ('the intent with which we run our business'); and cause ('the social good to which we aspire')." "A competence-based purpose (such as Mercedes's 'First Move the World') expresses a clear value proposition to [both] customers and . . . employees . . . . A culture-based purpose (such as Zappos's 'To Live and Deliver WOW') can create internal alignment and collaboration with key partners. A cause-based purpose (such as Patagonia's 'in business to save our home planet' or Tesla's 'to accelerate the world's transition to sustainable energy') promotes the idea that it is possible to do well by doing good. All three types can create a meaningful *why*."[1]

We believe that a consistent and original alchemy of these three approaches is at the core of a meaningful why—a combination of powerful elements such as the very reason a company exists, what it stands for, how it contributes to social good, why employees should be proud to work for it, what would motivate suppliers to favour my company over others, and why customers should emotionally connect with its brand, choosing *its* value proposition from among many possible alternatives.

We deliberately chose the order of words in the title of this chapter to emphasize that profit should never be prioritized over purpose, people, and planet. This "new" order is necessary because, until not long ago, the dominant paradigm was exactly the opposite. Case in point: Milton

Friedman's 1970 *New York Times* essay "A Friedman Doctrine: The Social Responsibility of Business Is to Increase Its Profits." Friedman—who just five years later won the Nobel Memorial Prize in Economics—delineated that a company has *no* social responsibility to society; its only responsibility is to maximize profits for the shareholders.[2] And that perspective was widely accepted until it became clear to many that any one company's legitimate profits must not come at the expense of society, the environment, or the people involved along its value chain. The acronym ESG is commonly used to refer to the attention that a business must devote to the environment, society, and its own governance, ensuring that its practices and performance are respectful of various ethical matters—including carbon footprint, water usage, gas emissions, biodiversity impact, deforestation, diversity, inclusivity, and working conditions along the value chain.

The Economic Imperative

But for the majority of established companies, the new standards both progressively required by institutions and demanded by the public pose a threat to their balance sheet. In order to effectively adhere to this new view, companies must (1) work to reduce the opacity that characterizes the current fragmented and geographically dispersed production system, (2) increase transparency and the level of control over the supply chain, (3) invest in the traceability of raw materials and semi-finished products, and, when possible, (4) promote collaborative consumption. The significant increase in costs this vision requires threatens to quash any attempt to move in this direction, especially in a historic moment when budgets are burdened by financial crisis and consumer spending power has been considerably reduced. A seasoned executive in the fashion luxury world (who wishes to remain anonymous) confirms this view referring to sustainability: "I am profoundly convinced that sustainability is crucial. The issue is figuring out how to maintain the same cost structure while implementing the new ESG policies, as in the short term it requires considerable investments. And we can't simply offset the extras to the customers." As a result, many executives struggle to allocate the considerable budget required in the short term in the hope that there will be a payback in the future.

And yet, data show that in the medium-to-long term there is clear payback for those who commit to the new paradigm. Tensie Whelan, Ulrich Atz, Tracy Van Holt, and Casey Clark at the NYU Stern School of Business analyzed more than 1,000 research papers authored between 2015 and 2020—and all the key findings confirm that there is a positive correlation between a purposeful approach to ESG and "operational efficiencies, stock performance, and lower cost of capital."[3] Professor Paolo Taticchi, another authority in this field, confirms that ESG initiatives have strategic value and believes that managing for a low-carbon future in particular can contribute to a competitive advantage in industry. As he puts it:

> *Numerous international executives I advise frequently ask me about ensuring the financial viability of these endeavours. While it's evident that investments in this domain are essential, the immediate influence on the P&L [profit and loss] often dissuades many. In all such instances, my response remains consistent: the expense of inaction will surpass that of taking proactive measures today. Beyond the recent years' buzz and the impressive assertions of*

> *various organizations, CSR and sustainability in particular should evolve into the fundamental business strategy for all companies aiming to flourish in the post-digital landscape you've depicted.*[4]

Andrea Baldo, the CEO of Ganni, a B-corp certified Danish ready-to-wear fashion brand ranked among TIME's 100 most influential companies in 2023,[5] suggested an additional angle to consider. He told us:

> *Over the past five years, private equity firms have integrated ESG factors into their evaluation procedures. This dimension now stands alongside the fundamental criterion of profit, which remains unequivocal. This change grants companies like ours, dedicated to purpose, a strategic advantage as it makes us more attractive for investors. Hence it serves as a means to strengthen the business, preparing it for the future, especially in anticipation of forthcoming government regulations.*[6]

And when it comes to consumers, they seem to have a very clear point of view on this topic. In a survey conducted by Wunderman Thompson, a global advertising firm within WPP, 61% of global consumers declare they value brands that have a purpose beyond selling products and services, while 60% said that they actively choose retailers and brands that are environmentally friendly. This percentage is relatively consistent across all age groups and countries.[7]

Taken altogether, we can deduce that a purposeful approach to corporate social responsibility is not a nice-to-have—it's an imperative. In concrete terms this means accepting as fact that (1) every business has an impact on its world that goes well beyond finance, and (2) management is responsible for a host of concerns, including minimizing the environmental footprint; and paying attention to diversity, inclusion, and human rights—down to how all people involved in the business are treated, be they subcontractors, partners, suppliers, or clients.

In 2002 Michael Braungart and William McDonough published the significant book *Cradle to Cradle: Remaking the Way We Make Things* in which the authors propose changing the dominant, linear model of "cradle to grave" to the circular model "cradle to cradle." The basic concept is to break away from the traditional "take, make, dispose" process, where resources are extracted, used, and then discarded. Instead, the ambition here is to create a more regenerative and sustainable system that benefits the environment, society, and businesses—where materials and products are continuously circulated and repurposed in a closed-loop system. Ideally, embracing this approach would lead to a zero waste world. As defined in a UN Economic Commission for Europe report of recommendations and standards: "An economic system can be defined as circular when products and services are marketed in a closed circuit, which triggers a virtuous circle that potentially eliminates waste."[8] Not surprisingly, the task of reviewing every link in the value chain necessitates abandoning the linear model. For example, conceiving a product with this approach means considering all means by which a product could be employed anew after its first cycle of use, both through upcycling (increasing the quality and economic value of the original product) and downcycling (decreasing the quality and economic value). In this way—ideally—obsolescence, either real or perceived, is no longer a problem, since nothing is in fact wasted. It also calls for carefully considering the impact of the entire process—conception, production, distribution, and consumption—on all the stakeholders involved, directly and indirectly.

This approach clearly resonates with what Michael Porter and Mark Kramer unleashed in 2011 in the famous *Harvard Business Review* article "Creating Shared Value: How to Reinvent Capitalism and Unleash a Wave of Innovation and Growth." They argue that companies must jettison the concept of prioritizing shareholders' values in order to systematically seek the creation of shared value for all the players in the value chain: both those "at hand" like employees, suppliers, business partners, external collaborators, and customers—but also society and the environment at large.[9]

As such, the challenge that many retailers and consumer brands face is how to reconcile the pressure to deliver short-term results—which is quite cogent considering the macroeconomic headwinds dominating the world—with the ambition to plant purposeful management practices at the heart of their business strategy.

Reflection Summary Questions

- What is the purpose of your company? Does it align with all the stakeholders involved along the value chain? Have you ever assessed your stakeholder's value set?
- Do you have an ESG strategy that combines short-term results with long-term transformation?

- Does your company have full commitment from the top of the hierarchy (shareholders and C-Suite) to actively engage in an ESG strategy?
- Is there alignment between your value set and the purpose of the organizations you are part of?
- How can you contribute to the shift toward this new approach?

3

The Direct-to-Consumer (D2C) Revolution: A Double-Edged Sword

One of the most intriguing effects of the digital revolution, at least over the last two decades, was the decoupling of "presence" and "location." It's now possible to be "present" in a particular environment without physically being there. During the pandemic we fully experienced the pros and cons of this decoupling, and today we're still trying to find the right balance between physical and digital presence in various domains. If we combine this process with the possibilities of Retail 3.0—purchasing goods and services through digital channels—we can fully appreciate the power of what is typically defined as "disintermediation." This is a process by which companies can leverage digital channels such as social media and e-commerce to bypass intermediaries so as to directly interact with the final customer. Though facility with this new opportunity calls for the development of specific skills and capabilities, the potential upsides—especially of increased profitability and access to first-party data—are very attractive.

This phenomenon has affected, and is affecting, incredibly diverse sectors, giving rise to new concentrations of power. In some cases, it has created new intermediaries like Alibaba, Airbnb, Amazon, Booking, Deliveroo, eBay, Farfetch, JustEat, Taobao, YNaP, and many others. In other cases, it has offered the opportunity for companies that were previously only B2B to establish a direct relationship with final customers; it has also enabled newcomers to design vertical business models conceived to function without any intermediation.

However, it is important to note that "running an online [direct to consumer] business requires more than just a Shopify storefront and ads on social media." So shared Tim Brown, cofounder and co-CEO, with Joey Zwillinger, of

Allbirds, which makes sustainable footwear and apparel with materials like merino wool and eucalyptus. The certified B Corp brand with revenue exceeding $100 million and worth more than $1.7 billion began as a pure digital player and then opted for a more traditional business model, developing its physical presence with both direct retail stores (at the time we are writing in August 2023 they have 54 locations) and a wholesale division (that sells to dozens of department stores, including Selfridges in the UK and Nordstrom in the US). Regarding why they opted for selling both online and offline, Brown explained: "Together, retail and wholesale represents new opportunities for young companies to reach new customers—especially as online advertising has grown exorbitantly expensive in recent years. Embracing these channels will be critical to navigating the new era of retail."[1]

Online advertising, usually combined with a strong social media presence, is the most common way to drive traffic toward an e-commerce website, and it was relatively inexpensive until a few years ago. The increase in cost can be prohibitive, so some D2C brands have had to accept that the original business model is unsustainable and have instead sought customers via more traditional channels. Physical stores tend to be perceived by shoppers as the proof that the once-pure digital brand is more "real." It reassures and, at the same time, offers an additional touchpoint where customers can experience products and services. And this, in turn, is likely to trigger a virtuous cycle with positive repercussions on the revenue. As we will note multiple times throughout this book, offering a compelling, frictionless omnichannel experience—one where shoppers can access brands though multiple channels—often results in better sales overall.

In many cases, as soon as a digital-native challenger opens a physical location, their traffic and sales climb both online and offline. This was the fortunate turn of events for Velasca, an Italian D2C company that makes artisanal shoes and clothing. They found that the vast majority of their online sales derive from the locations where they have brick-and-mortar stores.[2] As such, it would appear that utilizing a combination of channels is probably the best solution for D2C brands.[3] (For a visual comparing D2C with the traditional, wholesale B2B business models, see Fig. 3.1.)

Another interesting case study that emphasizes the evolution from pure D2C to more traditional channels is Glossier, which grew from being the spinoff of a 24-year-old blogger to a $1.8 billion company in just 11 years. In 2010 Emily Weiss was an assistant at Vogue. As a side gig she decided to share beauty recommendations via a personal

Fig. 3.1 The business-to-business (B2B) model versus the direct-to-consumer (D2C) model.

blog, *Into the Gloss*. After the blog became hugely successful, Weiss created her own D2C beauty brand. Despite the astonishing success, built on the intimate relationship with the customers that only a D2C business can expect to build, between 2020 and 2022 the company went through some turbulence—including layoffs, complaints about the lack of new products, claims of racist behaviour and tolerance, and strategic false steps that derailed the company from its core business. In May 2022, Weiss stepped down and passed the baton of CEO to her then chief commercial officer Kyle Leahy, who proceeded to hybridize the company's original business strategy. In February 2023, the company opened an immersive new flagship store in Soho, New York, and went live with a bold strategic partnership with the French beauty giant Sephora. Since then, shoppers can find the entire Glossier product line in each of Sephora's 600 locations across the USA and Canada.[4]

D2C companies typically excel at managing the relationship with their community of customers while also leveraging first-party data—both to nurture the existing customer base and to infer the precious insights necessary for sharpening their business strategy and refining their offering. For example, if a company has evidence that a cluster of their customers is more likely to buy a certain model, the company can reach out to them with specific product recommendations—and forward those suggestions to similar clusters based on their similar preferences. The stronger the bond with the community, the happier the customers and the higher the conversion rate of every marketing initiative.

According to the 2022 *Future Shopper Report* by Wunderman Thompson, the global consumers surveyed appreciate different factors in this approach, including

The top 10 factors that would encourage consumers to buy directly from brands:

1. Better price: 49%
2. Free delivery: 47%
3. Free returns: 35%
4. Fast and convenient delivery: 34%
5. Loyalty programme: 25%
6. Exclusive products: 23%
7. Better information about products: 22%
8. Access to full product range: 22%
9. Better all-round experience on brand owned sites: 17%
10. Bundled product deals: 17%

Fig. 3.2 The top 10 factors that encourage consumers to buy directly from brands.
(Source: Fletcher, Adapted from *The Future Shopper Report 2022*, Wunderman Thompson)

getting better prices, faster and cheaper delivery, and free returns; accessing a full range of products and bundles to get exclusive products and convenient deals; benefiting from a rewarding loyalty programme—and altogether getting a better customer experience (see Fig. 3.2).[5]

An Opportunity for Incumbent Brands

Apparently entrants into mature markets have a greater chance of succeeding with a D2C model, such as with the aforementioned Allbirds (sneakers), Glossier (cosmetics), and Warby Parker (eyeglasses)—as well as Casper and Resident (mattresses), Dollar Shave Club (shaving), and Peloton (fitness). The upsides of disrupting the status quo are potentially higher. According to TechCrunch, this potential upside has, since 2019, attracted upward of $8 billion in venture capital.[6] Notably, this model requires a significant digital advertising budget in order to cut through the noise, which raises the cost of customer acquisition. The potential profitability of the scheme has also inspired a bevy of new competitors in different markets. And yet this business model has attracted various incumbents with strong brand recognition and large budgets. Anheuser-Busch InBev (AB InBev), the world's largest brewer, offers their D2C service in more than 17 markets for a total of 69 million online orders and nearly $500 million revenue in 2021. PepsiCo operates PantryShop.com and Snacks.com to directly sell its drinks and snacks to the final customer; and Heinz, part of food conglomerate Kraft Heinz, owns Heinz to Home, a platform that—at the time we write in August 2023—is available in the UK, Ireland, and Australia and will likely expand to other countries. Jean Philippe Nier, head of e-commerce for the UK and Ireland, highlights that the strategic reason behind their D2C efforts goes beyond the short-term additional sales that they expect from this channel. "First and foremost, I would say brands should think of their D2C channel as a marketing and data insights channel, rather than just a sales channel. In doing so, there is more long-term gain for your business."[7]

Also, many carmakers, including BMW, Mercedes-Benz, and Stellantis, are transitioning from the current dealership-distribution model to an agency-distribution model, which should ensure more control on the sales funnel and provide direct access to customers' data. This shift moves away from a business model that's been relied upon for more than 130 years: it's considered that the first dealership dedicated to selling only cars (as opposed to selling cars and vehicles powered by literal horses) was opened in 1889 in Reading, Pennsylvania. At the other end of these new agency-distribution transactions, car buyers will benefit from a seamless experience, as well as more transparent prices across all channels.[8] Of course, it's still too early days to say if this is the right way to future-proof the automotive business model, but the fact that some major brands have initiated this transition proves that, even in this sector, D2C is an opportunity to be carefully considered.

Ultimately, the hybridization of once-pure digital players and the entrance of established incumbents in the direct-business arena have diluted the original concept of D2C. We saw earlier that Allbirds opted for a two-prong, online and offline approach. We also saw how digital Glossier opted for a physical footprint. A *Fast Company* article sharing that story cites two additional offline/online pairings: Pop-In@Nordstrom/Everlane's clothing and accessories, made with, according to their website, "exceptional quality [in] ethical factories [with] radical transparency"; and Target/Harry's ["Head-to-toe grooming, reimagined.")[9] Indeed, Target is a popular spot; Casper mattresses chose it for its pied-à-terre. Lola products—a D2C brand of sustainably sourced "feminine and reproductive care products made by women," selected Walmart as its "exclusive" offline retailer. And in the blog of Public Goods sustainable home products, Tyler Koslow shares "Why We Chose to Retail Our Products at CVS."[10]

Of course, this dilution of the original purpose and the subsequent pros and cons also involve new intermediaries. These "frenemies" (friends yet also enemies), as they are often called, force D2C and traditional brands to discuss several very relevant trade-offs. For example: Shall we have all customers buy though our website, or should we leverage the immense reach of an e-commerce platform? If we sign up with a partner—and thus compensate them—can we afford the loss of margin? Should we invest in our logistics, buy service from third parties (e.g., couriers), or join with an e-commerce frenemy so as to benefit from their distribution network? Are we willing to give up control on the customer experience? Can we afford to have only limited data about our customers? Do we have the resources (people, media budget, communication assets, content, etc.) to sustain a presence on multiple channels?

It goes without saying that maintaining full control allows brands to celebrate their products and curate their relationships with customers—which as we have seen is an essential characteristic of D2C brands, and a crucial asset for any company.

Another interesting case is Nike. For most of the company's history, it primarily operated with a quite traditional wholesale model. Customers could purchase products in sporting goods stores, department stores, mom-and-pop shops, and more. Of course, they also had some D2C sales, but those were just a fraction of their total sales. However, in 2017 Nike has progressively shifted its business strategy, focusing on its proprietary ecosystem of e-commerce, apps, and its 1,046 branded retail stores. They have eloquently named this strategy "consumer direct offense." In 2020, Nike doubled down on the effort, renaming the plan "consumer direct acceleration."[11]

These changes have led to Nike dissolving many seasoned wholesale partnerships, from Amazon to Zappos.[12] The only remaining option for stores to sell Nike products is an expensive consignment model that squeezes margins—a model that few players can afford. This scarcity in turn increases prices, which improves the brand's profit margins even more. The company's greater control allows it to establish a direct relationship with customers, triggering a virtuous cycle that makes its marketing and sales strategy even more effective and efficient. Clearly the only way to successfully make such a bold move is to rely on a strong brand equity built upon years of massive marketing investments. To wit: between 2017 and 2022, Nike's D2C revenue ramped up from $9.08 billion (out of $34.3 billion total revenue in 2017) to $18.73 (out of $46.7 billion total revenue in 2022)—meaning that 4 purchases out of 10 were made via a direct channel.[13] Although this strategy proved to be successful, Nike has decided to retain relationships with a selected number of wholesalers—which is itself a strategic call. As CEO John Donahoe shared in December 2022: "Our whole strategy is to offer [consumers] that choice in a seamless and premium way. And wholesale play is a very important part of that. It provides a very strong footprint, both physical footprint as well as digital."[14] We observe a similar dynamic in the technical consumer goods (TCG) industry. Hans Carpels told us, "Clearly when a brand goes D2C, they become a competitor." Carpels is the president and cofounder of Euronics, the EMEA (Europe, the Middle East, and Africa) market leader in TCG operating in 37 countries with 7,500 stores. "However," he added, "we welcome fair competition and equal opportunities. We communicate clearly with manufacturers: (1) they should acknowledge distribution channels on their platforms, and (2) they should avoid exclusive offers that exclude us. Good examples are LG in Europe and HP in the US, which prominently display retailer options. In parallel, we try to counter showrooming by focusing on staff training, exceptional customer experience, and unmatched after-sales support."[15]

The Benefits of the Hybrid Model

We can deduce that a combination of proprietary and intermediated channels is an optimal solution to meeting the needs of today's consumers, one that aims to exploit the pros of the direct interaction while minimizing the cons of intermediation. And this is true for Nike as well as for other retailers and brands. According to CEO John Donahoe, "a consumer who connects with us on two or more platforms has a lifetime value that's four times higher than those who don't."[16] Since every company is different, and every market has its peculiarities, finding the right combination of proprietary and intermediated channels would be crucial to maximizing the return on investment.

Let's say a company sells on a third-party e-commerce platform to maximize reach and sales, leveraging its existing infrastructure and state-of-the-art technology. Once it's had direct interaction with customers, it could later try to "earn" them: for example, with after-sales services that the end-client can access via a QR code on the packaging or in a brick-and-mortar store. The overall objective is always to engage the audience, drive traffic, trade value for data, foster brand equity, and cultivate the relationship to boost customer lifetime value.

At the same time, it's important to consider all the implications related to the ownership of the customer experience, including the considerable budgets needed to stimulate demand in a saturated market as well as the potential repercussions on the value chain. In fact, the moment an established manufacturer engages in a D2C shift that disrupts an existing scheme, chances are at least one of the parties involved (i.e., retail partners) will take exception—at minimum complaining about breach of trust and conflicts of interest. Needless to say, there is a risk of eroding the relationship and embarking on a price war.

Fortunately, it's possible to blend the benefits of both the B2B and D2C models in a hybrid model that strives to avoid head-on competition—most notably, vying to sell the same products to the same customers. A typical way to pursue this hybrid approach is to maintain the pre-existing relationship with the retail partners (and the established retail products) while simultaneously developing *different* offerings available only on D2C channels. This may include capsule collections, limited editions, new variants of existing products, or value-added services such as after-sale assistance or longer product guarantees. In parallel, the B2B bond could be nurtured by sharing data and insights gained in the direct channels, or by dedicating special promotions to the retail partners.

To recap, there are pros and cons that need to be carefully scrutinized if considering shifting to the direct-to-consumer business model.

The pros of the D2C model include:

- Potentially higher margins, since profit is not shared with intermediaries.
- Better control over sales funnels, customer experience, and brand identity.
- More-efficient marketing investments (better targeting and retargeting) thanks to the first-party data about D2C customers.

- Better demand-planning as a result of having a better understanding of consumer's desires, needs, and preferences.
- More-accurate feedback loops, which may enable a more-effective innovation process.
- More transparent and authentic brand-customer relationships—potentially leading to increased brand loyalty.
- Better inventory management (i.e., more-efficient replenishment).

The cons of the D2C model include:

- Losing the advantages of selling in bulk (including lower customer-acquisition cost, efficient financial planning, and the lower risks related to the stock produced), hence are more subject to demand volatility.
- Needing to invest to develop new skills, and needing to hack the operating model (logistics, information and communication technologies (ICT), human resources (HR), marketing, sales) to construct one that enables D2C.
- Jeopardizing the relationship with commercial partners in the transition from B2B to D2C.
- Losing competitive advantage, since the best suppliers and retail partners could be contracted by competitors.

In Summary

The digital transformation that started in the Retail 3.0 phase combined with the increased digital alphabetization that followed the Retail 4.0 phase have created conditions in which firms can explore the benefits of a direct-to-consumer business model. However, this model can be a double-edged sword: unlocking the model's opportunities requires assuming risks, making investments, and experimenting to find the optimal channel mix.

Based on the case studies we've analyzed in this chapter and the conversations we've had with various executives, we've deduced that in many cases a pure D2C business model does not allow for the flexibility that most post-digital customers desire—at least not once a brand reaches a maturity stage. At that juncture, consumers demonstrate a clear preference for brands that create a frictionless and seamless experience across multiple channels—enabling them to buy what they want how and when they want, regardless of the intervention of third parties. Customers don't see channels; they experience brands—and they expect consistency along their journey. This doesn't inherently imply that brands must be present across every available touchpoint; instead, they should be ubiquitous in significant areas of relevance (we will revisit this aspect in Part II).

This scenario poses several questions that need to be carefully addressed. As with all complex issues, there is no one-size-fits-all solution. In a post-digital BANI world, manufacturers, wholesalers, retailers, and consumer brands, challenged by the instability of the status quo, are legitimately tempted by the opportunities to be found in emerging technologies. We recommend that organizations adopt a continuous-improvement mindset: constantly experiment in search of that sweet spot of optimization. In the second part of the book readers will find specific principles to guide these decisions.

Reflection Summary Questions

- Considering your market, the competitive landscape, and the digital alphabetization of your current and prospective customers, what are the opportunities and threats of going D2C?
- Do you have all the necessary resources to embark in a full or even a partial D2C strategy?
- Is your brand equity strong enough to reduce or even eliminate your reliance on intermediaries?
- What would motivate you, as a customer, to buy from a brand-owned store? And what would prevent you from doing so?

4

Experiential Benchmarks

Companies once "enjoyed" a landscape where they had only their direct competitors in their shared industry to stand out from—but that time has passed. Today's customers are more demanding than ever, and so companies "need to be better than," as McKinsey & Company puts it, "the [many] sources of inspiration who are setting the standards for your customer."[1]

Once the bar of expectations of what is an "acceptable" delivery time or a satisfactory return policy gets set by the best-in-class players, who are often digital natives, all competitors, including established incumbents, must adapt. If they don't, they are immediately perceived as obsolete and risk being neglected by even the most loyal customers. We call this mechanism "experiential benchmarks." For example, imagine that a company wants to build a content platform to engage and entertain customers with branded content. The experiential benchmarks they must inevitably consider, beyond their direct competitors, are on-demand streaming platforms such us Netflix, Disney Plus, Amazon Prime Video, YouTube Premium—or Tencent Video, iQiyi, and Youku in China. Customers will expect the same breadth and depth of content, a personalized welcome page, proactive individual recommendations, an impeccable user interface, an efficient search bar, and so on. Delivering a state-of-the-art customer experience is the most important battleground for brands nowadays. Another example is what happened to the once very stable and predictable banking industry when digital banks and fintech start-ups began disrupting the sector, bridging the gaps along the value chain, and allowing people to access financial services that before required the intermediation of a banker. In this case, nondigital natives can't help but rapidly develop countermeasures to deliver similar products and services, working hard to defend their market share by delivering an equivalent customer experience.

In the first two decades of the new millennium—along what we have described as the Retail 4.0 age, dominated by digital transformation—similar dynamics happened in almost every industry. As Brian Solis, a digital anthropologist and futurist, puts it: "Innovation is all the work you do to conform to expectations and aspirations of people as they evolve instead of making them conform to your legacy perspectives, assumptions, processes, and metrics of success."[2] People's expectations are evolving faster than established companies are innovating. Gone are the days where companies could focus on "upstream activities" such as sourcing, production, and logistics; create new products; and then deploy vast marketing budgets to stimulate demand. In such a competitive landscape, the mantra is "customer-centricity," and the attention has definitely shifted "downstream" to the theatres where the customer experience ritual takes place, both online and offline. Niraj Dawar shares the following in *Harvard Business Review*:

> *For decades, businesses have sought competitive advantage in "upstream" activities related to making new products—building bigger factories, finding cheaper raw materials, improving efficiency, and so on. But those easily copied sources of advantage are being irreversibly eroded, and advantage increasingly lies "downstream"—in the marketplace. Today the strategic question that drives business is not "What else can we make?" but "What else can we do for our customers?" [As a consequence] the pace of change in markets is now driven by shifts in customers' purchase criteria rather than by improvements in products or technology.*[3]

The Ever-Higher Bar of Expectations

So, what are these "shifts in customers' purchase criteria"? While consumers have always cared about getting a good value for their money, now they also particularly value convenience and flexibility—experiential benchmarks that are forcing the entire industry to adapt. To appreciate the magnitude of the trend, consider the following from the Wunderman Thompson's 2022 *Future Shopper Report*: in 2022, 41% of global consumers expected their products to arrive in less than 24 hours; 24% expected them in less than 2 hours! This is a huge increase from 2021, when 30% expected delivery in 24 hours and just 4% expected delivery in less than 2 hours. Young people in particular are more impatient, with 29% of 16- to 24-year-olds and 29% of 25- to 34-year-olds expecting delivery in two hours. Regarding the impact of free delivery/returns, data show that 23% of everything that global shoppers order online is returned, and 39% of global shoppers admitted to over-ordering with the intent of returning part of the order. As for the number one reason consumers choose one retailer over another: "faster delivery."[4] This emphasis of the hyper-convenience of the "last mile" is unquestionably the result of the experiential benchmarks that the best-in-class players have established.

Of important note, once a new experiential benchmark has been set, it is virtually impossible that customers will thereafter consider suboptimal products, service, or experiences to be acceptable. And of course, in this era of widespread information, the chances of an unhappy customer leaving a negative online review are high.

Certainly, the ongoing reshaping of the bar of expectations, driven by the convergence of lowered barriers to entry across industries (including easier access to capital, democratized technology, and accessible distribution channels) along with disintermediation (as seen in the opportunities brought by D2C), is presenting significant challenges for established retailers and consumer brand companies. Changing your operating model is easier if you are a nimble start-up with digital technology at the core of your business strategy. But more traditional players have built their success around atoms rather than bits, and this can make them slow to adapt. Holger Blecker, CEO of the German fashion and lifestyle company Breuninger, confirmed that "the main objective is to inspire customers every day by offering them a comprehensive experiential destination that seamlessly integrates the best of online and offline. Our customers are at the heart of our operations, and we take pride in consistently providing them with unforgettable experiences. We truly believe in becoming a destination—much more than just a retailer."[5]

Un(Fair) Competition

With that being said, it's also important to consider the perspective of some incumbents who struggled to adapt to the challenges posed by newcomers. In fact, in our conversations with top managers all over the world, one question was repeatedly asked: "Is it fair to let less-regulated nimble-newcomers redefine the rules of the game?" This argument is built on the assumption that disruptors have often derived competitive advantage from circumnavigating the regulations in force. For example, many Airbnb hosts weren't required to comply with all the regulations of the hospitality sector,[6] at least for the first phase of Airbnb's launch—which led to an unfair competitive advantage over traditional hotels.[7] This happened because Airbnb, like other gig-economy ventures like Uber and Lyft, was changing the rules of the game, and governments weren't able to rapidly regulate the new market dynamics.[8] Therefore, customers developed an experiential benchmark regarding the cost of one night's stay, or the wait time for a ride, and this put a lot of pressure on the pre-existing players.

Another example of unfair competitive advantage often mentioned by top managers of global retailers and consumer brands is the impossibility of sustaining a free-delivery and free-return policy—which is the new standard defined by the largest e-tailers. In particular, traditional players with heavy brick-and-mortar operations tend to critique the practice of large e-commerce platforms offering hyper-convenient conditions as if there was no impact on the balance sheet and the environment—whereas, in reality, fast-and-free delivery and the "reverse logistics" of reabsorbing returns are both financially and environmentally costly. This is why, as reported in the *Washington Post*, major retailers are changing tack by charging for restocking fees and/or return shipping labels: "Anthropologie, Zara, H&M, Abercrombie & Fitch, and J. Crew charge $4 to $7.50 to restock merchandise." To "offset the back-end costs" of "bracketing—[customers] ordering several sizes of one item to see which fits"—retailers such as Footlocker, JCPenney, Dillards, and DSW are charging between $6.99 and $8.50; Big Lots charges 20%. In addition, "J. Crew, Bath & Body Works and Gap—including its sister brands, Athleta, Old Navy and Banana Republic—shortened their return windows."[9]

But how can the new-generation rivals possibly sustain covering the costs of such hypercompetitive conditions (free shipping and free return in particular)? Some might say that big conglomerates like Amazon or Alibaba have diversified into so many sectors that in this case they can afford to work with minimal operating margins—or even at a loss. According to this view, the largest holding companies operate some divisions with artificially low prices—which would be unsustainable for most players—with the precise intent of wearing down their competitors. They are able to sustain operating at a loss thanks to revenue from their higher-margin divisions. This unfair practice of deliberately altering the regular dynamics of competition has a name: it's called "dumping," and it's forbidden in many countries and subject to the intervention of national and international bodies. Our point is not to debate the details of a decidedly legal matter; we simply wish to point out the complexity of the forces that are reshaping the retail world, especially considering the enormous impact of experiential benchmarks.

So far, shoppers have proven to be quite opportunistic about this buyer's market dynamic. They have grown accustomed to enjoying free shipping and free returns, indulging in bracketing, expecting flexibility—and pay little heed to what happens behind the scenes in order to make it all happen. Many people prefer to avoid contemplating the environmental consequences associated with the constant movement of numerous packages—nearly one-third of solid waste in the USA originates from e-commerce packaging. E-commerce giant Amazon alone emits carbon dioxide on a scale comparable to that of a small country.[10] Many consumers also don't want to think about the meagre wages paid to those who pack the boxes or drive the trucks or restock the inventory once it's returned—the true cost structure of this favoured benefit. Why should they take into consideration the fact that some of the products they return need to be sanitized before being resold—or must be sold at a discount as "used" or "refurbished" or can't be resold at all, having become dud inventory that then needs to be donated or disposed of somehow? Due to this phenomenon, companies often incorporate the shipping cost into the retail price, giving customers the impression that they are not incurring any additional expenses to receive the item. From a perspective rooted in the psychology of consumption and behavioural economics, this approach is entirely understandable. Humans tend to prefer experiencing combined discomfort (aggregated pain), as they find it easier to endure all the associated inconveniences at once. Similarly, people take pleasure in experiencing separate benefits, as they enjoy celebrating each individual success (segregated gains).[11] Clearly this vicious cycle leads to a lack of transparency, which can potentially erode customer loyalty.

A New Market Modus Operandi?

We discussed this topic with Sandro Veronesi, the founder of Calzedonia group, the family-owned company behind brands like Intimissimi, Calzedonia, Falconeri, and Tezenis, whose products are distributed in more than 2,000 brick-and-mortar stores located in more than 50 countries for a total turnover of more than three billion per year at last count. He advocates for retailers and consumer brands to adopt complete transparency with their customers. This means providing detailed information, especially about the financial and environmental costs associated with practices like bracketing, free delivery, and free returns. By doing so, the goal is to raise customer consciousness and encourage more responsible behaviour.[12] This perspective offers the potential to transform the previously mentioned vicious cycle into a virtuous one, helping to address the challenges faced by the low-margin sector, further exacerbated by the competition from aggressive newcomers.

Another interesting case in this regard is represented by the Green Button Project, implemented by a prominent retailer in Mexico. When shoppers clicked the BUY button, they were presented with a series of thought-provoking questions. Each question aimed to gauge their willingness to embrace sustainable practices. For instance, one question inquired whether they would be open to slower shipping options in exchange for reduced CO_2 emissions. Another question explored whether shoppers would opt for slower shipping if it contributed to saving a specific number of trees. Interestingly enough, "when shown the tree option, 71% of shoppers agreed to the slower shipping."[13]

Although this perspective is definitely more sustainable, financially and environmentally, and the more-conscious consumers will be keen to embrace such options, the hypercompetitive nature of the market is such that it's unlikely these practices will become the new benchmark without an intervention of an international trade regulator.

In the post-digital age of Retail 5.0, companies will define their business models and exploit their value proposition not by how they play against traditional industry peers, but by how effectively they cope with the standards that are continually redefined by markets and regulated by institutions.

Furthermore, it will be increasingly important to educate customers on the dark side of experiential benchmarks so as to establish financially, socially, and environmentally sustainable best practices. These practices can become the new market modus operandi.

Reflection Summary Questions

- Have your experiential benchmarks as a customer (based on the products you buy, the services and experiences you pay for, etc.) in your personal life changed over time?
- Have your experiential benchmarks as a customer in your professional life changed over time?
- Does your company's analysis and monitoring of competition include the sources of inspiration that are setting the standards for your customers?
- Are you equipped to stay competitive in a fast-changing market where experiential benchmarks get constantly redefined?
- Are you leading the way in setting the bar of expectations in your sector or are you being carried away by the benchmarks defined by newcomers?

5

Making People Want Things Isn't Enough

Most people are inclined to think of marketing as a clever way to make people want things. We believe that this is only partially true, as it only puts the focus on one of the four Ps, Promotion, neglecting the importance of the other three levers of the marketing mix: Product, Price, and Place.

If we consider this holistic perspective and we add to the equation the vast availability of data that we have at our disposal, we can argue that marketing is actually not about "making people want things" but, today more than ever, it's about "making things people want."[1] As we have seen in Chapter 3, accessing first-party data can allow companies to realign their business model and deliver personalized recommendations. That data also enables more-accurate targeting and retargeting and eventually contributes to shaping the very research and development (R&D) strategy of the firm. If data are translated into valuable insights, they can suggest which products, services, and experience will more likely meet customers' preferences—as well as indicate customers' likely price ceiling (the highest price they're willing to pay). Armed with this information, marketers can potentially increase the overall profit margin of the company, select the most appropriate sales and communication channels, and determine which promotional efforts will be most successful. And the list goes on. More data means more insights on people's wants, needs, and desires.

This idea that the role of marketing is more about creating value than convincing people to buy products is not new at all. Peter Drucker wrote the following back in 1973:

> *There will always, one can assume, be need for some selling. But the aim of marketing is to make selling superfluous. The aim of marketing is to know and understand the*

> *customer so well that the product or service fits him and sells itself. Ideally, marketing should result in a customer who is ready to buy. All that should be needed then is to make the product or service available, i.e., logistics rather than salesmanship, and statistical distribution rather than promotion. We may be a long way from this ideal. But consumerism is a clear indication that the right motto for business management should increasingly be, "from selling to marketing."*[2]

In other words, according to this view, the more marketers leverage data to infer how to best orchestrate the four levers of the marketing mix to fine-tune supply and demand, the higher the chances of launching successful products, services, and experiences. In this view, marketing and innovation attend to very similar functions. Both revolve around comprehending and attending to customer needs and desires (in some cases when they are still latent). Innovation entails the creation of novel and enhanced products, services, or processes that fulfill customer demands or resolve their issues. Similarly, marketing seeks to recognize customer needs and devise strategies to proficiently convey the value of products or services to the intended audience. Which is why Drucker argued: "Because the purpose of business is to create a customer, the business enterprise has two—and only two—basic functions: marketing and innovation. Marketing and innovation produce results; all the rest are costs. Marketing is the distinguishing, unique function of the business."[3]

We may argue that this view is nowadays coming back into fashion because marketing return on investment (ROI) is much more measurable than it was in the past. Gone are the days when the business community echoed the quote supposedly said by John Wanamaker (1838–1922): "Half the money I spend on advertising is wasted; the trouble is I don't know which half." Today, businesspeople expect quantifiable metrics and reliable key performance indicators (KPIs). It would be naive arguing that marketing has become pure science, but it is absolutely true that today it is less about art than it was in the past—especially since digital advertising metrics such us clickthrough rate, acquisition cost, average time spent, conversion rate, return on advertising spent, and the like have become part of the agenda in every boardroom.

The availability of data and the possibility to make it actionable represents a great opportunity for both established companies and start-ups. However, it is essential to develop (or buy) the capability needed to collect, refine, analyze, and finally monetize that data. This may represent a threat for the more traditional players who are used to building their competitive advantage "upstream" (sourcing, production, logistics, R&D) and now realize that the battleground is indeed "downstream" in the marketplace, where customers have the final say. This is not to say that upstream factors are no longer relevant. They are still crucial, but they tend to be taken for granted by customers—and in most cases don't actualize a lasting competitive advantage.

Writing in the *Harvard Business Review*, Niraj Dawar discusses how "the strategic question that drives business today is not 'What else can we make?' but 'What else can we do for our customers?' . . . This new [downstream] centre of gravity demands a rethink of some long-standing pillars of strategy." The rethink needed is large enough to intimidate old-school strategists. Why? First, competitive advantage, which can't grow exponentially on its own steam, is no longer to be found inside one's own walls. So, where to look? Second, the how-to of competition is no longer static; to remain viable one needs to keep appraised of in which direction the most favourable customer winds (or whims) are blowing. That calls for pertinent, timely data—and the expertise to know how to benefit from it. And third, customers call the shots, basically. "The pace and evolution of markets are now driven by customers' shifting purchase criteria rather than by improvements in products or technology."[4]

Making Sense of Data

As the reader will notice, these three points are very much aligned with the traits of the post-digital era described earlier. In such a scenario, incumbents are struggling: on the one hand, they perceive the paradigm shift, and know it must be reckoned with; on the other hand, they know that to embrace it they'll need to rethink their business strategy and their operating model; and reskill or change their management. To fully grasp the magnitude of the change, it is important to emphasize that the skills that are required to process the quality and quantity of today's (and tomorrow's) available data are completely different from what served in the past: data-collection methods such as ethnographic research, in-depth interviews, focus groups, and surveys. However, the nature and the structure of the data that can be leveraged today require advanced competences, ranging from Microsoft Excel to HTML, to data visualization and data cleaning, to artificial intelligence, machine learning, web analytics, social media listening, project management, and so on. The overall ambition is to turn data into business intelligence—which TechTarget defines as "a technology-driven process for analyzing data and delivering actionable information that helps executives, managers, and workers make informed business decisions."[5] This is a very important point—data must become information. But what is the difference? Data per se is an objective representation of reality, not one that is interpreted; while information is a vision of reality derived after processing and interpreting the data.[6] Thus, data becomes relevant for a company only when it has been identified, validated, aggregated, cross-referenced, contextualized, analyzed, and then translated into explanatory or practical information.

Leveraging data to derive information also means merging online and offline sources with the aim of delivering a seamlessly integrated and frictionless omnichannel customer experience. Even in this case that's easier said than done. (We'll explore omnichannel in detail in the next chapter.) Traditional retailers and consumer brands having access to fresh in-store data has historically been an unrealized dream—let alone also having the ability to merge that offline data with online data. Adopting digital technologies—such as sensors able to interact with smartphones in brick-and-mortar stores: think Amazon Go, an innovative cashier-less shopping system, which utilizes a combination of computer vision, sensors, and artificial intelligence to enable customers to shop in physical stores without the need for traditional checkout processes. It can unlock several opportunities, including contextual advertising (personalized messages sent to a mobile phone based on various complementary user criteria such as location and search and browsing histories), instant gratification (i.e., promotional content aimed at stimulating an immediate conversion rate sent to the smartphone of a prospective customer), and immersive shopping (i.e., when the user can access augmented reality content through the smartphone camera). Data are also important for improving operations, enabling the customer to enjoy highly sought-after services such as identifying real-time inventory or locking in a specific product or appointment slot.

This apparently simple process requires a great deal of system integration plus changes in companies' operating models, which is one of the main reasons it is rarely implemented properly. Another reason is of course the investment required of money and time—which discourages many retailers, especially the small and medium enterprises.

As Matt Harker, VP of Global Marketing Strategy and Transformation at Walgreens Boots Alliance, puts it: "When you think about what matters to individuals, whether it's a product, service, content, or messaging, you soon realize that personalization—at our scale of hundreds of millions—is going to quickly overwhelm you. You need help from technology to orchestrate content and messaging to land with individuals in exactly the right moment and context."[7] In doing just that, companies will be able to consider their customers' perspective, demonstrate empathy toward them, and even assuage their frustrations.

The Privacy–Trust Equation

However, even when executives are determined to close the technological gap to pursue this opportunity, there is yet another barrier that prevents many companies from going all-in on data: privacy. Retailers are afraid of the reputational repercussions of a data breach or an improper use of customers' personal information. And consumers are alarmed by the quantity of sensitive data that they're giving up in order to maintain the flexibility they've grown accustomed to. And the European General Data Protection Regulation (GDPR) proves that those concerns are valid and that new regulation is needed. For retailers and consumer brands this is also an opportunity to build transparency and trust, which are the foundations of their business relationship. According to Adobe: "Responsible use of data is the price of admission for earning customer trust. Regardless of how quickly governments or businesses move to protect customer data, consumers want brands to act now." However, the same report shows that 71% of the customers interviewed in the 15 countries that were part of the research are "concerned with how companies are using their data, and 65% believe the information gathered from digital interactions only benefits the company, not the consumer."[8]

The ability to access first-party data is becoming even more vital given that the system currently in place is undergoing a significant shift. "Google's Privacy Sandbox aims to replace third-party cookies with a more privacy-conscious approach, allowing users to manage their interests and grouping them into cohorts based on similar browsing patterns."[9] This change will rewrite the rules in terms of how companies target clients, understand user behaviours, and optimize their value proposition and the user experience. As of this writing, Google plans to start rolling out its Privacy Sandbox in early 2024, and expects to have completely deprecated third-party cookies by the end of that year. Hence, the implications for the overall digital advertising ecosystem are still to be seen.

The retailers that successfully build trust in overcoming both internal and external barriers and merging online and offline data sets will be able to achieve a number of feats: building a competitive advantage vis-à-vis their direct competitors, strengthening customer trust and loyalty, finding new areas of efficiency, and benefiting from the extra profit that is typically associated with clients shopping on different channels. Furthermore, these savvy retailers will have the chance to make better use of their human capital, ensuring that sales associates focus on value-added interactions with customers.

Are we arguing that, thanks to the abundance of data, marketers have the power to determine what people want, need, and desire, and can make their companies successful simply by responding to that demand? Of course not. Marketing is still a combination of art and science—although in different proportions compared to the past. And, by the way, "it's not the consumers' job to know what they want," as Steve Jobs famously said.[10]

However, if equipped with the right skillset and technological infrastructure, a marketing team can today base every strategic decision on far more solid ground, aiming at realizing that ideal fine-tuning theorized by Peter Drucker 50 years ago. The idea is that human creativity and intuition, powered by technology, should be able to predict needs and desires before they get articulated into wants—or making things people want.

Reflection Summary Questions

- How much personal information are you willing to provide to a business? What do you expect in exchange?

- What is the line that should never been crossed when it comes to privacy?
- What is the role of data within your organization?
- Do you have a clear strategy in place to merge online and offline data?
- How can your brand leverage data to build trust and foster consumer loyalty?

6

Omnichannel Is Dead. Long Live Optichannel.

Imagine Lucie and her big family have planned a reunion for her grandmother's 90th birthday. Since they all live in different cities, this will be a wonderful chance to spend time together. Lucie wants to arrive early to help set up, so she bought her train ticket online months in advance. Since she was worried about the fact that she'll have to switch trains en route, she booked the first train of the day to make sure she doesn't miss the connecting train. When the departure date arrives, she goes to the station early to be sure to get a good seat. But once at the station she reads on the announcement screen that her train has been delayed two hours—which means she might miss the second train. Exasperated at this turn of events despite her careful planning, Lucie takes a picture of the screen with her phone to post it online, tagging the railroad company and expressing her frustration and ire. But before she can complete that a text message pops up, informing her that she can head to the customer service desk to learn what alternate travel options she might take. Ecstatic and relieved, Lucie runs to the desk and patiently waits in line for her turn. In less than five minutes she is speaking to a representative and learns she can use her current ticket to get on any train heading in the same direction. This is great news; an upcoming train heads straight to a city that's just one hour away from her original destination—and it won't be hard to convince one of her family members to pick her up there.

After getting settled in her seat on the train, a train conductor asks to see Lucie's ticket. When she shows him her original ticket he says that ticket isn't valid for riding on this train. She explains what happened, and what the customer service rep told her, but the conductor tells her this is not standard procedure. Her only options are to get off the train at the next station or stay onboard and pay a fine. Lucie is furious, but has no other choice but hand over her credit card to pay the fine. After giving her a receipt, the inspector suggests she call the company's help line to explain what happened and see if she could get a refund. Reluctantly thanking the conductor, she calls the help line, expecting a long wait spent on hold. To her surprise, in only 60 seconds she is speaking with a very kind operator. She learns that the customer service representative should have issued her a new ticket for the different train—and that the inspector should have applied a new "contingency" rule and waived the fine. In the end, Lucie can get the fine refunded by filling out and submitting a form available on the railway's website.

What happened to Lucie is the result of the typical disconnect that we all have experienced when dealing with service providers. The frustration we feel can be twofold: we find ourselves paying the consequences of a company's inability to coordinate all available channels (see text box for more) and deliver a consistent integrated experience; and, even more vexing, we often have to start from scratch each time we interact with different touchpoints across multiple sales and communication channels.

> A TOUCHPOINT is a moment of interaction with a business. A CHANNEL is the physical, digital, or virtual medium through which the interaction takes place. So when a customer buys a train ticket from a customer service representative, that interaction happens in a touchpoint. The train station is a channel.

The reason for this disconnect is simple: the range of touchpoints that companies make available to their customers are the results of years of stratification. A once-modern technological infrastructure becomes an obsolete legacy—but replacing it would be prohibitively expensive. A once-new available channel that the sales team wanted to exploit proved to be more confusing than helpful. The latest social network that the marketing team said the company must enter doesn't pan out as planned. Of course, at some point the new has to replace the old, but customers often embrace those innovative solutions long before the companies finally take the plunge. Furthermore, every additional layer often becomes a self-contained silo—with zero (or very limited) integration with the others. For example, it might make perfect sense to a customer (who wants to avoid paying return shipping) to be able to return to the flagship store the shoes they bought on that brand's website—but if that return procedure hasn't been established, the sales associates can only apologize and decline. As observed by Cyril Lamblard—former Global Head of eCommerce of Nespresso, now head of Business Development and Digital Ecosystem Food at Nestlé: "Customers are always navigating between digital and real worlds. . . . They don't differentiate between 'online' versus 'offline' behaviour in the way that executives often discuss it."[1]

All these operational deficiencies are exacerbated in the post-digital era now that innovation happens at lightning speed and touchpoints spring up regularly. As a result, the supply is condemned to catch up with the demand, under the pressure of experiential benchmarks defined by nimble digitally native newcomers.

From Multichannel to Omnichannel

This approach is known as MULTICHANNEL since it relies on multiple channels, online or offline, to engage with customers. The problem as we have seen is that each channel operates separately from within its organizational silo. In the fictional scenario at the start of this chapter, Lucie interacted with one company though different touchpoints—website, train station, social media, customer service, train car, call centre, and website again. It's entirely plausible that the customer service desk and the call centre would be managed by external suppliers. At minimum, an inefficient organization will frustrate its customers. Another consequence of this fragmented approach is that each channel's success is measured with independent metrics, generating a paradox that artificially mitigates the urgency to act. Imagine a checklist where the key performance indicators are as follows:

- For the website administrators: regularly seeking and fixing any glitches that could prevent people from buying tickets.
- For the social media team: responding to every user with a direct message within five minutes.
- For the customer service reps: informing customers of their various options—and efficiently, to minimize wait time.
- For the ticket inspector: issuing a fine to any passenger without a ticket.
- For the call centre: reassuring upset clients and offering the best possible solution.

If you look at Lucie's experience from this standpoint, you wouldn't realize that the company has a problem. From her original ticket purchase to her call to the help centre, each division performed their responsibilities fully. And chances are that the managers who run the departments responsible for each channel will get their bonus at the end of the year. This multichannel approach—which forces the customer to start from scratch at every interaction, and was acceptable in a more stable world with few channels and touchpoints in action—is clearly not suited to a BANI hyper-accelerated market, where attention is fragmented across dozens of touchpoints. The post-digital shopper demands a more holistic, frictionless, and integrated customer experience.

The recognition of this failed model led to an evolution called OMNICHANNEL. The term was first coined in 2011 by Darrell Rigby, a partner at the management consulting firm Bain & Company, who predicated that it was time to move from a perspective where channels are defined by the company to one where channels are defined by customers.[2] In other words, focusing on what we have defined in the previous chapter as downstream value. The idea is that companies should (1) embrace a customer-centric approach, (2) determine all the channels their customers want available to them, and (3) be everywhere (omni) customers want—whether that's a brick-and-mortar store, a desktop website, a mobile app, or a virtual world.

The fourth step is to ensure each shopper gets a personalized, consistent, frictionless, and seamlessly integrated customer experience across all these channels and their respective touchpoints. This last point is essential since customers don't see channels—they experience brands. In this holistic view, it doesn't matter which channel customers choose to start their journey; the company must develop the technological infrastructure to collect, process, and distribute data in such a way that customers are recognized and served as unique individuals regardless of which channels they might switch to during any one visit to that brand. All channels must be connected and synchronized, ideally in real time, in order to unlock all potential synergies. For example, a shopper might use their smartphone to localize a store, check the inventory in real time, and potentially book an appointment for a try-on or to reserve a curbside pickup. By combining all data coming from the different sources, the company would be able to derive a precise profile of each customer that will in turn enable a high degree of personalization. More personalized content and promotions means a higher conversion rate—hence, more revenue and more profit, all thanks to a more-efficient allocation of media resources.

We may argue that if an omnichannel strategy is orchestrated successfully the only KPI is the overall customer satisfaction. It wouldn't be relevant to appreciate great KPIs in one channel at the expense of another, since this would indicate there is a snag in the harmony of the system. A great customer experience is more than the sum of its parts.

Moreover, there seems to be a linear correlation between a successful omnichannel strategy and company profitability. As stated in a report by the management consulting firm McKinsey: "After it tightened the links between its digital and traditional channels, a large regional bank increased sales of current-account and personal-loan products by more than 25 percent across all channels. And a European telecommunications company saw a 40 percent increase in usage of its online service channel, reducing its costs by more than 20 percent while increasing customer satisfaction by more than five percentage points."[3]

In the US, a *Harvard Business Review* study of 46,000 shoppers showed that omnichannel customers spend 10% more online than do their single-channel counterparts. Better yet, "with every additional channel they used, the shoppers spent more money in the store . . . . [C]ustomers who used 4+ channels spent 9% more in the store, on average, when compared to" single-channelers.[4]

Salesforce adds to the data: 85% of customers "expect consistent interactions across departments"—and reward that consistency with brand loyalty.[5]

Unfortunately, all that glitters is not gold. Although omnichannel has been considered a panacea by the business community, many organizations are realizing just how much it's easier said than done. As much as happier customers are the golden fleece, that doesn't make the necessary behind-the-scenes maths more viable: the initial (considerable) investments needed to trigger that virtuous cycle won't necessarily do the trick. It's becoming apparent that the vast majority of companies don't have the bandwidth, personnel, operating system, media budget, or technical and technological expertise needed to fulfill the expectations of omnichannel customers. For example, click-and-collect purchases lose their appeal if customers have to wait at the curb to receive their merchandise. And even the best-in-class players capable of deploying huge investments are not always accurate in delivering timely personalized advertisements; promoting a product or service after the customer has already sealed a deal elsewhere doesn't impress the bean counters.

A seasoned executive who held multiple international roles at different large organizations lamented:

> *It's not sustainable being everywhere just because customers want that. If we were to sell our products on all available marketplaces, our supply chain would implode. Or, offering 48-hour free delivery would cost us a fortune—considering that, in some geographies, we don't have the capillary distribution required to make that happen. And that doesn't include the profit erosion we'd experience after aligning our prices to those offered on the most popular touchpoints. Our different channels would cannibalize*

> *one another. And even if we wanted to test viability, I'd have to allocate my entire team on the project for months, since going from multichannel to omnichannel requires a lot of trial and error and constant fine-tuning. So yes, I can understand that omnichannel customers are worth more than multichannel ones, but will the benefit of those hard-won customers match the investment required to attain them? And over what time period? How many other projects would I need to put on hold in order to pursue such an ambitious one?*

As he points out, the conflict among the various channels is another critical point to be considered. On the one hand, it is true that in today's channel-rich ultracompetitive marketplace it is not acceptable to either have few channels or deliver an inconsistent experience. And from a marketing and sales standpoint, omnichannel represents an unmistakably great opportunity. But on the other hand, the higher the number of channels, the higher the complexity in terms of operations, logistics, information technology (IT), and supply chain management. And maintaining positive customer relationships becomes very demanding given the system integration needed to make that happen—such as melding the user data from the app with the brick-and-mortar store database. Add to which, the software necessary to tie all channels together—including online and offline proprietary sources, and third parties—requires investments in the tens of millions.

We can conclude that, although it's absolutely true that a different approach was needed to overcome the limits of multichannel, omnichannel doesn't represent the solution that the business community hoped it was going to be. When operating across multiple channels, retailers must ensure an *optimal* integration of the incoming data and an understanding of why and how customers interact with each channel so they can avoid conflicts, attribute the most appropriate KPIs, and measure the marginal contribution of every channel. But pretending to be everything to everyone everywhere is not the solution. As Martin Lindstrom explained during one of our conversations: "The reality is that brands can't afford to be 'friends with everyone.'"[6]

To summarize, while omnichannel retailing has many benefits, it also carries major threats:

- Cost: the cost of implementation, especially for smaller retailers. Significant investments in staffing, technology, and logistics are required to seamlessly integrate the different channels and deliver a consistent customer experience across all touchpoints.
- Complexity: the complexity of managing multiple channels, including physical stores, e-commerce websites, mobile apps, and social media platforms. New processes and systems must be put in place to manage inventory, order fulfillment, and customer service.
- Data management: the challenge of collecting, organizing, storing, and then finding, extracting, refining, managing, and analyzing data coming from multiple sources in order to make the data both actionable and monetizable.
- Channel conflict: the conflict linked to managing competing priorities among channels, integrating inventories, and aligning employee's incentives (especially in siloed organizations where different people lead overlapping channels—for example, head of sales for brick-and-mortar stores and head of e-commerce sales).

- Customer expectations: the pressure to compete with experiential benchmarks defined by nimble digital-native competitors and the necessity of dealing with expectations of a personalized seamlessly integrated customer experience.

From Omnichannel to Optichannel

So, how can we reconcile the fact that customers demand frictionless choice, guidance, personalization, and transparency with the financial difficulty and the operational complexity of dealing with so many channels and touchpoints? And how can companies help customers navigate a market overloaded with branded content, advertisements, promotions, and abundant options?

The best solution to this complex equation appears to be the shift to what has been defined as "optichannel": the ideal optimization of all available channels and touchpoints, such that the customer is put at the centre of a consistent holistic brand experience while the channel mix allows the company to maximize synergies among touchpoints. In this view, the point is not being everywhere, but being where it matters the most for the right customer at the right time. To achieve this, a business has to take into account the entire customer journey, blending demographics, transactional data, purchase history, past preferences, behavioural patterns, and contextual information. Armed with this information, it's possible to drop the least-performing channels and double down on the best-performing in a constant feedback loop. Therefore, instead of prioritizing *breadth*—in terms of channels and touchpoints—retailers and consumer brands embracing this approach would prioritize *depth* so as to create truly meaningful interactions. In pursuing this approach, they would also consciously factor in the potential decision to reduce the overall number of clients/transactions: essentially, aiming for fewer but more profitable interactions and a higher customer lifetime value. The promise of optichannel is a personalized (hence simplified) and more meaningful customer experience—there being fewer interactions enables those interactions to be relevant and perfectly integrated. Of course, access to the right data, plus the ability to process it, is the vital requisite for unlocking the potential of this alchemy. In the words of Brian Cornell, Chairman and CEO of the American retail giant Target: "The days of only one function driving any successful initiative are behind us. Everything we do requires strong coordination of cross-functional teams . . . . [F]rom digital to store operations to merchants and more, everyone plays an integral role. And it all starts with a clear understanding of consumer expectations and the right prioritization."[7]

Optimizing Your Channel Strategy

MULTICHANNEL: Providing customers with multiple nonintegrated channels. Every channel is a stand-alone silo of interaction. Customers need to start from scratch as they move from one channel to the other.

OMNICHANNEL: Providing customers with a seamlessly integrated holistic experience across all channels and touchpoints. Information is shared in a way that allows customers to build on previous interactions regardless of the channel.

OPTICHANNEL: Providing customers with ideal optimization of the available channels and touchpoints. Customers benefit from an optimized customer journey where they interact with fewer, seamlessly integrated, more relevant touchpoints.

Being optichannel in a post-digital world requires a perfect mix of a selected number of channels and touchpoints: the physical (brick-and-mortar stores, paper catalogs, and brochures, events, etc.), the digital (apps, websites, e-commerce, social media, etc.), and the virtual (virtual reality and virtual ecosystems like the metaverse). In the next chapter, we'll focus on how the customer journey is evolving, and what organizations should do to fully benefit from this business strategy.

Reflection Summary Questions

- How important is it for you to have a seamless experience across multiple channels when dealing with the same company?
- As an organization, do you have access to data on all available sales and communication channels?
- Does your company define and measure cross-functional KPIs?
- Is your company ready to assess the pros and cons of the current omnichannel strategy and potentially evolve into optichannel?

7

The Post-Digital Customer Journey

"The purpose of a business is to create a customer" as Drucker famously stated in his 1954 book *The Practice of Management*.[1] But as we've seen in the previous chapter, there is no way a company can succeed in this mission unless it understands what its prospective customers need and desire. And even more important: a company must understand how those desired customers behave along the journey from the moment they first realize their want to the moment they obtain (or don't) what they want. Understanding customer behaviour and tracking the customer journey is a vital element of a company's very existence.

The customer journey has always been determined by personal, social, and cultural factors, "as well as being influenced," according to Katherine N. Lemon and Peter C. Verhoef, "by consumer motivation, perception, emotions, and memory. This, in turn, influences the customer buying process—a journey that entails the recognition of a need, a search for the best means to fulfill that need, and evaluation of the available options to finally arrive at the ultimate decision of what, when, where, and how much to buy, and how to pay for these purchases."[2] Due to the explosion of channels and touchpoints that we've experienced from the Retail 3.0 phase onward, and the unprecedented quantity of alternative products and services available, this journey has become far less linear and predictable than it was in the past. People still start the journey by recognizing a need or a want, later search for information to identify the "right" product or service, evaluate alternatives, decide whether or not to buy something applying the personal, social, and cultural filters, and finally—depending on the previous decisions—they experience certain post-purchase behaviours.[3] However, the complexity is such that companies struggle to determine (1) what the most relevant interactions are, (2) how to influence the journey, and, as a consequence, (3) on which touchpoints they should allocate their media budget. Although most of the sales still happen in-store, the very concept of "point-of-sale" (POS) or "point-of-purchase" (POP) has become obsolete in a context where the transaction can virtually happen anywhere. The ubiquity of online and mobile tools means that people no longer view the brick-and-mortar store as a primary shopping destination—only as one of the many available touchpoints.

An effective way to visualize and analyze the customer journey is the Five A's framework (Fig. 7.1) we introduced in the book *Marketing 4.0*.[4]

It's important to notice that the shape of the funnel can vary depending on the type of product, the industry,

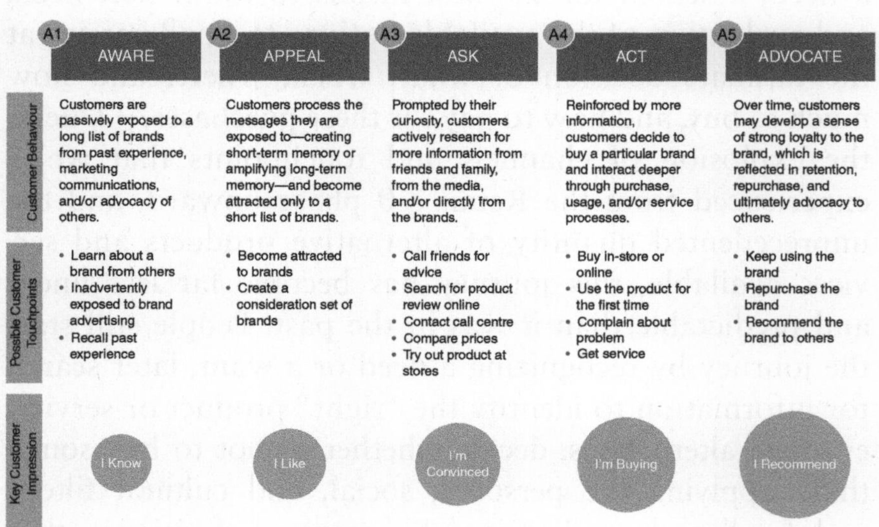

Fig. 7.1 The Five A's of the customer journey.
(Source: Kotler et al., Adapted from *Marketing* 4.0, 2016)

the customer's profile, and so on. For traditional products, like staples, we can assume a quite linear progression where the number of people targeted narrows down stage after stage. For luxury products, we observe a completely different flow, more similar to a butterfly than to a funnel: many people are aware of the brand or product and like it; only few people actually asked for information, let alone bought the product; but nevertheless many people tend to have a good opinion about and foster the reputation of the brand or product. Furthermore, nowadays customers typically enter the so-called funnel from anywhere, using online or offline touchpoints—sometimes even skipping some of them (i.e., when they click a BUY-NOW button embedded in a piece of content, jumping from "aware" to "act").

Traditionally, loyalty has been associated to the customer lifetime value and measured with metrics such as customer retention and repurchase rate. But in a connected world, loyalty must take into account the huge potential of people to advocate for a brand (or to destroy its reputation). The more people feel emotionally connected to a brand, the more they are inclined to partake in its initiatives, be loyal, and promote the brand itself. Take, for example, Lego, the largest toy manufacturer in the world. The company is committed to building a strong and loyal customer base establishing an intimate connection with its fans and customers. It invests in marketing initiatives that promote creativity and imagination. It advocates for the importance of play and creativity in childhood development, supporting non-governmental organizations (NGOs) such as UNICEF. And it hosts events and contests that encourage customers to showcase their creativity and share their stories about the role that Lego has played in their lives.[5] In doing so Lego goes beyond selling its famous bricks; it creates the conditions for its customers to become natural brand ambassadors. We will discuss this topic in depth in Chapter 20, "Be Loyal."

A Hybrid Journey

Another trait of the digital (and post-digital) world is the diffusion of hybrid purchasing and consumption behaviours. People are browsing on their smartphones while visiting a physical store or entrusting entire stages of the customer journey to digital only—to then pop into the store to try on a piece of clothing or check the quality of the fabric. Other people will prefer to begin the journey in a department store, then explore the websites of individual brands and perhaps complete the purchase on the site of a multi-brand e-tailer after reading reviews and making comparisons. We often use the terms "showrooming" and "webrooming" to describe, respectively, the practice of researching offline and purchasing online (showrooming), and the practice of researching offline and purchasing online (webrooming).

The habit of alternating digital and physical channels led to various acronyms coined to describe customer behaviour:

BOPIS: Buy Online, Pick up In Store (also known as click-and-collect)

BOPAC: Buy Online, Pick up At Curbside

BORIS: Buy Online, Return In Store

BOLSFS: Buy Online, Ship From Store

BASAH: Browse Anywhere, Ship At Home
BISFA: Buy In Store, Fulfill Anywhere
ROPIS: Reserve Online, Pick up In Store (also known as click-and-reserve)
COPUS: Customize Online, Pick Up in Store
MOPUIS: Manufacture Online, Pick Up In Store (made-to-order)

During Retail 4.0, digital and physical merged and fertilized each other in a permanent hybrid that has been defined by Professor Luciano Floridi as "onlife,"[6] and gives the title to the fourth of our 10 guiding principles described in Part II. In our vision, if companies want to thrive in Retail 5.0 and fully embrace onlife, they need to seriously consider an additional dimension—the virtual world. Whether it's in the realm of gaming, virtual reality, or one of the metaverses, the possibility for people to virtually interact with each other and with brands is here to stay, and will grow. Therefore, retailers and consumer brands should start considering a three-dimensional customer journey, where channels and touchpoints can be physical, digital, and virtual.

Asmita Dubey, Chief Digital and Marketing Officer at L'Oréal, confirms this approach:

> *We believe that the future of beauty will be physical, digital, and virtual, as consumers are craving more experiences, and more consumers are able to access those experiences. If you look at gaming, out of these five billion people online, almost three billion people do some kind of gaming. We are doing a lot of work with gamers and gaming influencers, which we call "glam-ers." It's a sizable audience. If you look at augmented reality, like our work with Modiface, the field of AR is quite sizable already.*

> *Where the subject is growing every day is in virtual reality, the immersion, the new devices, and the new tech platforms that are getting on blockchain. All these experiences will come together. What we want to do is use our 100 years of expertise to power our web3 with technology and continue to nurture it with creativity.*[7]

And Walmart, the largest mass-market retailer in the world, launched in 2022 an AR "view in your space" feature that lets customers see how furniture purchases would look in their homes. Similarly, the multinational furniture company IKEA, launched in 2017 its ARKit app to create lifelike pictures of furniture in people's home. In both cases, people can use the camera of their devices to visualize how specific items would fit into their spaces before they complete the purchase and without going to a brick-and-mortar shop.[8]

Interestingly enough, it turns out that the more time people spend in a virtual world in the shape of an avatar, the more their virtual self plays a role in their customer journey and can command specific buying decisions. According to the global marketing communications agency Wunderman Thompson, "60% of consumers would be interested in buying the same products for themselves and for their avatars."[9] And retailers from all over the world have tried to capitalize on this tendency.

Chipotle Mexican Grill, the American fast-food chain, released a new dish, Garlic Guajillo Steak, via mobile and online delivery across the US and Canada, as well as on Roblox (a virtual world), through the Chipotle Grill Simulator experience. The chain explained that learning about the dish beforehand in the metaverse and "tasting" it virtually has been a great way to enhance the tasting experience in the brick-and-mortar restaurants.[10]

Even the American fashion company Ralph Lauren jumped on the bandwagon. It has partnered with Fortnite, an online video game, to create branded avatars wearing digital apparel and accessories inspired by the Ralph Lauren's Stadium Collection and Polo Sport lines from the 1990s. The digital collection is exclusively designed for the platform, but all the products are also available for purchase online and in store.[11]

It's All Real

All these examples demonstrate that we are already witnessing a three-dimensional customer journey that seamlessly blends physical, digital, and virtual touchpoints where people can become part of the journey at any stage and from any point. As you might have noticed, we haven't used the word "real" to describe the physical touchpoint. The reason is very simple—in the post-digital world, digital and virtual are as much real as the physical world itself. Of course, there are still relevant differences, but the more people embrace connected technologies and spend most of their active life online or in a virtual world, the more it's becoming anachronistic to think of digital and virtual as not real.

Having said that, they are by no means the same thing. "Digital" basically means having to do with digits (fingers or toes)—as such, performed with a finger. When we access an e-commerce website from a smartphone while we wait for the train, we are simultaneously inhabiting the real world and the digital world. "Virtual" is an immersive dimension that we can assess through digital devices. A video game is a virtual experience; the metaverse is a virtual experience. If we wear a specific headset, then the degree of immersion into the virtual world increases enormously.

To summarize, virtual technologies have the potential to further revolutionize the customer journey by adding a third dimension to the current physical and digital touchpoints. Some of the key ways in which they are impacting our life are:

- **Virtual product experiences:** Augmented and virtual reality can allow customers to visualize products, spaces, and experiences in an immersive and interactive way. (Besides the Walmart and IKEA case studies discussed earlier, see, for example, a feature released by Google Maps that allows users to remotely navigate in 3D their future destinations, and visualize on their smartphones 3D renders of monuments and restaurants.)
- **Virtual human interactions:** Videoconferencing platforms, avatars, and chatbots can enable retailers and consumer brands to provide customers with remote assistance and a personalized customer service. (See, for example, the boom that livestreaming platforms had in the last few years. In China, livestreaming e-commerce sales skyrocketed from $62.30 billion in 2019 to $623.29 billion in 2023—accounting, respectively, for 3.5% to 19.4% of total retail sales in the country).[12]
- **Virtual try-ons:** Tools like virtual fitting rooms, virtual makeup, and virtual glasses can allow customers to simplify the customer journey by trying on products before they get into a physical store or buy on an e-commerce site. (Many retailers, including Warby Parker and consumer brands such as RayBan, offer

users the ability to wear digital product renders using AR try-on on their website. Cosmetic brands like Sephora and L'Oréal launched their AR feature to allow customers to virtually try on makeup; Prada, Gucci, Farfetch, and Cartier all offered the same through Snapchat).[13]

Virtual events: Retailers and consumer brands can interact with their customers in engaging and interacting contexts such as gaming platforms, virtual fashion shows, and virtual events to launch new products. And in some cases these events become hybrid. (For example, global marketing communication agency Spring Studios partnered with the e-commerce retailer Revolve Group to launch the first AI Fashion Week in April 2023, allowing digital creators to showcase their virtual creations at Spring Place, a cultural space located in Tribeca, New York.[14] [Disclaimer: coauthor Giuseppe Stigliano is CEO of Spring Studios.])

Virtual worlds: A plethora of metaverses and virtual gaming platforms, in some cases powered by brands, allow immersive interactions with other avatars. In some cases there is a human being behind an avatar; in other cases it's all AI (As we've seen above with Chipotle and Ralph Lauren, virtual worlds can represent an opportunity for brands.)

Overall, virtual technologies have the potential to create a more engaging, convenient, and personalized customer journey, allowing companies to provide an optichannel, seamlessly integrated experience across all touchpoints. However, considering that there is a whole new world of touchpoints to be considered, retailers and consumer brands need to carefully develop a strategy that aligns customer expectations with their resources and goals.

As we will discuss in detail in Part II, progressive companies are approaching the customer journey in a more holistic way, trying to see their customers in their full lives as multifaceted, constantly evolving individuals who simultaneously play different roles every day. We will describe this approach in Chapters 14 ("Be Onlife") and 16 ("Be Human") using the concept of customer personas (also known as "buyer personas" or "marketing personas"). They are fictional characters or, as Gartner Glossary defines them, "archetypal representations of existing subsets of your customer base who share similar goals, needs, expectations, behaviours, and motivation factors."[15] They are built upon research, data, and insights and typically include demographics (age, gender, education, income, marital status), psychographics (belief system, interests, values), and behavioural traits (shopping habits, preferences, media consumption). The purpose of creating customer personas is to help businesses better understand their target audience and develop more effective marketing strategies.

In the previous chapters we have often stressed the role that technology is playing in reshaping both the market landscape and customer behaviour. One of the main challenges for retailer and consumer brands, therefore, is figuring out what portion of the customer journey should be delegated to technology and which activities should instead continue to be handled by humans. What is the balance between high tech and high touch? Let's find out.

Reflection Summary Questions

- As a customer, think of the different ways you engage with brands. Is it a linear journey? Are all touchpoints either physical or digital? How does the virtual world change your behaviour?
- Given the different personas of your particular customers, what are their ideal journeys?
- Are you effectively exploring the potential of AR/VR and virtual technologies? How should you evolve your operating model to fully embrace the potential of a three-dimensional customer journey?
- Are you prepared to fully exploit all the synergies of physical, digital, and virtual?

8

High Tech + High Touch

I'm a frequent flier [Giuseppe Stigliano speaking here]. One of those individuals who spends approximately 400 hours a year on an airplane. I interact the most with the flight attendants, who, despite their best efforts, invariably mispronounce my surname, which is quite hard to pronounce for non-Italians. But one day something remarkable happened. A gentle flight attendant, who was not Italian, greeted me by saying my name with an almost perfect pronunciation—"stee-lee-YA-no"—smiling as if she'd known me from our infancy. That incredibly simple, warm moment made my day; it also made the seven-hour flight more agreeable, and strongly influenced my attitude toward not just the entire crew, but also the airline brand. So, how did she do that? She heavily relied on technology in advance, finding my name in the computer-generated passenger list, and perhaps consulting the Internet to learn the correct pronunciation. She then heavily relied on her human skills: perhaps spending a few seconds practicing pronouncing my name, she put her tablet away before approaching me, looked into my eyes, greeted me, and smiled while offering me a glass of champagne—and my most memorable experience as a customer. To quote a chapter title from *Marketing 5.0*: machines are cool, but humans are warm.[1]

We ended the previous chapter noting the significance of determining the ideal optimization of the customer journey. As Kroger CEO Rodney McMullen puts it in the *Harvard Business Review*, "We are now at the point where competitive advantage will derive from the ability to capture, analyze, and utilize personalized customer data at scale—and from the use of AI to understand, shape, customize, and optimize the customer journey." He shared that Kroger is focusing on delivering "seamlessness and personalization." Many retail giants—including Home Depot, JPMorgan Chase, Starbucks, and Nike—are doing the same.[2]

With "high tech + high touch" we mean the harmony between seamless technology and the personalized, value-added human interaction that can create a perfectly balanced customer experience (CX). But, as is often the case, there is no one-size-fits-all means of reaching that sweet spot. The perfect balance depends on various factors—ranging from the industry to the type of business to the digital alphabetization of the audience. But one helpful rule of thumb is knowing that it's not always necessary to leverage technology every time. For example, chatbots are ideal for providing customers with quick answers to frequently asked questions—such as tracking shipments, store hours, or product availability. With these sorts of activities the value that can be added by a human employee is relatively low. The human value is much more pertinent in a brick-and-mortar store, or when the complexity of the transaction calls for a tailored approach, such as personalized recommendations or explanations of fine-print details—whether or not that human is interacting in person.

To reiterate, when personalization is informed by technology but performed by a person, its full potential is unleashed. A good example is the fitness app Future, defined by *Wired* as a "winning blend of old-school personal training and modern-day mobile technology." Future is a fitness tech platform that collects and tracks users' data related to their workouts, sleep, and other biometrics. The data is then analyzed by the platform's proprietary algorithm to create a personalized workout plan, which is proposed to the user in combination with a certified personal trainer, who provides ongoing support, motivation, and guidance. Trainer and trainee are constantly in contact via the app, and can fine-tune the workout based on the individual's needs and goals.[3] Future thus demonstrates how game-changing the right combination of technology and human input can be.

But we must ensure the combination is carefully managed. If, for example, a business decides to automate a phase in the journey in which the client would prefer to engage with a human, there is a big risk of creating a friction that will upset the balance, sometimes with significant negative repercussions. (Those repercussions could be the loss of a single customer or, worse, "negative advocacy"—if that customer chooses to widely share their displeasure.) No doubt you've experienced the frustration of being forced to interact with a robot when what you need is a human to attend to your unique situation—the website with a buried (or nonexistent) "contact us" option, or the phone tree that stalls rather than immediately fulfilling your request to be connected to customer service. Companies would be wise to ensure that human interaction is available every time empathy, creativity, humour, out-of-the-box problem solving, ambiguity management, and other human-only capacities are called for. This human support can be vital to fixing a situation or even "just" enhancing a customer's experience. Business leaders have the responsibility to understand what to deploy and when, leveraging data and their own emotional intelligence to understand what can best serve their customers' need. As Greg Hoffman, keynote speaker, author, and former chief marketing officer of Nike, shared with us: "Data has given us more knowledge about our customers than we could have ever imagined. But, without applying the creativity that often resides in the right side of the brain, we are often left with creating solutions that only satisfy rational needs, not emotional ones. It takes both left and right-brain thinkers, working together to deliver the most meaningful value to our customers."[4]

We believe that in this post-digital age, the position that a company occupies on this ideal continuum—between fully analog and fully digital/virtual—will determine its ability to thrive. The distinction between what tasks technology should do and what tasks humans should will be one of the most important differentiators to building brand personality.

In other words, in situations where efficiency is more called for, customers might vastly prefer a purely digital experience, such as for scheduling a routine appointment, or initiating a return. This is exactly the value proposition of self-service kiosks, let alone fully automated stores—such as Amazon Go in the US and UK, Hema Fresh and BingoBox in China, and 7-Eleven in Korea—that utilize a combination of check-out-free technologies, sensors, cameras, scanners, computer vision, and deep learning algorithms in order to provide a seamless and efficient shopping experience.

But, if, as Hoffman told us, "we rely only on technology and not also on human ingenuity, then brands will end up being perceived as equal and equivalent, and lack distinction." So, for example, if a company decided to position its brick-and-mortar locations as fulfillment centres (as opposed to experiential stores), it would be essential that customer service representatives be specifically trained to deliver a service that leverages a distinct emotional connection with clients. Essentially, if a company's value proposition is based on the value-added service delivered by its highly qualified employees, then investments in technology should be confined to other stages of the customer journey. This approach is confirmed by Cristiano Fagnani, CEO of Off White and CEO of NGGH++, which manages (among other brands) the full Reebok business in Europe and the luxury business of Reebok worldwide. He confirms: "In an increasingly tech dominated world every brand must have a strong 'human' component at some point of the customer journey or it would go through a dangerous process of commoditization."[5] (For more use cases, see Fig. 8.1.)

When we discussed this topic with Stéphane de la Faverie, executive group president at the Estée Lauder Companies, he recalled:

> *Mrs. Estée Lauder had a quote, "Touch your customer and you're halfway there." When she founded her brand in 1946, she knew exactly what her customers wanted. She believed you had to touch the consumer, show her the results on her face, and explain the products. That was the beginning of the company's high-touch service, and it is still at the heart of everything we do today. We strive to deliver outstanding personalized service that creates a strong connection with our consumers, and a memorable experience that sets our brands apart.*

In this case we clearly see that the role of humans is non-negotiable—indeed, that role is vital to accurately delivering the brand ritual.

Behind the Scenes

Several opportunities to leverage the power of digital technology and automation also reside along the supply chain. Everything run behind the scenes is an opportunity to not

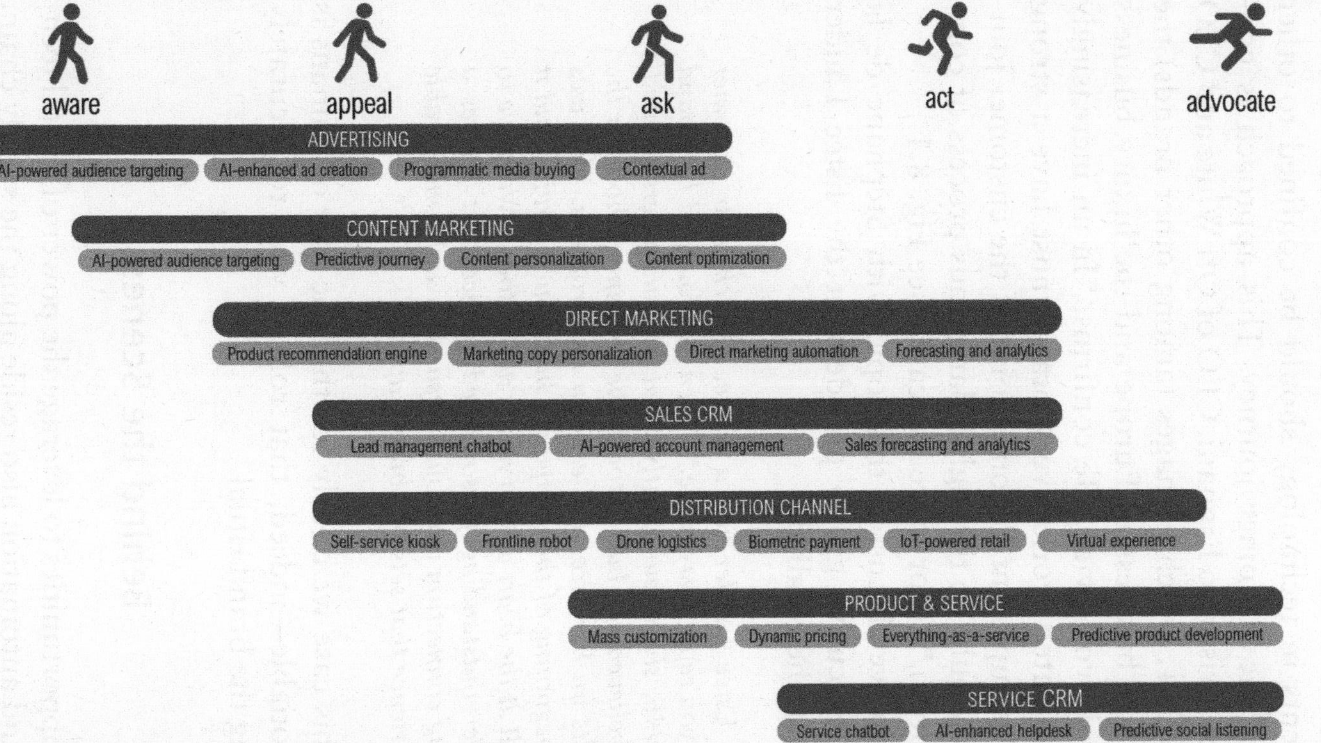

Fig. 8.1 Marketing-technology use cases in the new CX.
(Source: Kotler et al., Adapted from *Marketing* 5.0, 2021, p. 124, fig. 7.4)

just improve efficiency but also to free time that employees can devote to more rewarding activities. It's not surprising that Walmart is a pioneer in this field, employing a workforce of around 25,000 tech specialists, which is comparable to the total combined employee count of four prominent tech companies: Pinterest, Snap, Spotify, and Zoom.[6] The president and CEO Doug McMillon detailed to us how "there are opportunities to use automated storage and retrieval systems in ambient distribution centres, food-distribution centres, e-commerce fulfillment centres, and . . . market-fulfillment centres next to stores."[7] With the Market Fulfillment Centre (MFC)—a "compact, modular warehouse built within, or added to, a store," which Walmart first rolled out in late 2019—instead of being tasked with tracking down and fetching various items in storage, employees are able to enlist the help of Alphabot, whereby an "autonomous cart" delivers items to the employee, who then packages and completes the order. This solution is a win-win: Walmart is able to utilize its (perhaps less-visited) stores as fulfillment centres—which enables them to efficiently complete sales whether the customer shops online or in person.[8]

Amazon famously uses humans, robots, and advanced technology in its fulfillment centres—in part to improve efficiency, and in part to maintain safety, especially considering the weight of heavy pallets or the dangers of a complex, fast-moving conveyor system. (In fact, engineers keep watch from the safety of a multi-screen command centre. For more, check out Amazon's guided video-tour through a fulfillment centre.)[9] As for the efficiency angle, the *Harvard Business Review* article "What Robots Can Do for Retail" relates that "Amazon says robots have helped it store 40% more inventory in its centres." Not to be outdone by Walmart or Amazon, the Kroger Company, "America's largest grocery retailer," teamed up with Ocado, the grocery e-commerce innovator, to create Kroger Delivery customer fulfillment centres (CFC) that combine "vertical integration, machine learning, and robotics to provide an affordable, friendly, and fast fresh food delivery service."[10]

Not surprisingly, this revolution is already having an impact on the job market. Many jobs will likely be replaced by robots, new jobs will be created, and a lot of investments will be allocated to upskill and reskill the workforce. According to Goldman Sachs, "as many as 300 million full-time jobs around the world could be automated [and] 18% of work globally could be computerized, with the effects felt more deeply in advanced economies than [in] emerging markets."[11] The trade-off between creation and replacement is hard to predict, but we are optimistic that, if businesses follow the right guiding principles and the institutions play their role in regulating the application of emerging technologies, the pros will likely overcome the cons. (For more, see Part II.)

As for what we already know: high tech and high touch clearly offer different benefits and drawbacks, depending on the combination of the two elements, creating both great opportunities and complex challenges for retailers and consumer brands (see Table 8.1).

We can conclude that, in a post-digital world, a brand value proposition is a function of (1) the combination of high tech and high touch, (2) the characteristics of the market, (3) the experiential benchmarks that set the expectations of the audience, and (4) the traits of the customer

Table 8.1 The Pros and Cons of High Tech and High Touch.

	High Tech	High Touch
PROS	**Efficient**: Technology can automate and scale many tasks and processes.	**Emotional connection**: High touch enables a strong emotional connection between employees and customers.
	Consistent: Technology can remove human discretion and ensure a consistent experience across the various channels.	**Flexible**: Humans are excellent at coming up with creative solutions to unexpected problems.
	Personalized: Leveraging data, companies can deliver a personalized customer experience.	**Personalized**: A warm personal touch (even when informed by technology) can be a key differentiator for a business.
CONS	**Impersonal**: A lack of emotional connection can lead to customer complaints.	**Inefficient**: Service quality depends on individual employees and can't be standardized.
	Expensive: The cost of building and maintaining a high-tech ecosystem can be prohibitive.	**Inconsistent**: People can't continually deliver identical service.
	Complex: High-tech ecosystems require complex system integration and skilled people.	**Training**: Employees need to constantly be trained, upskilled, and reskilled.

personas that interact with the brand itself. Striking a balance between high tech and high touch can provide the best of both worlds and allow retailers and consumer brands to thrive.

Reflection Summary Questions

- As a customer, what are the touchpoints that you believe should remain "human"? In what cases would you be happy to interact with a robot or an AI?
- Where is your business positioned in the high-tech versus high-touch continuum?
- Which areas of your business should be informed by technology versus performed by a person—and vice versa?
- What is your strategy to create the best combination of the two approaches?

9

Shopping Malls Apocalypse?

Shopping malls have been part of the retail landscape for decades. For many they offer a safe hub where people can shop for everything they need, get a haircut, pick up or drop off items for the drycleaner, or simply hang out with family and friends—maybe sharing a meal or watch a movie together. Malls are often considered the connective tissue of local communities, especially when they're located far from urban areas.

But many malls, particularly in the US, have struggled to maintain their relevance in our high-tech era, largely because of changing consumer behaviour and the rise of e-commerce. In fact, although brick-and-mortar stores still account for the lion's share of consumer retail spending, many people today consider the idea of browsing in a giant mall obsolete—instead relying on digital channels to discover new products and services. Additionally, fewer people are inclined to concentrate all their shopping into one expedition to a more distant location, perhaps for reasons of having less time for errands in general—a trend that benefits smaller stores situated along work commutes.

Shopping malls in the US started as open-air affairs perhaps as early as 1922. Aside from some suburban malls from the late 1940s, it seems the two oldest "fully enclosed, indoor" malls opened in Wisconsin in 1955 and Minnesota in 1956. In the 1980s, the heyday of the large iconic shopping mall, there were 2,500 in the US. As of 2022, there are just 700—and by some estimates that number may dwindle down to less than 200 in the next decade. (Note we're referring to the largest malls; the total number of shopping *centres* is more like 115,000. Note, too, that figures vary from source to source depending on different variables.) To understand the economic magnitude of the shopping mall, consider that "in 1987 there were 30,000 malls accounting for over 50% of all retail dollars spent (about 676 billion dollars, 8% of the labour force, and 13% of our gross national product)."[1]

The model through which malls were developed is based on the so-called anchor tenant, a large retailer whose reputation drew in customers—who then partook of the smaller retailers clustered around the anchor magnet. However, the crisis of the sector, exacerbated by the long isolation period of the COVID pandemic, has sent some of these anchors into bankruptcy, triggering a vicious cycle. In some cases, malls are marred by empty hulls of once vibrant stores now advertising only a FOR LEASE sign. In other cases, the mall develops a sort of patchwork Frankenstein model. As *The Economist* reported in June 2022, those empty hulls that once were Macy's or JCPenney are in many locations being repurposed for schools, offices, cinemas, even health-care facilities—all of which "can make good use of large stores and malls because many hospitals were built . . . where there is little room to expand. Malls offer a lot of parking space . . . [and] in suburban areas malls are often well placed for aging populations that need more doctor's appointments [than they need] new shoes."[2]

Regional Differences

However, the decline of shopping malls is not uniform across all regions of the world. It's also subject to several different factors, including population density, digital maturity, climate, purchasing power, availability of modern delivery services, local retail market dynamics, legislation, and trade context. In much of Europe, where people have a stronger culture of city centres, high streets, and independent retailers, the decline is relatively less pronounced—in part because there are fewer malls to begin with. For every one mall in Europe there were nearly 10 in the US. RegioData reports that, "in most Western European cities, the shopping centre share reaches a maximum of 25%, while in CEE/SEE cities the value can easily be more than 50% of the total trading volume."[3] There are two notable exceptions: Scandinavia has a higher concentration of malls for reasons of both the weather and city centres being less retail-oriented; and Eastern Europe saw a high growth rate during its development phase following the breakdown of the communist system.

But in various emerging economies in South America, Southeast Asia, China, or the Middle East, malls are still prospering, since they play a key modernizing role. According to Alejandro Camino—CEO at Parque Arauco Perù, one of the largest commercial real estate developers in Latin America: "Many Latin American cities have poor infrastructure, poor delivery services, and few public spaces where people can hang out or go to enjoy an exhibition. Therefore a private, safe space like a shopping mall is a very important resource for people. If you also consider that there is still a barrier to placing orders online, you understand the importance of such a format."[4] Another reason why shopping malls are still relevant in some regions is the capability of mall stores to serve as a conduit with e-commerce—both fulfilling orders and accepting returns.

In many emerging economies the aforementioned modernizing effect of shopping malls has accelerated that development. For example, most of the malls in Asia have all been built in the last couple of decades. *The Economist* notes how, "until near the end of the 20th century, the region's monumental architecture was dominated by imposing projections of imperial, communist, or newly minted post-colonial state power," whereas today, "Asia's glass-and-concrete malls sucking city dwellers indoors mark a huge architectural and cultural break." Indeed, out of the world's largest malls, eight are in Asia. One notable attraction is the fact that, in some of these locales, malls offer escape from unbearable weather conditions, especially heat.[5] Based on our consulting experience, we've seen that China, Thailand, Philippines, Singapore, South Korea, and the United Arab Emirates have recently experienced a boom in mall development.

Of course, significant portions of Asia and Africa maintain the traditional retail formats, where street markets, bazaars, and mom-and-pop shops continue to dominate.

Beside the geographical peculiarities, we can argue that successful shopping malls in the post-digital era should extend their value proposition way beyond product distribution centres or places where people can casually browse. In fact, the most successful malls offer first-class entertainment, highly sought restaurants, and value-added services that are relevant for the local communities, including hosting meaningful events such as product launches, fashion shows, seasonal celebrations, live performances, workshops, festivals, children's activities, and so on. In our conversation, Camino of Parque Arauco Perù highlighted that commercial real estate developers should carefully cater the right mix of stores, services, and experiences to the taste of the place. "It's not just about filling spaces," he shared. "We need to carefully curate the whole experience, taking into consideration what people need and desire in each specific location." (We will return to this idea of retailers as curators in Chapter 17, "Be a Destination.")

Mixed-Use Developments

One challenger with the potential to mitigate or eliminate the effects of the trend described above is standard mixed-use development—a blend of commercial and residential real estate complemented by office space and useful services such as gyms and sport courts, food courts, even schools. This approach can play a significant role in stimulating the development of a remote community, especially in low-density countries. When well executed, these live-work-play environments have the potential to create efficient, virtually self-sustaining communities.

Consider the London, UK, development Canary Wharf, an extensive mixed-use environment with a self-sufficient enclave incorporating a shopping mall, offices, leisure facilities, and a school. In the course of just a few years this spot became one of the most prominent business districts in the world, housing multinational corporations, financial institutions, professional-services firms, and tech companies. The Canary Wharf Shopping Centre houses a wide range of retail outlets, including luxury brands, fashion retailers, department stores, speciality shops, and restaurants—with offerings suited to residents, workers, and visitors alike. The same can be said of the multiplex cinema, fitness centres, and art galleries. There is a primary school—Canary Wharf College—and University College London has installed its School of Management on the 50th floor of one of the Wharf's many towers. Finally, there are several high-rise residential buildings. Canary Wharf is not immune from the dynamics of the post-digital era, in particular the tendency toward e-commerce and working from home. (We can't help but wonder: might suburban malls benefit from the decline of the traditional five-day commute, since suburban residents thus spend more time outside the urban centre?) And the fact that the consequences of Brexit is triggering many financial institutions moving their offices out of the country poses an additional threat to the prosperity of the district. Time will tell whether a different mix of facilities and services in this new landscape will prove to be sustainable.

This is not the right place to discuss in depth the sociological implications of this dynamic, but it's important to mention that these developments often become artificial self-contained enclaves for privileged people—oases that are completely detached from the outside world, where sometimes people live in very different life conditions. Of course, this gap is more pronounced in emerging economies and poor countries.

Continuing with London's ever-changing retail landscape, a May 2022 *Financial Times* article begins with: "Along a short stretch of high street in Croydon, south London, it is possible to trace the collapse of British retail in less than 10 minutes." This is because, despite the Amazon-led successful foray into e-commerce—note that the guided video-tour through an Amazon fulfillment centre referenced in Chapter 8 was filmed in part in Birmingham, UK—"malls were still attracting serious interest from investors," including "French company Unibail-Rodamco, [which] bought Westfield, owner of shopping centres in London and New York, in late 2017 for $25 billion." Five years later, Unibail-Rodamco-Westfield [was] selling off billions of pounds worth of European malls to bring down its debt."[6]

Ultimately, in our post-digital world—where experiential benchmarks command stellar customer-experience standards, and digital literacy and accessibility continues to mature in many economies—shopping malls will need to figure out innovative ways to blend physical, digital, and virtual in order to attract, engage, and retain the foot-fall that sustained them for so long.

Reflection Summary Questions

- What could the future of shopping malls look like in a post-digital world?
- How can a company be strategic about the right combination of product, service, and experience?
- How can your company get the most out of the shopping mall ecosystem?
- How are people going to shop in the future, considering the opportunities offered by digital and virtual?
- Will mixed-use developments become a dominant trend in a world where people tend to work remotely more than before?

10

The Perfect Storm

We opened Part I emphasizing the risks of both running backwards and allowing our experience of the past to guide our decisions about a fast-approaching future. We have argued that the world changes faster than our companies and institutions can adapt, and humans are more prone to defend the status quo than to forge unexplored paths outside their comfort zone. Therefore, the majority of established companies struggle to maintain their position vis-à-vis new-generation competitors and emerging technologies. Over the course of these chapters, we've focused on some of the most relevant challenges that retailers and brands currently face. But additional challenging elements need to be added to the discussion, including the macroeconomic headwinds that are impacting the retail industry from the outside in, and the inside-out dynamics that interact with those driving forces. In the next pages we will turn to these angles, although with a caveat: since the complexity of the global economy, combined with the disruption the retail industry is experiencing, could never be covered in one book, we offer a curated exploration.

The title of this final chapter of Part I came from a series of conversations we had in May 2023 with a flagship consumer brand Global Retail Director, who asked to remain anonymous. He explained that many retailers are today dealing with the perfect storm that has resulted from a convergence of unfavourable conditions, which we lay out here:

- the spiral of constantly rising operational costs
- the debt many retailers accumulated both before and during the COVID-19 pandemic

- the toxic cocktail of recession plus the high interest rates that many economies face
- the supply chain's disruption caused by lockdowns and wars
- a work environment where more and more employees work from home at least part time and
- a generalized lack of personnel in the retail world due to more attractive alternatives, lower than average salaries, and long working hours.

Rising operational costs are the result of some endogenous factors—such as risk-averse culture and siloed organizational structures—that led to the postponement of many strategic decisions that have become long overdue. For example, now that once-emerging technologies are an integral part of the competitive advantage of best-in-class players—the risk-averse retailers need to fork out high investment costs just to catch up. Additional endogenous factors include the chronic suboptimal use of available consumer data; limited digital knowledge, skills, and capabilities; and a generally scarce collaboration culture.

There are also exogenous variables to be factored in. The most important is probably the exponential growth of digitally native players who have fully embraced digital transformation from a technological, operational, and cultural point of view. Take Amazon for example. The annual budget they allocated on R&D for 2022 was $73.213 billion, a 30.62% increase from 2021 ($56.052 billion), which was a 31.15% increase from 2020 ($42.74 billion), which had increased 18.95% from 2019.[1] How many companies in the world can compete against this muscular power?

Among the external forces, a predominant role has also been played by an impressive series of black swans (as per the concept popularized by Nassim Nicholas Taleb: rare events that are virtually impossible to predict or foresee[2]) that have radically destabilized the global economic environment, including the attack on the Twin Towers in 2001, the global financial crisis in 2008, Brexit's referendum in 2016, and the COVID-19 pandemic. But there is another exogenous dynamic that has continually come up during our conversations with retail and brand's executives: the pressure inflicted by commercial landlords, especially for prime locations. In fact, many of the most sought-after retail locations on the high streets of the world's commercial capitals are owned by large real estate developers or private equity firms who tend to apply, in the words of our anonymous interlocutor, "astronomical rates that are far from being sustainable for a brick-and-mortar flagship store." These owners' business model is built on the assumption that they will be able to pay back the debt they incurred to acquire a property with the future rent paid by the tenant—and they often use the property itself to back the debt.[3] Due to the nature of this model, such companies must aim to maximize their returns on investment no matter what, and are driven by short-term financial results. As a consequence, the exorbitant rental rates of many of the top sites inevitably create significant burden to retailers. This is even more painful in a mature e-commerce world where ever-changing consumer preferences force companies to constantly refresh their value proposition.

One last dynamic that's worth mentioning is the fact that, for the first time in human history, there are five generations living, working, and consuming at the same time—Generation Z (born between 2001 and 2020); millennials (born between 1981 and 2000); Generation X (born between 1965 and 1980); Baby Boomers (born between 1946 and 1964); and the Silent Generation (born between 1925 and 1945). Inevitably, this coexistence of people with very different backgrounds and ambitions creates additional turbulence in the effort to understand customer personas and map the customer journey. For example, it is estimated that millennials and GenZ will make approximately 75% of the luxury spend by 2026.[4] Brands must figure out new ways to engage with these segments, because they conceive "luxury" in a less materialistic way, are driven by a different set of values and, in many cases, have different priorities compared to previous generations—including social and environmental sustainability, inclusiveness, equality, and gender fluidity. High-end product resale and rental are also relevant options for this cohort, which tends to research and engage with brands predominantly online and is more prone to embrace virtual technologies and augmented reality during the customer journey. Another example is the business opportunities for retailers and brands connected to a healthier and wealthier Silent Generation—ranging from mobility aids, health-care products, and personalized wellness solutions to tailored travel packages, guided tours, senior-friendly accommodations, and entertainment options.

Where Do We Go from Here?

And here is the perfect storm—an articulated mix of impossible-to-control variables that are making the life of retailers and consumer brands a rollercoaster. As a result, on the one hand we have managers complaining about the strong pressure to deliver short-term results and demonstrate the ROI of every initiative before they have the chance to show the real potential of a project. And on the other, we have shareholders, company owners, and CEOs complaining about an ill-prepared workforce that struggles to compete with the digitally native dynamic competitors.

Decades of managerial and consulting experience have taught us that both positions are actually valid. When we're in the middle of a storm we can't help but anxiously focus on—or obsess over—all performance indicators and metrics. It's in our DNA: amid instability, humans cling to what proved effective in the past—everything that is reassuring and reduces uncertainty. When we fear our lives/livelihoods are in danger, we're less inclined to experiment and patiently wait for long-term results. Additionally, when a paradigm shift occurs, it's natural that we would feel out of place and uncertain.

As we have observed earlier in the book, we need to cut company executives some slack: the majority of them were hired for a different economic reality, selected for their particular leading style, and evaluated on the basis of their previous performances; the old model was "command and control" no matter what, and there was very limited space for leaders who understand the importance of including soft skills in the mix. And, given the magnitude of the paradigm shift we're in the midst of, their past experience might not only be less relevant—in some cases it's counterproductive, especially if it's eschewed the digital innovation of the last few decades. But the reality is that the most dangerous thing one can do in this turbulent phase is to stand still, feverishly iterating known patterns. (We will come back to this aspect later in the book.)

Considering the risk of being the first to face obsolescence, how could such leadership teams foster the necessary conditions for the radical change that's currently needed in the majority of established companies? How can shareholders pretend that the leadership they appointed for a very different world will be able to guide their companies in a post-digital world? How can managers effectively persuade shareholders to make significant investments in people and technology during a sluggish economy? How can we reverse-engineer the *leveraged* dynamic that has shifted the balance of power toward real estate developers and private equity firms—making the retail equation seemingly impossible for the brands interested in prime locations?

In Part II, we outline a comprehensive framework of ten guiding principles that we firmly believe will enable business leaders and managers to steer their ship in the right direction amid the winds of change.

Part II

The 10 BEs of Post-Digital Retail

> Change is the only constant.
>
> —Heraclitus, ancient Greek pre-Socratic philosopher, active around 500 BCE

By the late 1980s it had become clear that the economic conventions favoured by policymakers for three decades—including liberalized trade, maximum efficiency, and the supposed superiority of open markets—could not protect against disruptions and black swans. Policymakers are now looking to secure supply chains and prioritize trusted partners for trade relationships, even when doing so is somewhat less efficient. However, the path forward remains unclear, since elements of the previous economic orthodoxy are still in the process of being set aside.

Given the clear evidence that many elements of the previous status quo are no longer viable, with this section we hope to inspire world business leaders in the search for a new path forward.

In particular, we outline a strategic framework built upon 10 guiding principles that we believe can serve as compass and radar to navigate the complexity and uncertainty of the post-digital era. We developed these principles from our hundreds of conversations with executives from different industries and countries. And while much of them are widely applicable, there are a few key factors to consider when using the framework for your purposes:

- Socio-cultural nuances: Different regions and cultures have unique consumer behaviours, preferences, and market dynamics. These nuances also play a role when it comes to socio-cultural values and environmental concerns. So it is crucial to align the framework with local sensibilities and norms.
- Economic factors: Economic conditions, purchasing power, and market maturity vary across regions. Hence, the competitive landscape is populated by different players and is influenced by different market dynamics. And so it's essential to tailor our framework by gathering insights and mapping your market environment. Adjust your retail strategies to align with your local economic factors, competitive landscape, and consumer spending patterns.
- Technological infrastructure: The level of digital literacy, technological advancement, and infrastructure differs across regions. So organizations must consider the availability of technology solutions while tailoring the framework to their needs.
- Regulatory environment: Since market dynamics are influenced by various regulations, it will be important to fine-tune the framework to comply with local laws and regulations so as to ensure sustainable and compliant operations.

The 10 "BEs" that we recommend to guide retailers and brands in a post-digital world are divided into two sub-groups.

The first three are "overarching" because they apply to the mental posture that every business leader and manager would be wise to embrace in a BANI world.

Be Humbitious: "Humbitious" is a portmanteau of the words "humble" and "ambitious."[1] Humbitious leaders value vulnerability, recognize the value of collaboration, and possess the humility to acknowledge their limitations and learn from others. At the same time, they maintain a strong ambition to set goals, inspire others, pursue personal and professional growth, and make a positive impact on the world. They are convinced that pure humility may limit bold plans, while pure ambition may lead to hubris.

Be Purposeful: In an ever-changing complex world, both clarifying and expressing the true purpose of your company and its role in the world offers a unique opportunity to build resilience, differentiate from competitors, foster stakeholder trust, nurture brand reputation, and attract, engage, and retain talent.

Be Ambidextrous: The term "organizational ambidexterity" was coined by Charles O'Reilly and Michael Tushman.[2] Inspired by the concept, we argue that business leaders and managers, especially in established businesses, should be able to effectively integrate two seemingly contradictory approaches: exploration and exploitation.

The following seven principles focus on more specific focal areas and outline the optimal path for retailers and consumer brand leaders to achieve success.

Be Onlife: Coined by Professor Luciano Floridi,[3] the "onlife" concept highlights the blurring boundaries between digital and physical worlds. It recognizes that our online activities and digital footprint are intertwined with our offline experiences, relations, and behaviours. In the chapter, we argue that we should add a third variable to the equation, since virtual touchpoints are going to gain a lot of attention in the next few years, opening the way for a 3D customer journey.

Be Personal: Individuals are by definition attracted by personalization. It makes us feel unique and valuable. From a business standpoint, personalization allows companies to increase efficiency and effectiveness while also maximizing the likelihood of offering products, services, and experiences that are highly relevant for the users. Leveraging technology in this direction can be a game-changer, but the decisions to be made require a thorough assessment and consideration of complex trade-offs.

Be Human: While technology and automation are increasingly more pervasive, humans still play crucial roles that cannot be fully replaced by machines. Moving forward, understanding which activities should be automated or digitized versus which should be performed by humans will determine the unique proposition of a company—as well as create the conditions for its competitive advantage. Given the multitude of variables involved—including geography, industry, market conditions, digital maturity, and local culture—there is no single approach that fits all situations. Finding the right balance will require thoughtful consideration and case-by-case evaluation.

Be a Destination: The post-digital world is characterized by a fragmentation of touchpoints, and we are constantly inundated with stimuli urging us to try new products, services, and experiences. In this saturated environment there is limited space for merely transactional have-to-go touchpoints. And so it is crucial for brick-and-mortar stores, e-commerce websites, content platforms, social networks, and all other touchpoints to be strategically designed and curated to captivate and engage people—and compel them to return.

Be Exponential: This concept is inspired by the book *Exponential Organizations* by Salim Ismail, Michael S. Malone, and Yuri van Geest.[4] This type of organization leverages exponential technologies and strategies to achieve rapid growth and outperform traditional linear competitors. Exponential organizations are often structured in a decentralized way, relying on networks, platforms, and ecosystems. They leverage external resources to extend their capabilities and access a wide range of expertise.

Be Invisible: While technology is more ubiquitous with each passing day, it should always be seen as a means to an end; it should seamlessly integrate into our lives and experiences without drawing unnecessary attention to itself. Invisible technology is intuitive, effortless to use, and conducive to our daily routines.

Be Loyal: Companies should prioritize and act in the best interests of those invested in their success. This means their loyalty should extend beyond their shareholders to also include their stakeholders and customers. Every single link in the value chain includes direct and indirect third parties that should be not only taken into account, but also deserve loyalty. Note, since this vision is relatively new, it might require a painful restructuring of the P&L, especially for legacy firms.

For each of the 10 principles we will present the concept, detail the background thinking, reflect on its applicability, and analyze both desired outcomes and potential unintended consequences. We have discussed elements of the 10 BEs with hundreds of top managers and thought leaders, and have woven their perspectives, real-world experiences, and useful examples into the chapters.

Again, we encourage you to adapt the framework to your needs, applying its guiding principles to your specific business reality. We also hope you will share your feedback with us on our website (redefiningretail@giuseppestigliano.com). We will later elaborate on the comments we receive and circulate the feedback with the community to foster knowledge and nurture the debate.

Enjoy the journey!

11

Be Humbitious

As noted earlier, the term "humbition" fuses humility and ambition in promoting the value of balancing a humble mindset, which is indispensable when navigating unexplored paths, and a strong drive for success, which is a vital antidote to impervious arrogance.[1]

Being a humbitious leader means recognizing that ambition alone can lead to a "hubris syndrome." The term "hubris," which derives from Greek mythology, encapsulates the overconfidence that can lead individuals to their downfall. It's today associated with a psychological and behavioural condition characterized by excessive self-confidence and the tendency to act on confirmation biases, which in turn can perpetuate arrogance and a sense of invincibility. As a result, leaders develop an "inflated ego" and "lose touch with the people we lead, the culture we are a part of, and ultimately our clients and stakeholders."[2] This view is confirmed by Paolo Gallo, keynote speaker, author, and coach who explains: "Leaders with hubris are obsessed with visibility. Their image counts more than everything. They usually appoint a director of communication who is totally focused on promoting the persona, their image, their presence on social media more than the company they are supposed to represent. Humble leaders don't care about their visibility, as they are focused on credibility, impact, and reputation."[3]

But one can avoid that perilous path by embracing humbitiousness, which encourages leaders to maintain a grounded perspective, acknowledge their limits, share their vulnerability, ask for help, and treat others with respect and empathy. This attitude typically paves the way for a positive, equal, inclusive, and diverse work environment—where collaboration and collective success are valued and rewarded, and psychological safety is the norm. For example, consider Microsoft executive chairman and CEO Satya Nadella, who is widely recognized for his humble and inclusive leadership style and his business acumen, such as: "Success can cause people to unlearn the habits that made them successful in the first place. Stay grounded. Be a learner, not a know-it-all."[4]

Humbitious leaders typically welcome feedback and constructive criticism from anyone, regardless of seniority or status. They are receptive to new ideas and diverse perspectives, and encourage personal development. Since this mindset helps everyone in an organization feel both empowered to explore innovative ideas and comfortable to take calculated risks, humbitious leaders foster adaptability and the ability to navigate uncharted waters. By leading with humbition, leaders also create a sense of purpose in creating a better future for the company, its employees, and society at large. What's more, while the "ambition" angle of this mindset is vital when an organization needs to reinvent itself amid new market conditions, the "humility" angle helps in accepting setbacks, learning from failures, and trying again. Fully embracing humbition translates into a constructive, growth-oriented mindset that fosters a culture of continuous improvement.

In her *Wall Street Journal* article "The Best Bosses Are Humble Bosses," Sue Shellenbarger reports that Patagonia, the American retailer of outdoor recreation wear known for its vision regarding sustainability, "begins scrutinizing job applicants for humility as soon as they walk through the door for interviews"—to the extent that the way a candidate behaves with front-desk employees can be a deal breaker.[5]

In his 1977 book *Servant Leadership*, Robert K. Greenleaf, a retired AT&T executive, explains how, to his mind, leaders of this ilk are "the servant as leader," since they prioritize the needs and development of the people they lead from the mindset that this approach unlocks the success of the organization—as well as their own success. Rather than exerting their power, they share it. As Vaneet Kashyap and Santosh Rangnekar write in *Review of Managerial Science,* "Instead of the people working to serve the leader, the leader exists to serve the people." Humbitious leaders are de facto servant leaders who are humble enough to admit that they can benefit from the ideas, insights, experience, skills, and expertise of anyone. However, note that, as Dan Cable shares in the *Harvard Business Review,* "humility and servant leadership do not imply that leaders have low self-esteem, or take on an attitude of servility. Instead, servant leadership emphasizes that the responsibility of a leader is to increase the ownership, autonomy, and responsibility of followers—to encourage them to think for themselves and try out their own ideas."[6]

The American multinational food, snack, and beverage corporation PepsiCo seems to pay this approach a lot of attention. Indra Nooyi, CEO from 2006 to 2018, advocated a leadership philosophy to empower employees and make them feel safe. At the same time, she recognizes the importance of being a role model: "As a leader, I am tough on myself and I raise the standard for everybody; however, I am very caring because I want people to excel at what they are doing so that they can aspire to be me in the future."[7] And Mauro Porcini, senior vice president and chief design officer at PepsiCo, extends the concept, emphasizing that in this historic moment leaders should be even more human-centric: "The starting point, the cultural level in every company, needs to be the needs and wants of human beings and, therefore, the needs of our planet, our society, and of everything else that [matters to us] as human beings. This is the starting point, and I think it's the biggest challenge right now because we're in a moment of transition, and many companies are not yet understanding how important it is to focus on this."[8]

To become humbitious leaders, we need to ask ourselves several questions: Are we confident enough to remain humble? Are we humble enough to serve the people we lead and to admit to them, our superiors, and ourselves that we don't have all the answers? Are we modest enough to accept that we need their help to deal with the complexity of today's world? Are we willing to subordinate our personal ambitions to the success of the people around us?

Different Leaders for Different Corporate Cultures

So, is humbition the best possible leadership side in a post-digital turbulent world? If humility is so important, why is it a relatively rare trait in modern business, and why are so many arrogant leaders still so successful and celebrated?

To answer this question, we need to acknowledge that traditional leadership models—derived from the military and from factory operations—have often emphasized and celebrated attributes such as assertiveness, decisiveness, and a strong sense of authority. As a consequence, humility has traditionally been seen as a sign of weakness and insecurity. Also, in many corporate cultures there is a strong pressure to deliver ambitious targets and meet shareholders' high expectations—which can lead to showcasing one's own achievements while downplaying the contributions of others. Furthermore, it might be challenging for experienced managers to admit that the very qualities instrumental to their past success may not necessarily be helpful to their future success; this is because people tend to defend the world they contributed to build. As we saw in Chapter 10, the majority of leaders and managers who are in charge today were hired for a different economic reality. But, given the magnitude of the shift we are going through, the experience of current leaders might not only be less relevant—in some cases it's even counterproductive. For more, see the sidebar.

How Managerial Bias Can Hold Back an Organization

1. Managers who have spent decades in traditional brick-and-mortar retail might be hesitant to fully embrace digital transformation strategies—as well as underestimate the potential of e-commerce and online platforms. Those who are accustomed to traditional marketing methods might overlook emerging digital marketing channels—limiting the company's reach to newer customer segments.
2. Seasoned managers might assume that only a certain type of person would make an ideal employee—not realizing that the broader experience of a diverse workforce can be the trick to remaining competitive.
3. Managers accustomed to overseeing in-person teams might struggle with fully trusting and effectively managing remote workers—leading to reduced collaboration and fewer candidates.

4. Managers with extensive experience may rely more on their intuition and established practices rather than embracing data-driven decision-making—potentially missing out on more accurate insights.
5. Managers used to traditional hierarchical structures might resist adopting agile methodologies—hindering the organization's ability to quickly adapt to changing market conditions.
6. Managers who don't focus on sustainability might downplay the importance of ESG (environmental, social, and governance) practices—missing opportunities to align with changing consumer preferences.

In all fairness, although we strongly advocate for leaders and managers to be humbitious, and we believe that top-down, know-it-all, authoritative, command-and-control leadership philosophies are anachronistic in a world dominated by novelty and change, it is important to acknowledge that sometimes a more directive approach can still be effective. In other words, there can be critical situations, such as those that call for quick decision-making, in which the balance between the humility and ambition must tilt toward the latter—at least until harmony is (re)established.

For example, if a company is in the middle of a transition period, or appears to be foundering in some way, it might be best for the person at the helm to assert a more decisive approach to reassure all stakeholders, (re)gain everyone's trust, and then steer the ship in the right direction. Take Sergio Marchionne, for instance. He served as the CEO of Fiat Chrysler Automobiles (FCA) from 2004 until his passing in 2018. When he took the driver's seat, the company was on the brink of bankruptcy, but he put in place a turnaround strategy that led to the merger of

Fiat and Chrysler—and a revitalization of the business. He was known for his hands-on approach and for creating a performance-oriented culture that focused on efficiency, productivity, and profitability. His many bold moves to restructure the company were instrumental in its financial recovery and subsequent success. Was Marchionne a humbitious leader? Definitely not. As one of his former directors reports (who asked to remain anonymous) described him to us: "Although he was a fan of cross-functional teamwork, Sergio was probably the antithesis of humility. In his case the balance was 100% toward ambition. He was smart, driven, determined, workaholic, and notoriously brusque. But he was exactly what the company needed at that time. Sometimes an organization needs an electroshock to resurrect. And in those situations, you've got to be a bulldozer."

Another circumstance where the humbitious approach might not be (quite) the perfect fit is when maintaining rigorous organizational standards is of utmost importance. For instance, if a start-up needs to demonstrate to investors the viability, profitability, and scalability of its business model. Or when a well-established organization embarks on a realignment process and needs to comply with a specific roadmap. In truth, at most junctures when enforced compliance and strictly controlled metrics are called for, the leadership team may be legitimately tempted to shift toward a more authoritative approach. The trouble is, the structural volatility of the post-digital world makes it virtually impossible to see a linear cause-effect relationship. In fact, to achieve the sought-after economies of scale, scope, and learning that typically allow organizations to build standard metrics and then maximize efficiency and effectiveness, the *conditio sine qua non* is stability. How can you obtain rigorous organizational standards in a complex world where standards are constantly redefined?

* * *

As previously noted, the most appropriate leadership style at any particular time and place varies depending on contextual factors, including macroeconomic conditions, market trends, competitive landscape in the specific sector, organizational size and culture, and so on. Interestingly, the different stages in which a company or organization can find itself also play a crucial role. It would be a mistake for leaders dealing with a new challenge to simply rely on the skills and strategies that worked for them in the past. Instead, they should start by gaining a deep understanding of the current situation and then adapt accordingly. In some cases, it might even lead them to realize they aren't the best fit for that particular context.

To aid in precisely assessing the situation and determining whether a leader possesses the apt skills to tackle existing challenges, Michael D. Watkins, the author of *The First 90 Days: Proven Strategies for Getting Up to Speed Faster and Smarter*, devised the S.T.A.R.S. framework. Each letter in the acronym corresponds to a distinct phase in an organization's life:

S for Start-up: This stage is relevant when stepping into a leadership role for a new venture or when initiating a fresh initiative within an organization.

T for Turnaround: The turnaround stage comes into play when an organization is in crisis or confronting issues demanding significant corrective actions. (See the FCA situation described above.)

A for Accelerate Growth: This stage revolves around amplifying the organization's growth trajectory, often by expanding successful initiatives and broadening market presence. This happens, for example, when a company evolves from start-up to scale-up once it has validated the business model and identified recurring revenue streams.

R for Realignment: Realignment involves fine-tuning the organization's value proposition to remain in sync with evolving market dynamics or internal shifts.

S for Sustain Success: This stage revolves around sustaining the organization's achievements, streamlined operations, and ongoing innovation.[9]

Each stage requires different leadership styles, and it's impossible to identify the "right" one per se. Nonetheless, our work with companies all over the world suggests that, in a fast-changing, ever-evolving market reality, retailer and brand leaders must accept that what made their success in the past is not necessarily what will make their success in the future. They must be humbly open to constantly reinventing themselves, learning from experience, valuing other's opinions, and actively seeking constructive critics. This is why the advice of being humbitious is the first overarching guiding principle for leaders and managers who want to navigate the complexity of the post-digital world.

Reflection Summary Questions

- What kind of business leader are you?
- Which leadership style is more appropriate to the organization you belong to? Does that style suit the internal culture?

- Are you prepared to question yourself? Is it possible that some of the skills instrumental to your past success won't lead to future success?
- Do you have the confidence to fuse humility with ambition while exploring the uncharted territories of a post-digital world?

12

Be Purposeful

As we highlighted in Chapter 2, "purpose" is an abused word these days. The growing importance of the concept applies to personal as well as professional lives—despite the traditional business modus operandi to prioritize shareholders' profit over anything else. The concept of "people before profit" was anathema to Nobel-laureate economist Milton Friedman, who was figuratively crowned for saying, back in 1970, that corporate social responsibility is a "'fundamentally subversive doctrine' in a free society. . . . [T]here is one and only one social responsibility of business—to use its resources and engage in activities designed to increase its profits so long as it stays within the rules of the game, which is to say, engages in open and free competition without deception or fraud."[1] In other words, according to this view, there is no such thing as corporate social responsibility, as the only responsibility of a company is toward its shareholders and consists in maximizing their return on investment (a.k.a. profit). Allocating money on a social cause wouldn't be in the interest of shareholders as it would reduce their profit.

However, today it is widely accepted that any business has a responsibility to go beyond serving the interest of just the owners. (Indeed, *Fortune* magazine published an article on September 13, 2020, titled: "50 years later, Milton Friedman's shareholder doctrine is dead."[2]) Many believe companies should strive to create value for their customers, invest in their employees, maintain fair and ethical relationships with partners and suppliers, and contribute to the well-being of the local communities in which they operate—as well as to the well-being of society at large. This holistic approach allows a business to create a positive impact that extends beyond its financial success. The social responsibility of a company has transformed from a mere option to a critical business opportunity as a consequence of a world characterized by deeper social consciousness, a stronger environmental commitment, and a dedication to equality, diversity, inclusion, and human rights in general. Both workers and consumers expect organizations to actively demonstrate their commitment to making a positive difference in the world. And this commitment will pave the way for what is a fundamental bargaining chip in a turbulent and uncertain context—trust. In fact, according to the Salesforce Research *State of the Connected Customer* report, "66% of customers have stopped buying from a company whose values didn't align with theirs"—with four of the top five issues being treatment of employees, environmental practices, actions on economic injustices, and actions on racial injustices—up from 62% in 2020.[3] As we will see, advocates of this approach are convinced: it's not only compatible with the generation of profit for the shareholders; in the medium-to-long term, it can even have a multiplier effect.

We've argued in Chapter 2 that the purpose of an organization is a combination of powerful elements, such as the very reason a company exists, what it stands for, how it contributes to social good, why employees should be proud to work for it, what would motivate suppliers to favour this company over others, and why customers should emotionally connect with its brand, choosing its value proposition from among many possible alternatives. In the words of Javier Quiñones, president and chief sustainability officer of IKEA US: "Being a purpose-led brand always starts with the 'why' behind what we are doing. People will not only buy from but also buy into brands that stand up for their values." In other words, as we have stated elsewhere: "A good company offers excellent products and services. A great company also offers excellent products and services but also strives to make the world a better place."[4] If this purpose is appreciated and valued by customers, then the company will be seen as a leader and will likely prosper.

The authors of the Monitor Deloitte report *The Purpose Premium: Why a Purpose-Driven Strategy Is Good for Business* point out that there should be a clear correlation between what a business does and its ability to provide the world with concrete solutions: "A company's purpose is the role it serves in society connected to long-term value, including the differentiated needs it addresses for all its stakeholders. Business leaders can protect their company's future success by adopting strategies to solve the problems of people and planet profitably—and not profit from causing such problems."[5]

One of the most emblematic case studies in this regard is the American retailer Patagonia, which operates stores in more than 10 countries globally. The company and its founder are a living example of the philosophy described above. Patagonia.com proclaims: "the best product is useful, versatile, long-lasting, repairable, and recyclable." Their ideal is "to make products that give back to the Earth as much as they take." Chouinard became a "reluctant" billionaire thanks to the success of the brand he founded in 1973 to provide fellow climbers with the best active wear. True to form, in 2022, "on the eve of [their] 50th anniversary,"[6] Chouinard surprised the world by giving the $3 billion company to a trust and nonprofit that will use future profits (of about $1 million per year) to help fight climate change. In describing his rationale, the 83-year-old founder and CEO said: "We will influence a new form of capitalism that doesn't end up with a few rich people and a bunch of poor people."[7]

In this chapter, we will further explore the concept of purpose and consider both the opportunities and implications it has for retailers and brands.

The Benefits of Being Purposeful

In principle, when a company is purposeful—when it "[does] well by doing good," advice attributed to Benjamin Franklin—there are multiple positive effects, including the potential of creating a meaningful legacy. For example:

Focus: A clear purpose helps align and focus the efforts of everyone within an organization. Purpose provides a shared sense of meaning that helps to naturally align all decisions, preventing the company from taking false steps.

Engagement: A strong purpose stimulates a sense of belonging within an organization, fostering engagement and motivation. The more stakeholders are motivated by this purpose, the more likely they are to be committed, enthusiastic, and proactive in their respective roles.

Trust: In a BANI world, trust is the most important bargaining chip between people (all stakeholders) and organizations. The trust that can derive from shared purpose can cement relations, enhance reputation, and create competitive advantage.

Talent: In an ever-changing world, the ability to attract and retain talent is more crucial than ever. Crafting the right purpose positions a company to attract those who share the same values.

LOYALTY: When customers identify with a company's purpose and believe what it stands for, they are more likely to be loyal and even advocate the brand.

SUSTAINABILITY: In a transient world, purpose-driven retailers and brands are more inclined to have long-term perspective—which can maintain their relevance and sustain their business model.

To be purposeful is to strive to create a positive and meaningful impact on society—whether directly, through its products and services; or via environmental sustainability efforts, social initiatives, or contributions to local communities. To be purposeful is also to prioritize the well-being of employees, foster a supportive work culture, provide equal opportunities, promote work-life balance, and ensure fair practices. This mindset applies to broader stakeholder relationships as well (investors, suppliers, customers, employers, local communities) in the fostering of mutually beneficial partnerships. In operations work, being purposeful calls for transparency, integrity, ethical standards, responsible sourcing and supply-chain management, and fair-trade practices—in addition to honest marketing communications and accountability for the company's actions.

It's important to highlight that we are not only referring to the practice of compensating, offsetting, or in the most virtuous cases limiting one's negative environmental, economic, and social impact. This is certainly a very good start, but long-term benefit involves more than just compensating for, or reducing, the negative consequences of the current model. We must also move decisively toward a complete overhaul of this model in search of a new scenario in which all phases are truly sustainable. Metaphorically speaking, this is like refraining from buying "indulgences" (the Roman Catholic practice of receiving forgiveness for a sin in exchange for a monetary donation), to a complete change of behaviour, with the goal of no longer sinning.

Michael Braungart and William McDonough cowrote a book that proposes changing the dominant model, cradle to grave, to a circular model: *Cradle to Cradle: Remaking the Way We Make Things*. They posit that if we can transition from a linear process to a circular one, we could oversee sustainable management of all stages—conception, production, distribution, and consumption—with the ambition of making the entire process a zero-sum game, where all waste is reused as technical or biological fuel to power other processes. Similarly, an economic system can be defined as circular when products and services are marketed in a closed circuit, which triggers a virtuous circle that potentially eliminates both waste and the passive disposal of waste.

This viewpoint strongly aligns with the perspective put forth by Michael Porter and Mark Kramer in their influential *Harvard Business Review* article "Creating Shared Value: How to Reinvent Capitalism and Unleash a Wave of Innovation and Growth." Porter and Kramer contend that companies must move away from solely pursuing value creation for shareholders and instead actively strive for the systematic generation of shared value across the entire value chain. This includes considering the well-being of employees, suppliers, business partners, external collaborators, and customers—as well as broader societal and environmental concerns. In summary, companies should actively pursue shared value opportunities so as to harmonize social and environmental progress with financial prosperity.[8]

A Difficult Harmony

This seems very clear in theory, and numerous entrepreneurs and business leaders claim that this harmony is effectively achievable. But in almost every conversation we had with shareholders, entrepreneurs, and managers all over the world, we got to a point where they said something like: "Taking for granted that everything you have described in this guiding principle is paramount, how can I contemplate all those variables while also generating profit margin in the short term?" The underlying assumption is that if a company has been built on a different basis, often in a different market reality, the structure of its P&L can't absorb all the investments required to embrace all the legitimate requests of today's society. And at the same time the incremental demand pushed by conscious customers wouldn't be sufficient to pay back the investments required to change the modus operandi.

The business community appears to be aligned on the fact that being purposeful is a concrete opportunity to realign the business vision in the medium to long term. However, our experience suggests that restructuring companies' operations to prioritize shared value creation can yield significant short-term impacts. And this is obviously perceived as a big issue considering that most organizational leaders are typically evaluated on short-term performance indicators. Put yourself in the shoes of a CEO of an established retailer or consumer brand currently in the process of finalizing budget allocation for the upcoming year. With limited resources at your disposal, you are faced with a critical decision: invest funds in an operational transformation to achieve carbon neutrality within five years, or hire additional sales people who are highly likely to generate incremental revenue and profit. Opting for the latter would please shareholders and probably result in higher bonuses for you and the management team, and the achievement will potentially have a relevant impact on your career. But, this sunny outcome would come at the expense of pursuing carbon neutrality. This hypothetical scenario captures a dilemma that many executives face every day—which just underscores the importance of aligning the organization's vision and purpose with shareholders' expectations and management's incentive structure. Policymakers play a key role in this scenario as well, since leaving the markets to regulate themselves has been only partially effective. In fact, unless all these elements harmoniously converge, the transition toward more purpose-driven businesses will require the initiative of inspired individuals—in both figuring out how to make it work and being willing to sacrifice profit. For this vision to become standard practice, singular guidance is highly needed—such as could be enforced by governments and international bodies.

How can we reconcile the pursuit of profit with the necessity of integrating ESG (environmental, social, and governance) priorities? What is the right balance between "value" and "values"? How can a business be both profitable and purposeful?

It's not an exaggeration to say this topic is decisively top of mind for all companies these days. *The Economist* has calculated that the number of times S&P 500 companies have used the term "ESG" in quarterly earning calls skyrocketed from 2020 onward.[9] But for all the discussion, there is no simple answer to these questions, nor a clear roadmap on how to proceed. As noted earlier, the fact that there are socio-cultural, economic, technological, and regulatory variables at play makes the search for a global standard solution even more complex. In fact, although there are guidelines, such as the UN's 17 Sustainable Development Goals,[10] retailers and brands are wary of investing in a specific direction. If national, regional (such as, EU versus US standards), and global regulations are not aligned—as can happen—doubling down on one standard could risk wasting resources, breaching local regulations, incurring fines, and tarnishing the brand's image. Then again, an image can be tarnished if a company is found guilty of "greenwashing," when the claim of planet-saving pursuits proves to be just window dressing. Cynics would say every brand can find a way to make ESG claims appear virtuous.

This silo effect is a double-edged sword. The absence of global standards and certifications discourages and disincentivizes retailers and brands to take action, slowing down their efforts to become more purposeful. Meanwhile, the seeming business-as-usual mentality creates confusion and disenchantment in public opinion, which becomes increasingly skeptical about the ability to conciliate profit and purpose.

Toward a Common Standard

Despite the lack of standardized norms, the growing number of virtuous companies is raising the bar for the market, continually pushing the boundaries of what is considered unacceptable practices. A valuable method of identifying these inspiring purpose-driven companies is through the B Corp certification, established by B Lab, a global nonprofit organization committed to facilitating the certification of mission-driven companies based on their positive impact on the planet and society. This certification entails a rigorous accreditation process where a company's performance is evaluated using a points system across five key categories: customers, community, governance, workers, and the environment. To achieve certification, a minimum of 80 points is required. An additional examination is administered consisting of 150 to 200 questions (depending on the company's size and sector) that assesses the company's operational practices. This comprehensive process not only reveals areas with room for improvement but also provides a clear roadmap for implementing sustainable and socially responsible practices to continuously strive for excellence.

Note that obtaining a B Corp certification is not a one-time accomplishment; businesses must undergo recertification every three years, and are expected to enhance their score. Furthermore, these certified companies are legally obligated to consider the impact of their decisions on all their stakeholders—employees, customers, suppliers, community, and the environment. This certification enables the recognition of brands that possess exceptional values and are dedicated to constant improvement for their workforce, the planet, and the well-being of all. The list includes some well-known brands—such as illycaffè, Patagonia, and The Body Shop—but also more recent stars, such as the previously mentioned footwear and apparel company Allbirds and Aesop. (As an aside, Aesop is an Australian luxury cosmetics brand that was acquired by L'Oréal for $2.5 billion, making it the biggest brand acquisition ever made by the French beauty giant.[11])

Danone is a publicly traded multinational corporation that actively engages with the B Corp movement across various fronts. Since 2015, Danone has partnered with B Lab to help define a meaningful and manageable path to certification for multinationals and publicly traded companies. As we write, 74.2% of Danone's worldwide sales have attained B Corp certification, signifying remarkable strides toward Danone's aspiration of becoming one of the first fully certified multinationals by 2025.[12]

Another brand that deserves a special mention in this chapter is the Japanese clothing retailer UNIQLO. Its founder, Tadashi Yanai, is famous for saying, "Without a soul, a company is nothing."[13] He's also famous for the 23 management principles that he has distilled and applied to every aspect of his company. At the core of these principles is customer-centricity, an idea of giving back to society and being self-disruptive. The latest available report reveals a remarkable achievement for the company, as it showcases a substantial surge in both revenue and profit during the initial nine months of fiscal year 2023.[14] These business results demonstrate the company's commendable performance in generating substantial financial gains while also maintaining a strong commitment to its purpose. A tangible example of UNIQLO's approach is represented by RE.UNIQLO STUDIO. In UNIQLO stores in several cities customers can pay $5 to get buttons and zippers repaired or replaced, holes patched, and seams mended. (UNIQLO will also "collect secondhand UNIQLO clothes in stores for reuse and deliver them to people in need worldwide . . . . Clothing that cannot be reused is recycled as fuel or soundproofing material.")[15] The repair service has been implemented by an array of other companies, including the likes of Apple, Barbour, Gucci, H&M, Louis Vuitton, Nike, and many others. When we discussed this topic with Riccardo Stefanelli, CEO of the Italian luxury fashion brand Brunello Cucinelli, he acknowledged the importance of prolonging the lifespan of garments, but also stressed the importance of embedding a more virtuous approach in the whole process. He told us: "Our objective is to develop products that possess inherent longevity, constructed with a focus on durability, designed to maximize their lifespan, and engineered to withstand the test of time in both physical robustness and functional relevance. Throughout this process, we diligently uphold the principles of preserving the moral and economic dignity of individuals involved."[16]

These examples offer constructive models for other companies to emulate while also serving as benchmarks that indicate what more and more people admire and are coming to expect—something the less reactive players should pay heed to.

The Business Correlation

In 2023 McKinsey and NielsenIQ conducted an impressive study aimed at examining sales growth for products that claim to be environmentally and socially responsible. The study utilized five years of sales data from the United States, covering the period from 2017 to June 2022. This extensive data set encompassed 600,000 individual product SKUs, representing a substantial $400 billion in annual retail revenues. The products originated from 44,000 brands spanning 32 categories, including food, beverage, personal care, and household items.[17]

While the study provides evidence that the demand for environmentally and socially responsible products extends beyond niche audiences, it also highlights the fact that not all brands making ESG-related claims witnessed a positive sales impact. Interestingly, in 59% of the studied categories smaller brands appeared to possess a greater aura of credibility, leading to disproportionate growth for such claims—which may explain why corporations often acquire smaller brands that prove to be strong in this regard. Moreover, the study suggests that a comprehensive integration of ESG-related issues throughout a brand's portfolio could foster stronger consumer loyalty toward the brand as a whole. Additionally, products with multiple claims spanning various ESG themes demonstrated faster growth compared to other products. In fact, "in nearly 80 percent of the categories, the data showed a positive correlation between the growth rate and the number of distinct types of ESG-related claims a product made. Products making multiple types of claims grew about twice as fast as products that made only one." In other words, consumers are more convinced by multiple ESG-related claims. In addition, "brands might be wise to reflect on their commitment to ESG practices and to ensure that they are thinking holistically across the interconnected social and environmental factors that underpin their products."[18]

In the pursuit of a purposeful strategy, there are also potential challenges that demand careful consideration. Some companies have been accused of "woke washing" (the appropriation of ethical values as a form of advertising), and some brands have received flak for lacking ties with local communities. This risk can sometime be amplified if a famous influencer is involved, since the company cannot dictate the actions of the celebrity. For example, in 2022 the renowned rapper Kanye West made controversial and antisemitic remarks on various social media platforms. As a result, in the span of two weeks, all brands that had established business relationships with him publicly distanced themselves and swiftly terminated contracts worth billions of dollars. One notable giant affected by this turn of events is the German sportswear manufacturer Adidas, which found itself in possession of $1.3 billion worth of unsold "Yeezy" shoes. Initially contemplating the destruction of the remaining inventory, the company has ultimately chosen to sell the products and donate "a significant amount" of the proceeds to organizations such as the Anti-Defamation League and the Philonise and Keeta Floyd Institute for Social Change. (Philonise Floyd is the brother of George Floyd, whose 2020 murder by a police officer in Minnesota sparked widespread outrage and protests.) Adidas CEO Bjørn Gulden shared: "We believe this is the best solution as it respects the created designs and the produced shoes, it works for our people, resolves an inventory problem, and will have a positive impact in our communities . . . . There is no place in sport or society for hate of any kind, and we remain committed to fighting against it." The public responded well to the decision: "The value of Yeezy shoes in the resale market has rocketed since, with some more than doubling in price."[19] To better appreciate the magnitude of the issue, consider that in 2020 the partnership (which was due to expire in 2026) had generated nearly $1.7 billion in revenue for Adidas.[20]

We believe that the management of Adidas (among other brands that distanced themselves from West) behaved in line with this guiding principle: being purposeful also means transparently admitting any false step, and responsibly taking stands against harmful and hateful actions.

As highlighted earlier in the chapter, being purposeful also means respecting people and society at large. Purposeful organizations create inclusive environment where employees, partners, suppliers, and of course customers and clients are treated equally no matter their race, sex, social status, disability, religion, or any other characteristic. Purposeful organizations value different points of view, backgrounds, and skillsets—because that diversity will be essential to success in a complex post-digital world. However, especially for established organizations that might have operated for years based on different priorities, it is paramount that the transition toward a more purposeful position is handled with care.

In April 2023, the American brewing company Anheuser-Busch found itself entangled in a significant controversy. The spark was a sponsored Instagram video post by transgender influencer Dylan Mulvaney, who at one point in the video holds up a can of Bud Light beer with her face on it, marking her "day 365 of womanhood."[21] The post generated a flurry of both conservative and progressive reactions: some applauding inclusivity and others fueling anti-trans sentiments and even calls to boycott Bud Light products. Where did the brewing company go wrong?

Anheuser-Busch had embarked on a public relations initiative to connect with a younger audience, one more attuned to supporting LGBTQ+ rights. However, their execution went off course. The brand's objective to align with this cause led them to deviate too abruptly and drastically from their core values—since for years Bud Light had relied on humourous advertising campaigns to nurture its identity as a light beer, often with a pro-sports angle. (While this campaign was light and humourous, it was also glamourous and a bit campy, with tongue-in-cheek references to sports.) This deviation caused a dissonance that reverberated across the consumer landscape and even among Anheuser-Busch employees. In an effort to quell the storm, the CEO made a vague post aiming to please everyone by declaring support for all Americans—without addressing the company's stance on the transgender community—which just added to the confusion and alienation. The aftermath was palpable: Bud Light sales sank 17% in just one week (concluding on April 15, 2023) compared to the preceding year. Executive personnel were placed on leave, and the brand's reputation took a noticeable hit, since the initiative has been perceived as "rainbow-washing"—superficial actions to attract an audience sensitive to LGBTQ+ rights.[22]

A different example from a few years earlier demonstrates how a company can embrace the "be purposeful" principle while maintaining a resolute commitment in the face of challenges. In a 2018 television advertising campaign, the sportswear behemoth Nike offered its latest installment of its three-decade legacy "Just Do It" slogan. This time the call to just do it spoke to pursuing impossible goals—like playing basketball in a wheelchair (Megan Blunk) or pro football with just one hand (Shaquem Griffin). This is standard Nike messaging; what wasn't standard was the controversial choice of narrator, former football quarterback Colin Kaepernick, who exhorted: "Believe in something, even if it means sacrificing everything." The use of "sacrifice" spoke to Colin Kaepernick's polarizing decision in 2016 to kneel during the pre-game national anthem to protest police brutality, about which he said: "I am not going to stand up to show pride in a flag for a country that oppresses Black people and people of colour"—the fallout of which led to the San Francisco 49ers canceling the quarterback's contract.[23] Nike must have expected the boycotts and protests that followed their 2018 campaign, which came from Nike fans, who denounced Kaepernick's lack of patriotism—and burned Nike shoes in protest—as well as advocates of the Black Lives Matter cause, who accused Nike of "woke-washing." Like the commercial's narrator, Nike did not back down from their position. As it happens, "despite Fox News and parts of the social mediasphere predicting the Swoosh's downfall, the company claimed $163 million in earned media, a $6 billion brand value increase, and a 31% boost in sales." And in 2019, that Nike ad won an Emmy Award for outstanding commercial.[24]

Although it is still unclear how to track the long-term influence of these events in the grand scheme of brand equity—never mind the impact on the P&L in the medium-to-long term—it is clear that such incidents immediately impact how people chose which brands to work for and buy from. They also serve as two poignant reminders in the realm of brand-consumer relationships for those aiming to avoid repercussions by upsetting both current and prospective customers. First, to avoid the clash between intentions and actions, it is essential to meticulously align a brand's DNA with the values it aims to uphold. Authenticity, credibility, and consistency are crucial when embracing a cause with the aim of being purposeful. Second, when navigating the storms of cultural change, staying anchored to one's course—unless the management realizes they have unequivocally made a mistake—is a cardinal compass that guides brands to emerge with integrity and credibility intact.

Public/Private Collaboration Required

The dynamic described in this chapter emphasizes how complex issues can only be addressed if private and public sectors collaborate closely. We advocate both (1) coopetition (collaboration between competitors) between retailers and consumer brands, and (2) collaboration between the business community and international institutions. Selvane Mohandas du Ménil, managing director of the International Association of Department Stores (IADS), agrees:

> *Many retailers might worry that teaming up with their potential competitors could eat into their market share. But here's the thing—there are opportunities for collaboration that don't harm anyone's competitive advantage. In fact, they create a domino effect throughout the supply chain, where consumers, suppliers, and regulators can all get on the same page. Working together, they learn from each other and reach a critical mass that makes it easier to see what needs to be done, what areas need the most attention, and where collaboration can really make a difference in driving meaningful change.*[25]

There is no doubt that, in order for companies to comply with the ESG standards described and follow the principle of being purposeful, they will have to make significant structural investments, acquire specific skills, and equip themselves with innovative technologies to monitor the supply chain. This will have a major impact on the cost structure. In such a complex moment in history, aggravated by the aftermath of the pandemic, it is pertinent that international institutions establish regulations that both dictate compliance with higher ESG and create the financial conditions for businesses to comply without losing profitability. We believe that in order for businesses to be purposeful it will be necessary for policymakers to keep promoting several measures aimed to help companies mitigate the investments required. These measures include:

- a new international (or global) regulatory framework: mandatory reporting on sustainability metrics, setting emissions reduction targets, or requiring social responsibility practices
- financial incentives: tax breaks, grants, subsidies, and so on
- R&D support: funding to support innovative approaches to ESG-related matters; training and education programmes to improve the understanding and the capabilities required to enable companies to effectively integrate ESG practices
- market-access support: facilitated access to markets for virtuous companies, preferential treatment in public procurement processes, and so on
- collaboration platforms that incentivize the collaboration between businesses, NGOs, and governmental agencies to address ESG challenges collectively (shared resource, knowledge sharing, networking opportunities, etc.).

While we have endeavoured to outline the boundaries of action that retailers and consumer brands should embrace on their path to being purposeful, and offered inspiring case studies, it is crucial to reiterate that there is no such thing as a perfect plan. Waiting indefinitely to draft the perfect strategy is not just counterproductive in terms of competitiveness—it's also dangerous for our society and the planet.

Instead, we urge business leaders to take action, initiating incremental yet meaningful steps. By doing so, they can demonstrate to all stakeholders their active commitment to embarking on a journey toward a more harmonious future—one where profitability is a natural outcome of their focus on purpose, people, and the planet. Embracing this approach enables businesses to make tangible contributions and inspire positive change. We also urge policymakers to foster collaboration at all levels, working toward the establishment of common rules that aim to protect the world and its inhabitants without compromising the ability of businesses to thrive.

In the post-digital world, progress is achieved through collaboration, continuous adaptation, learning from experience, and iteratively refining strategies. It is through persistent efforts, even in the absence of a perfect plan, that each of us can make significant strides and contribute to a more sustainable and prosperous future.

Reflection Summary Questions

- What is your inner motivation? What drives you to accomplish your duties? Is it aligned with the purpose of your organization?
- Is your organization striving to create value for all its stakeholders?

- Are you prepared to consider profit a function of a focus on purpose, people, and the planet?
- Do you have a clear understanding of the equilibrium between "value" and "values"? And an idea of how can your organization be profitable and purposeful at the same time?

13

Be Ambidextrous

We've already mentioned Janus—the two-faced ancient Roman god associated with beginnings, transitions, doorways, and passages capable of simultaneously looking to the past and the future—as a metaphor to inspire the attitude that leaders and managers should embrace in a post-digital world.

Charles A. O'Reilly and Michael L. Tushman use the same image to introduce the concept of "organizational ambidexterity." They explain that whoever oversees organizations in today's complex world should pursue exploration and exploitation simultaneously. In their opinion, every business "must constantly pursue *incremental innovations,* small improvements in their existing products and operations that let them operate more efficiently and deliver ever greater value to customers." At the same time, though: "businesses need to come up with discontinuous innovations—radical advances . . . that profoundly alter the basis for competition in an industry, often rendering old products or ways of working obsolete."[1] In some cases, companies may even explore a completely new market space that would make competition irrelevant—what book authors W. Chan Kim and Renée Mauborgne define as a "blue ocean strategy."

According to this vision, companies shouldn't insist on working in existing markets ("red ocean"), trying to exploit the current value proposition in a saturated space where, typically, products are perceived as equivalent, price is king, and profit margins tend to deteriorate over time. Instead, they should constantly explore (and potentially create) new markets, where they have more freedom to pursue innovation and growth ("blue ocean").

Although this approach is valid for any kind of organization, it's particularly relevant for legacy businesses that must reinvent themselves amid the digital transformation that radically altered market dynamics over the course of the last couple of decades. The risk otherwise is to be disrupted by newcomers empowered by new technology and more inclined to meet emerging customers' needs and desires. The anectodical examples are: Kodak—which failed to jump on the bandwagon of digital cameras despite having invented the underlying technology in the 1970s; Nokia and BlackBerry—which were once prominent players in the mobile phones industry and missed the transition to smartphones, leaving the leadership to Apple, Samsung, Huawei and Oppo which today stand at the forefront; Blockbuster—once a leader in the home entertainment industry which ended up going bankrupt when the world transitioned to on-demand streaming services; and Toys "R" Us—a once major toy retailer that struggled to adapt to the shift in consumer behaviours toward online shopping, and filed for bankruptcy in 2017.

However, there are also successful examples of established players that managed to surf the wave of innovation instead of being overwhelmed.

Nintendo, a Japanese multinational video game company—founded in 1889 as Nintendo Karuta—proved its ability to reinvent itself multiple times amid adverse market conditions. The firm's original focus was manufacturing playing cards; the business grew continually from its foundation until 1964, when card sales began to decline due to shifts in Japanese interests toward bowling and other activities. At that point the company had the opportunity to leverage its experience in the tabletop game industry, which it had developed in parallel, and released its first electronic toy—the Beam Gun, an optoelectronic pistol. It was a breakthrough innovation in a new market space—a blue ocean—far from the core business but adjacent to the collateral business the firm had cultivated as a diversification opportunity. Thereafter, Nintendo kept exploiting the original business while simultaneously exploring alternatives. And when the wind changed again, it headed into the video games that the company is best known for. With some ups and downs along the way, Nintendo entered the new millennium occupying a prominent position in the crowded videogaming industry. After a not-so-successful product launch with the GameCube console, once again the company leveraged its capacity to pivot in a new direction. Instead of competing head-on with powerful and technologically advanced consoles like Sony PlayStation and Microsoft Xbox, Nintendo targeted a broader market of casual gamers and non-gamers by launching its latest blue-ocean strategy, the Wii console. Thanks to the motion-sensing controllers and several family-friendly easy-to-play games, the Japanese giant created a new market space of interactive and accessible gaming experiences. The Wii was first released in November 2006, and since then several innovative accessories were released including a remote controller equipped with accelerometer system and infrared sensors that detect the player's position in a three-dimensional environment. As of 2022, the Wii is the seventh-best-selling home console of all time.[2]

Nintendo is thus a model adaptable-legacy firm that systematically alternates between exploitation and exploration—and doubling down on innovative products as soon as the emerging business line begins to gain traction.

Another very interesting case study in this regard is Walmart, the multinational American retail corporation that is also the world's largest company by revenue. The company was founded in 1962 and operates a chain of more than 10,000 stores with different formats, including hypermarkets, discount department stores, and grocery stores in 24 countries ranging from the United States, Canada, and South America to India and South Africa. In 1972, Walmart made its debut on the New York Stock Exchange, and by 1989 it emerged as the largest retailer by revenue and the most profitable.[3] Needless to say, such a gigantic traditional retailer faced significant challenges when digitally native e-commerce players like Amazon—that completely lacked physical outlets—disrupted the landscape with a more agile and scalable business model. However, after certain initial backlashes and challenges to realigning the operating model, the company managed to adapt and embarked on a digital transformation journey that led it to maintain the leadership position. In 2016 Walmart invested $3.3 billion to acquire the e-commerce website Jet.com, and revealed a partnership with IBM and Tsinghua University in Beijing to implement blockchain technology for tracking the pork supply chain in China in an effort to unlock incremental profit by automating supply-chain tracking. Continuing their strategic expansions, in 2017 Walmart announced two impressive acquisitions: Moosejaw, a prominent online retailer specializing in active outdoor products; and Bonobos, a renowned men's apparel company that had started in 2007 as a web-only clothing manufacturer and later opened innovative brick-and-mortar showroom stores with no inventory. In parallel, Walmart heavily invested in advanced technologies to optimize inventory management and fulfillment processes, and leveraged automation, data analytics, and AI-powered systems to improve operational efficiency and bridge the gap between digital and physical. They also focused on leveraging the Jet.com platform to enhance available online product assortment and combine it with flexible delivery and pickup options.[4] Thanks to this combination of investments and updates in the operating model, and a strong commitment to reinvention and adaptation—while defending the established business as much as possible—Walmart is still the largest retailer in the world, and its e-commerce business has constantly grown over the last few years. In 2023 the e-commerce sales of Walmart reached a total of $53.4 billion, reflecting a growth of approximately 12% compared to the previous year. Walmart operates through three distinct business segments: Walmart US, Walmart International, and Sam's Club—its wholesale wing. Though Walmart is still very far from the volumes traded online by Amazon—its direct competitor and the world's second-largest retailer[5]—it is nonetheless a legacy player that embraced organizational ambidexterity to survive and thrive amid a remarkable disruption of its business.

What lessons can we draw from the adaptability of Nintendo and Walmart in response to a radically changing context? How did they approach their realities differently compared to companies like Kodak, Nokia, BlackBerry, and Blockbuster?

Here are some very relevant takeaways:

One: In a hypercompetitive and volatile world, companies can't rely on the exploitation of their competitive advantage over the long term. In her book *The End of Competitive Advantage*, Rita Gunther McGrath suggests that to stay relevant organizations should focus on developing transient advantages that can be quickly adapted and constantly updated to continuously reconfigure the value proposition—until they reach a strategic inflection point when it's time to constructively disengage (before it's too late).[6]

Two: The context is such that companies need a more agile, iterative, and experimental approach, where learning and adapting through discovery become central to the planning process. We are not arguing that every business innovation should be disruptive or a breakthrough per se. In some circumstances incremental improvements are absolutely acceptable. However, companies need to develop the ability to recognize inflection points and swiftly adapt, which involves creating flexible structures, empowering employees, fostering a culture of experimentation, and embracing continuous learning and adaptation. Drawing from our experience, we acknowledge that this shift poses severe hurdles to established companies and requires a radical transformation, from the mindset of the management all the way down to the operations.

Three: When incumbents embrace ambidexterity and exploit their dominant position in time, they can actually be better positioned than newcomers to surf the next wave. In fact, leveraging their substantial resources, established organizations are well equipped to make significant investments in R&D, creating a significant gap between themselves and smaller emerging competitors. An impressive illustration of this dynamic can be seen nowadays in the tech giants—Alphabet, Amazon, Apple, Meta, and Microsoft—who jointly poured a staggering $200 billion into R&D just in 2022. This remarkable figure constitutes 80% of their collective profits and accounts for 30% of the total R&D expenditure among publicly listed American companies. This financial prowess puts them in a position to steer innovation, promptly seize opportunities arising from breakthroughs, and consistently lead the charge in adopting emerging technologies. Another relevant approach combines internal R&D with a smart M&A strategy. Under this perspective, established players demonstrate ambidexterity by forging strategic alliances with start-ups and, in certain instances, even acquiring them—often before their growth scales too extensively. As an example, in the past decade in the US alone a whopping 74% of venture-capital "exits" have been achieved through acquisitions by incumbents. This fruitful collaboration efficiently brings start-ups' innovations to market while providing incumbents with cutting-edge innovations to offer their customers.[7]

Four: In the pursuit of ambidexterity companies need to recognize that they are embarking on a journey where the outcome is often unknown. Hence, they should accept failure as an organic consequence of this experimental approach, and in parallel they should ensure that they don't put all their eggs in one basket. We could say that companies should opt for a "multiple bets" strategy, as opposed to "going all-in." McGrath too promotes the idea of managing a portfolio of initiatives rather than focusing on a single strategy. Other advocates of this approach are authors such as Clayton Christensen and Eric Ries who recommend companies to simultaneously manage a balanced portfolio of diverse projects with varying levels of risk and potential returns.[8]

The majority of the managers we engaged in discussions on this topic agree that adopting an ambidextrous approach is wise. According to Stéphane de la Faverie, executive group president at the Estée Lauder Companies: "In the midst of this ever-changing landscape that you have described as a post-digital world, organizations cannot afford to stand still or adhere to familiar patterns. Instead, they must embody flexibility and agility, constantly adjusting their compass while remaining steadfast to their North Star."[9] In this regard, de la Faverie seems to echo Jeff Bezos who famously said: "What we need to do is always lean into the future; when the world changes around you and when it changes against you—what used to be a tailwind is now a headwind—you have to lean into that and figure out what to do because complaining isn't a strategy."[10]

Overcoming the Obstacles

But why is it so difficult for many companies to walk the talk? What blocks the desire to become more agile, embrace versatility, and stay vigilant and ready to surf the next wave? What ultimately causes ambidexterity to fail?

First and foremost—it is undeniably difficult to turn a ship around, or even just to change course. Even when the leadership team values organizational ambidexterity, and understands that the firm should develop agility and organize teams to protect the business as usual while exploring new ventures, the number of variables needed to work in harmony is quite high. This is why O'Reilly and Tushman emphasize the importance of cross-fertilization among business units and the third parties involved (suppliers, complementors, partners, etc.), as well as the importance of preventing cross-contamination. In their words: "The tight coordination at the managerial level enables the fledgling units to share important resources from the traditional units—cash, talent, expertise, customers, and so on—but the organizational separation ensures that the new units' distinctive processes, structures, and cultures are not overwhelmed by the forces of 'business as usual.'"[11] Another difficulty is highlighted by Nicola Zotta, a seasoned international top manager who is today the CEO of Artsana, an Italian multinational manufacturer of products for children:

> *We are currently in the middle of a transformation process and are pursuing organizational ambidexterity. Inevitably we find ourselves facing conflicting priorities and pursuing multiple goals at the same time. Although this is absolutely normal given the situation, I must admit that it is counter-intuitive for most of the managers, as they are measured on the basis of specific KPIs and are used to delivering results according to a clear business plan. Another challenge lies in the capacity to maintain the discipline to prioritize and selectively choose opportunities, accepting trade-offs, and have the courage to simply say 'no' to some ideas. Being ambidextrous requires a huge effort, as it forces us to put into discussion most of what we've learned and to behave in a less straightforward way.*[12]

Zotta highlights some points we made earlier in the book—that the instability of the landscape requires a different managerial mindset, and the importance of having the capacity to make prompt decisions with very limited visibility on the future outcome.

Joseph Pistrui and Dimo Dimov explain how to accomplish both goals:

> *For almost 100 years, management has been associated with the five basic functions outlined by management theorist Henri Fayol: planning, organizing, staffing, directing, and controlling. These have become the default dimensions of a manager. But they relate to pursuing a fixed target in a stable landscape. Take away the stability of the landscape, and one needs to start thinking about the fluidity of the target. This is what's happening today, and managers must move away from the friendly confines of these five tasks.*[13]

A concrete step toward igniting ambidexterity and stimulating a cultural shift is to hire key people with different backgrounds and let them organically create a positive internal tension leveraging the power of diversity. In an article released by McKinsey & Company, Sergei Goncharov, CEO of the Russian chain of convenience stores Pyaterochka, confirms the potential of this move:

> *A very interesting thing started happening after we hired tech talent. As I said, they have a different mentality from people in the traditional retail industry; they're not as risk averse as traditional retailers. Some of them are actually quite risk loving. And they started changing the culture around them. Their risk-taking mentality started trickling down into the organization. We started to see a lot of people in the traditional retail departments changing their attitudes and mentality. So, I think we're all benefiting from this mindset. It has become one of our competitive advantages, for sure.*[14]

Other companies approach the shift by creating internal cross-functional innovation teams—with employees from marketing, sales, operations, R&D, and technology plus, potentially, consultants with specific complementary skills—tasked with developing innovative business ideas that could allow the company to explore both adjacent and breakthrough growth areas. Of course, it is crucial in this case that the teams are provided with the freedom and the means necessary to deliver the expected results. There are other ways to inspire change with an outside-in approach, but in all cases the ambition is to create a shock that would trigger a chain reaction capable of accelerating the transition toward ambidexterity.

In conclusion, we can assert that organizational ambidexterity serves as a vital guiding principle for every company operating in volatile and complex landscapes. It allows retailers and brands to survive and thrive, thanks to the parallel exploitation of the existing business and the exploration of multiple new sources of potential growth. However, it also requires dealing with cultural misalignments. For example, employees tend to naturally gravitate toward one approach over the other, and a siloed organizational structure can jeopardize both strategy roll-out and thorough resource allocation. These obstacles are even more problematic during an economic slowdown and in the presence of conflicting priorities. However, the fact that a number of established companies have successfully navigated these challenges means that they are not insurmountable. This perspective has the potential to constitute a sort of revenge for the incumbents, since it challenges the notion that innovation mainly originates from newcomers and that incumbents are inevitably sluggish to adapt and prone to failure due to their legacies. Being ambidextrous will be key to successfully guiding the business decisions of both start-ups and seasoned businesses in a post-digital world.

Reflection Summary Questions

- Are you and the leadership team at your organization in a position to simultaneously pursue incremental and radical innovation?
- How is your company dealing with the reduced length of time in which a competitive advantage can be exploited? Does the team continuously explore potential innovations?
- Are you ready to surf the "next wave" of innovation—or is your organization's legacy such that you and your team will face challenges in keeping up?
- Are you equipped to avoid the traps that can cause ambidexterity to fail (resource allocation, cultural misalignment, resistance to change, governance issues, conflicting priorities, overemphasis on short-term results, skill gap, etc.)?

14

Be Onlife

In Chapter 6 we discussed the importance of integrating various channels, both online and offline, to provide a seamless and cohesive customer experience. The ambition of retailers and consumer brands embracing this approach is to fulfill today's diverse customer preferences by offering convenience, personalization, and flexibility. We've also pointed out that the effective approach is not trying to be "everywhere" customers want, but instead to pragmatically be where it matters the most. We have hence proposed replacing the omnichannel with optichannel, an approach that "takes stock of individual channel performance and then makes optimizations based on customer expectations, personal preferences, and the anticipated return on investment. . . . By optimizing the customer experience through what's preferred and not just what's available, brands can effectively refocus their efforts and resources to fully understand *how* people come to a brand and *why* they stay engaged."[1]

This more focused approach allows businesses to meet customers' expectations by ensuring a consistent and integrated experience, regardless of the channel or device used. It starts from a comprehensive understanding of customers' behaviours and preferences. By leveraging this data, businesses can then tailor their offerings, promotions, and communications to better suit each customer. As we have argued, customers don't see channels, they seamlessly experience brands. Ultimately, optichannel aims to enhance customer satisfaction, increase engagement, and build long-term loyalty by providing a personalized experience that aligns with their preferences, regardless of how they choose to interact with the brand.

Building on this concept and extending this idea of a personalized customer journey, in Chapter 7 we argued that a third dimension should be considered when planning an optichannel strategy—the virtual world. Hence, if retailers and consumer brands want to imagine a truly seamless customer experience, they need to consider a three-dimensional customer journey.

In this chapter we introduce the concept of "onlife" to describe the interconnectedness of physical, digital, and now virtual lives in the post-digital era. The onlife concept recognizes that technology and the Internet have become deeply embedded in our daily lives, influencing how we communicate, work, buy, consume, learn, entertain, and even define our identities. It emphasizes that our online activities and interactions have a direct impact on our offline lives and vice versa. And we can expect the same in our interactions in virtual worlds.

The term "onlife" was first coined by Luciano Floridi, professor and founding director of the Digital Ethics Center at Yale University. Over the course of his career, he has devoted a lot of attention to the ethics of information and its impact on society in order to describe the interconnectedness between our online and offline lives. In this guiding principle we propose an extension of the original idea, adopting "onlife" to describe the fluidity of a post-digital world, one in which the lines connecting physical, digital, and virtual blur in a frenetic continuum. For retailers and consumer brands executives, being onlife means acknowledging the profound influence that digital platforms, social media, mobile devices, artificial intelligence, augmented and virtual reality, and the Internet of Things (IoT) have on shaping our behaviours, perceptions, relationships, and societal dynamics. And it encourages individuals, businesses, and society to navigate this interconnected landscape mindfully, considering the ethical, social, and psychological implications of our actions and choices in physical, digital, and virtual realms. Retailers and brands that understand the dynamics of an onlife three-dimensional customer journey value optichannel because they understand the impossibility of aspiring to ubiquity. However, they typically need to overcome various challenges to fully roll out the strategy.

Facing the Most Common Threats

As we highlighted in Chapters 6 and 7, one of the biggest questions is how to ensure profitability when implementing optichannel. In fact, achieving a successful optichannel strategy, given the need to make choices between a considerable number of channels and touchpoints across three dimensions, requires a thorough analysis in order to overcome some relevant challenges. In our experience, established companies that embark in this journey must deal with five categories of threats:

Organizational structure and culture: Traditional retail organizations tend to have separate teams and departments responsible for different channels, leading to a lack of coordination and collaboration. Walled-off mindsets and resistance to change can impede the implementation of a cohesive strategy.

Technology complexity (siloed systems and data): Implementing and integrating the necessary technologies in pre-existing legacy systems can be complex and costly. Companies must invest in robust e-commerce platforms, customer relationship management (CRM) tools, inventory-management systems, and other software to enable an effective sharing of data across all departments. Retailers, especially the most traditional ones, often struggle with integrating various systems and data sources across different channels. Legacy systems and outdated infrastructure may undermine the smooth flow of information and create silos, making it difficult to provide a seamless experience across channels. In fact, without a fluid integration of all available data, it's impossible to create a unified view of the customer. For example, it can be difficult to determine which factors lead a customer to use one channel over another, as well as to calculate the actual marginal contributions of each touchpoint to the overall customer journey. A successful optichannel onlife strategy requires data cleansing, normalization, and integration processes to avoid discrepancies and inconsistencies in customer information.

Operational challenges: Managing inventory and logistics across multiple channels can be challenging. Companies may encounter conflicts between their physical stores and online channels. For example, online sales may cannibalize sales from physical stores, leading to decreased profitability. Narrowing down to the optimal channels, ensuring seamless synergies, maintaining accurate inventory levels, coordinating order fulfillment, securing timely delivery, and managing returns and exchanges in an optichannel environment require streamlined operations and extremely accurate supply chain management.

Consistency in customer experience: Ensuring that pricing, promotions, communications, product information, and customer service are consistent and synchronized across all touchpoints can be a complex task, requiring coordination and alignment across the organization.

To these complexities we need to add the fact that customer expectations are constantly evolving, their experiential benchmarks rising by the day. All combined, our only viable option is to abandon the omni concept of serving the customer in every possible touchpoint across the three dimensions. We must instead embrace a more realistic concept that focuses on optimizing the most relevant touchpoints, the ones most likely to provide the "ideal" onlife customer journey. Businesses will still need to adopt a holistic approach, focusing on strategic planning, organizational alignment, technology investments, and a customer-centric mindset. They will still need to invest in the right infrastructure, implement robust data integration solutions, foster cross-functional collaboration, and prioritize the customer experience. But instead of aiming at being omnipresent, they will design the journey around relevance so as to maximize the value of their proposition.

In recommending that businesses embrace optichannel as a core strategy, the "be onlife" mindset builds on a profound understanding of the delicate interconnectedness among all the dynamics in play. Being onlife means focusing on the most relevant touchpoints rather than chasing ubiquity.

Consider, for example, how digital transformation has greatly reduced the foot traffic at the conventional brick-and-mortar branches of banks around the world. The most successful banks didn't try to maintain their physical presence intact while also developing their digital presence; they focused on the evolving needs of their customers and optimized the overall number of touchpoints. Most of these successful banks drastically reduced their number of branches while launching mobile applications that enabled customers to easily complete their most frequent tasks. This is not to say that optichannel always implies a reduction in the number of touchpoints. The point is just to consider the onlife nature of the post-digital journey, which implies an optimization that may or may not lead to reducing the points of contact depending on what makes more sense in each specific situation.

Another relevant example of a retailer that has leveraged technology to develop an entire ecosystem of services around emerging customer's needs is the Chinese e-commerce giant Alibaba with its Hema supermarkets (the English name is Freshippo). Hema stores rely entirely on the Hema app, which acts as a tool to check prices, navigate in store, get product nutritional information, and pay without any interaction with either a physical cashier or even a checkout line (with technology that is almost identical to that in AmazonGo stores). Jack Ma, Alibaba Group's cofounder, described it as "the integration of online, offline, logistics, and data across a single value chain." Other than serving customers, the 257 stores (as of 2021) act as fulfillment centres for Hema's online grocery orders—in fact, more than 60% of Hema's gross merchandise value comes from online orders. The Hema app utilizes machine learning to analyze and remember shoppers' purchasing patterns, enabling personalized product recommendations tailored to each customer's preferences. Talking about this perfect integration of online and offline, the president of Alibaba Group

Michael Evans said: "Consumers don't think about the world online versus offline. Neither should brands and retailers."[2]

There are also interesting examples where the physical world seamlessly blends with the virtual world. Ubisoft Entertainment, a French video game publisher, released a free in-game feature for its popular game *Assassin's Creed*, allowing owners of the "Origins" game version to access the "Discovery Tour" mode. In this edutainment mode, players can travel around the game's world in ancient Egypt, ancient Greece, and the Viking Age. Now, imagine you're the owner of a family resort in Egypt and you want to attract tourists by promoting both the ancient beauties of your land and your resort. Embracing the "be onlife" guiding principle would lead you to focus on the ideal customer journey of a segment of young gamers who live thousands of miles away and are moving from the Aware to the Appeal phase of their journey, as they discover Egypt through an immersive video game. What is the ideal next best action for this customer persona? How can you, as a resort owner interested in intercepting that emerging demand, target that audience as they enter the Ask stage? Is the next best action still in the virtual world (e.g., an in-game call to action) or rather in the digital world (e.g., retargeting the gamers via email or perhaps digital advertising)? We will further discuss how brands can leverage data to personalize the customer experience in Chapter 15 when we will introduce the guiding principle "Be Personal." However, it appears very clear how savvy businesses that acknowledge the importance of "being onlife" and understand the dynamic of a three-dimensional customer journey can unlock additional opportunities to fine-tune supply and demand.

The Five A's—Awareness, Appeal, Ask, Act, and Advocacy

In Chapter 7, "The Post-Digital Customer Journey," we explored the five A's—Awareness, Appeal, Ask, Act, and Advocacy. These stages enable business leaders to map out the customer's needs and priorities during their purchasing process. The journey begins with **Awareness**, where the customer becomes conscious of a new brand, often through advertisements, word-of-mouth, reviews, or an interest in similar brands. If we find ourselves drawn to what we discover, we transition into the **Appeal** stage, where we seek further information to validate our initial impression—this is the **Ask** stage. Here, we might read reviews from other customers, explore the brand's website, visit their social channels, and even seek opinions from trusted peers. If we like what we find, we naturally progress to the **Act** stage—the core of the customer experience. This is when direct interactions with the brand occur during and after the transaction. If the company delivers a satisfying experience, brand loyalty is fostered, and we become eager advocates, recommending the brand to others. In the Retail 4.0 era, the **Advocate** stage gained tremendous significance, as each of us possessed the ability to reach a vast audience through the combination of mobile devices and online social networks. This exponential reach emphasizes the importance of delighting customers and providing exceptional experiences, as such can significantly impact brand reputation and customer acquisition through word-of-mouth. In both our personal and consumer lives, this journey of connection, validation, and advocacy shapes the nature of our relationships. Understanding and navigating this process is pivotal for businesses seeking to create lasting bonds with their customers in the ever-evolving landscape of Retail 5.0.

Similar questions should be raised when brands partner with video game developers or make digital products known as non-fungible tokens (NFTs) that can be spent in one of the metaverses. For example, Epic Games, a prominent American video game and software developer, collaborated with Moncler, a renowned Italian luxury outerwear company, to introduce exclusive in-game outfits for *Fortnite*, one of their highly successful products. Drawing inspiration from Moncler's physical ready-to-wear collection, the Moncler Classic Set offers gamers a unique avenue for self-expression.[3] In their case, the appropriate questions are: "Given that some gamers will discover the brand through the game, how can the brand continue the relationship with them? What is the ideal follow-up in an onlife optichannel customer journey?"

Regarding the metaverse, the American research firm Gartner predicted that, by 2026, one in four people will spend at least one hour per day in this space, whether for work, shopping, education, socializing, and/or entertainment. Attracted by this prospect, many brands have decided to join one of the many popular platforms (Axis, Illuvium, Infinity, Decentraland, Roblox, Sorare, TheSandBox, etc.) to familiarize themselves, experiment, learn, and try to capitalize on a first-mover advantage. The list of these inquiring brands spans all sectors and includes the likes of Adidas, Balenciaga, BMW, Burberry, Chipotle, Coca-Cola, Disney, Estée Lauder, Gucci, Hermès, H&M, Hyundai, Kroger, Louis Vuitton, Nike, Prada, Samsung, Walmart, Zara, and many others. These companies are experimenting in a number of different directions, from logistics to reimagining the way customers shop, to hosting virtual events. Some are even creating digital "twins" of their facilities so they can simulate how best to streamline and optimize processes. Regardless of the type of activity or the nature of the interaction, for the purpose of this book we want to highlight the plethora of additional contacts that retailers and brands can establish with their customers—because these virtual worlds have in effect added a third dimension to the customer journey. In venturing beyond the second dimension, the risk is, once again, not retaining a silo mentality, failing to understand that all channels and touchpoints are intertwined, and savvy consumers move across them seamlessly.

When we discussed this guiding principle with Mauro Porcini—author, senior vice president, and chief design officer at the American F&B corporation PepsiCo—he emphasized the necessity of designing the onlife journey with "real" human beings in mind. Over time, businesses have shifted their focus from product to service to experience. Now it's time to turn attention to "the specific needs, wants, and dreams of individual human beings." According to Porcini, regardless of which new technology appears on the horizon:

> *companies should primarily focus on understanding genuine human emotions, and only afterward figure out how to leverage technology to amplify the relationship with a brand. On the contrary, the majority of firms get stuck in a loop of short-term financial outcomes, market share supremacy, and viewing technology solely as a means of competitive advantage—rather than as a catalyst for creating delightful experiences. They only see people as "customers in a channel" and tend to design the journey as if people were completely rational machines.*[4]

A very similar perspective is promoted by Accenture Song's executives David Droga, global CEO and creative chairman, and Baiju Shah, chief strategy officer. Discussing the broader scope of customers' contemporary lives, they argue: "Over time, businesses have moved from a product-centric approach focused on performance to a customer-centric strategy meant to prioritize experience. But now, the dynamics are more complicated. Companies need to accept their customers as ever-changing, complex people deeply impacted by unpredictable external forces." And they advocate this approach because it allows businesses to "achieve relevance by bridging the interplay between these life forces and their customers' everyday decisions. And they maintain that relevance by perpetually evolving their products, marketing, sales, and service experiences as life continues to shift."[5]

Giovanni Valentini, general manager for Lancôme USA and member of the L'Oréal Luxe USA leadership team, confirms the importance of this broader perspective when reflecting on the target audience:

> *The modern consumer goes beyond the limitations of in-store, mobile, digital, and virtual experiences, surpassing the traditional boundaries of marketing. As a result, understanding consumers requires a more comprehensive and holistic perspective. At our company, we are committed to continuously monitoring and observing how customers engage with technology across multiple channels, including in-store, online, and now even in virtual worlds. Additionally, we place great emphasis on leveraging cutting-edge technologies that enable our customers to interact with our products in innovative ways. We firmly believe that staying attuned to the ever-evolving behaviours and preferences of our customers is crucial for our success.*[6]

Embracing an Onlife Optichannel Strategy

Focusing on individual human needs and seeing customers in their full onlife lives calls for understanding how technology is changing culture and our entire lives—and how much the journey that people embark on as customers is impacted by this cultural shift. At this delicate juncture, how well a company optimizes its value proposition to fine-tune this dynamic could be the difference between success and failure. However, before retailers and brands eagerly embark on implementing their optichannel capabilities, it is crucial for them to pause and deeply reflect on the fundamental drivers of value creation specific to their business. Without this thoughtful consideration, retailers may find themselves overwhelmed by a plethora of approaches, technologies, channels, and touchpoints to choose from. The risk, as we discussed earlier while explaining the downsides of the omnichannel approach, is to be victims of a "fear of missing out" (FOMO) and implementing innovative technologies or platforms just for the sake of it, without first thoroughly considering the venture. On this specific point Greg Hoffman, an author and the former chief marketing officer of Nike, suggests always keeping in mind a few significant questions: "It's very important for business leaders to not get seduced by 'the new toys' of technology. Everyday there is a new digital platform or a news social network that claims to bring brands closer to consumers. I believe it is ultimately about staying true and asking yourself questions like—What is the problem I'm trying to solve for my customers? How can I bring to them a truly meaningful benefit? Why should they care?"[7]

Leaders in this realm carefully assess the journey of the most relevant customer personas and then make an action plan that meticulously takes into consideration every aspect of their organization, mapping the gaps between the "as is" and the "to be" scenario, in order to avoid the five challenges that we described at the beginning of the chapter. It's very important to focus on "personas," as that enables businesses to describe segments of the population in a more nuanced and comprehensive manner than traditional demographic-based segmentation allows. It is a way to consider "people" rather than "customers." To avoid dangerous resource misallocations, it is also very important to develop a robust understanding of the gap that often exists between what people say versus what they actually do. Manuel "Manolo" Arroyo, the global chief marketing officer of the soft drink behemoth Coca-Cola Company, shared with us a counterintuitive truth: "I no longer trust blindly consumer research on brand perception." He articulated:

> *Over the past two decades, we've been closely monitoring brand love metrics, but the issue lies in the fact that research has largely been reliant on consumers' declared perception disconnected from their actual, real, behaviour. In our sector, we've discovered that increases in consumer positive perception do not necessarily translate into consumer behaviour. In truth, it works the other way around—consumption, real behaviour, always translates into positive perception, thus driving brand love. By strategically adapting our research, data and analytical approach and gaining a deep understanding of what our customer personas consume on a regular basis, we managed to effectively influence brand real growth performance and building brand love.*[8]

In our experience the most successful companies follow these three macro-steps:

Understand the onlife journey of your most relevant personas. Utilize all available resources to deeply comprehend how the people you aim to serve navigate across various channels—physical, digital, and virtual.

Instead of viewing them as passive customers, observe the intricate nuances of their multifaceted journey. Identify the touchpoints where your audience naturally interacts with your brand and analyze their behaviours, preferences, and pain points at each stage. This profound understanding is crucial to avoid future investing in cutting-edge technological innovation, such as in-store sensors or smart mirrors, that could fail to resonate with your audience.

Establish clear and realistic objectives. Evaluate the structural limitations of your organization, the competitive landscape, the experiential benchmarks, and the digital literacy of stakeholders involved. Based on this assessment, define attainable objectives and desired outcomes for your seamless optichannel strategy. Determine what you seek to accomplish, whether it's enhancing customer experience, increasing sales, or improving brand consideration or brand loyalty. Utilize the insights gained from phase one to carefully identify where technology can bring efficiencies and where a human presence should be maintained. Consider the nature of your organization, the skills and capabilities of your team, and the realistic budget available for employee training, hiring new talent/consultants, and investing in new technologies and systems such as CRM or inventory management tools.

Plan the onlife optichannel strategy. Ensure a smooth and frictionless transition across channels and touchpoints with attention to each next-best action. Avoiding channel friction is essential for crafting a truly integrated optichannel strategy. Without strategic alignment, organizations often fall into fragmented investments, allocating resources to conflicting priorities in store operations, e-commerce, marketing, sales, IT, HR, and supply chain. Always keep in mind that the core business of any organization is to serve a customer, which in complex and saturated markets often implies simplifying their lives by reducing the number of options or time needed to complete a task. A good rule of thumb in this regard, as suggested by Hoffman, is to keep asking yourself "Why should they care?" Ensure the plan is adaptable and includes key performance indicators (KPIs) and metrics to gauge success. Share these ex ante metrics with key stakeholders to maintain alignment and minimize the risk of misalignment along the process. Align incentives to ensure that all parties involved are focused on the same direction. And prioritize interoperability so that all departments can simultaneously access the same data set and facilitate real-time information circulation. Finally, ensure you leverage data to bridge the gap between customers' statements and actual real actions.

Retailers and brands that successfully follow these three steps and manage to overcome the threads described above understand the risk of indulging in delusions of grandeur. They value the importance of starting small, aiming at achieving early wins—which is especially important in a resource-constraint scenario and in a sector like retail that traditionally suffers from acute margin pressure. In doing so, wise companies obtain two crucial results: (1) they motivate the stakeholders involved as they create momentum focusing on the few low-hanging fruits that can be realistically achieved in a short amount of time; and (2) they gain the trust of the top management and the shareholders (who would be harder to keep motivated if the process required upfront massive investments, as well as an expanse of time before seeing results). Another smart move we've observed in successful transitions toward optichannel is the creation of cross-functional teams composed of representatives from different department channels—along with supporting functions such as IT, marketing, sales, and operations—who collaborate to pilot new initiatives. These nimble teams, who operate as independent cells, typically achieve relevant results in a fraction of the time that would be required of the entire company.

In a post-digital world, where individuals are influenced by ever-changing external factors and behave inconsistently, a rigid, one-size-fits-all approach would be unsustainable. Therefore, agility, adaptability, and continuous optimization are all necessary. Successful organizations reap the rewards of aligning their value proposition with market demand, resulting in the conquest of new customer segments, increased sales, and improved operational efficiency. This pursuit focuses on quality over quantity, emphasizing the notion of "less but better" that connotes an onlife optichannel strategy.

Reflection Summary Questions

- Based on your experience as a customer, have you always encountered seamless transitions when interacting across different channels?
- What are the channels and touchpoints that hold the most significance for you? Which ones do you consider to be primarily transactional, and which ones do you believe should not include commercial calls to action?

- How can we navigate the challenges and complexities associated with the virtual world and the evolving customer expectations in a three-dimensional customer journey?
- How can companies ensure profitability while implementing optichannel and making choices between numerous channels and touchpoints?
- How can you effectively manage inventory and logistics across multiple channels considering potential conflicts between physical stores and online channels?
- How can your organization maintain consistency and synchronization in pricing, promotions, product information, and customer service across all touchpoints in an optichannel environment?

15

Be Personal

Think about the sense of satisfaction and gratification that you experience when you enter your favourite café and you order "the usual." Or when the server anticipates your needs and serves your favourite cappuccino without your saying anything. The benefits of feeling a personal connection remain deeply ingrained in the essence of commerce—from ancient marketplaces where merchants called clients by name and tailored their offerings, to modern-day CRM tools that utilize advanced data analytics to deliver personalized experiences. At the core of the current tech-led optichannel personalization there is a very basic human need of being recognized as individuals.

The element of personalization in commerce acknowledges that each person has their own distinct characteristics, desires, and buying behaviours. By understanding and addressing these individual differences, businesses can create more meaningful and engaging interactions with customers. This involves tailoring offerings, recommendations, and communication based on a deep understanding of individual preferences, previous interactions, and demographics. In the contemporary business landscape, personalization has been further empowered by advancements in technology, data analytics, and customer insights. With access to vast amounts of data, businesses can now leverage sophisticated algorithms and machine learning to better understand customers and provide highly relevant, timely, and personalized experiences. However, the importance of the human touch in a post-digital world can still play a crucial role. By embracing personalization, businesses can forge stronger connections with customers, foster loyalty, and potentially drive growth. This approach also enables businesses to deliver more targeted marketing efforts—as well as improve conversion rates, customer retention, and overall efficiency of the system.

It's important to distinguish between "customization" and "personalization." "Customization" refers to the process of adapting or tailoring a product, service, or experience to meet the specific preferences or requirements of a particular group of customers (a cluster). It typically involves offering options or features that customers can choose from to create a combination that suits their preferences. Hence it is a "reactive" technique based on what people actively choose, and it doesn't lead to the creation of one-of-a-kind products. Whenever we receive a newsletter with content and offers that are identical to others in the same group who share our preferences, we encounter this same sort of customization. Though the message has been "tailored" to match our preferences—and even if the message begins with "Dear Philip"—it's not unique.

"Personalization," on the other hand, goes beyond customization. It involves creating individualized products, services, and experiences that either allow customers to make a one-of-a-kind bespoke product or leverage data and insights about an individual's preferences, behaviours, and characteristics to infer what they might need and want. Marketers utilize the same data points to deliver tailored content, recommendations, or interactions that are relevant to the individual. Personalization aims to provide a more seamless and intuitive experience that feels uniquely designed for each person. Nike, the world's largest supplier of athletic shoes and apparel, uses customer data and AI-driven algorithms to personalize the shopping experience both online and in-store. They analyze customer behaviour, preferences, and purchase history to offer personalized product recommendations and content tailored to each individual's interests. For example, if a customer frequently buys running shoes, Nike's website and app will showcase new running shoe releases and related content whenever that customer visits the site.[1]

Needless to say, personalization offers the advantages of one-to-one relationships, but it's also inherently inefficient due to its lack of scalability. And though customization is more scalable, it can come across as less authentic. Hence a combination of both is recommended. Wise marketers distinguish between the two and deliberately choose which touchpoints deserve personalization—perhaps enhanced by a human touch—and which touchpoints get enough value from customization. Since the more granular approach of personalization typically requires more time and resources, it's best adopted when the expected return on investment is higher.

Although optichannel personalization doesn't equal technology, it is true that the most advanced implementations of generative AI could lead to astonishing transformations in the way we shop, buy, and consume—and could potentially lead to the holy grail of mass personalization. For example, consider the AI-empowered virtual try-on introduced by Google in the summer of 2023. In a potentially ground-breaking move set to revolutionize the shopping experience, the company has photographed a diverse group of 40 men and 40 women, encompassing various sizes, body shapes, ethnicities, hair types, and skin tones. Leveraging this data set, Google has developed a tool that allows users to see how different products look on real models, offering a more realistic and inclusive representation. Unlike other brands that have faced criticism for using fictional or digital models, Google's method promises to avoid ethical concerns by superimposing digital garments on to images of actual people. This development is particularly significant as the fashion industry grapples with high return rates (e.g., US consumers were estimated to return more than 20% of all online purchases in 2022) and the environmental impact of overproduction and discarded inventory. (Textile production alone is estimated to be responsible for about 20% of global clean water pollution.)[2]

Indeed, consumer expectations around personalization are increasing. Some 88% of consumers say they're more likely to shop with retailers that deliver personalized and connected optichannel experiences. While 73% of shoppers worldwide expect brands to understand their unique needs and expectations (up from 66% in 2020), 62% want companies to anticipate their needs (up from 56% in 2020) and 56% expect offers to be always personalized (up from 52% in 2020). Interestingly, 56% of respondents in the same survey declare that most companies treat them as a number, down from 65% in 2020.[3] This last data point seems to prove that companies overall are making progress in the way they leverage data to customize and personalize the relationship with customers.

Matt Harker, VP of Global Marketing Strategy and Transformation of the Walgreens Boots Alliance, says: "When you think about what matters to individuals, whether it's a product, service, content, or messaging, you soon realize that personalization—at our scale of hundreds of millions—is going to quickly overwhelm you. You need help from technology to orchestrate content and messaging to land with individuals in exactly the right moment and context."

It's true that recent advancements in customer data platform (CDP) technologies, featuring user-friendly "out-the-box" and low code capabilities, provide organizations with a valuable opportunity to accelerate their optichannel personalization efforts. By successfully integrating their unified data from a CDP into their legacy systems, organizations can effectively leverage the insights derived from the data and deliver customization or personalization depending on the context. These technological developments have the potential to bring the relationship with customers to a completely new level.[4]

The Benefits

In today's crowded marketplace, supply exceeds demand in almost every sector, and people are constantly overwhelmed by the paradox of choice. In this context, personalization can play a crucial role in creating meaningful connections with customers and enhancing their overall experience. Businesses can leverage data to gain valuable insights into customer behaviours, preferences, and trends. These insights can drive informed marketing strategies and decision-making, unlock future growth opportunities, and pave the way to customize and personalize the relationship with customers. Mastering this process can create a powerful differentiating factor and lead to a competitive advantage.

By understanding customer preferences and delivering tailored experiences, businesses can stand out, be more engaging, better anticipate (hence better respond to customers' needs), attract new customers, and retain a loyal customer base. In the absence of a profound understanding of customers, businesses run the risk of treating their less valuable customers better than they "deserve," while neglecting their more valuable customers, which can be a significant gamble in a competitive landscape where customer experience expectations are elevated. To avoid falling behind, businesses must strive to comprehend their customers on a deeper level and meet or exceed their expectations.

In our experience, successful retailers and brands leverage personalization to seek the following core-benefits:

- **Customer Satisfaction:** When customers receive personalized experiences that cater to their specific interests and preferences, they feel valued and understood. This leads to increased satisfaction, loyalty, and advocacy for the brand.
- **Customer Engagement:** Personalization allows businesses to tailor their marketing messages and offerings to individual customer preferences, needs, and behaviours. By delivering relevant and customized content, businesses can capture and maintain customer attention, leading to higher engagement levels.
- **Customer Retention:** Personalization builds stronger relationships with customers, fostering loyalty and reducing churn (the regular fluctuations in the customer pool). By consistently delivering personalized experiences and relevant recommendations, businesses can increase customer retention and customer lifetime value.
- **Conversion Rate:** Personalization helps businesses deliver targeted and timely messages and offers to customers, increasing the likelihood of conversion. By presenting customers with relevant products or services based on their preferences and purchase history, businesses can drive higher conversion rates and

revenue growth—in addition to driving traffic toward physical and digital stores.

To maximize these benefits, companies should seek to implement optichannel personalization at each step of the customer journey—from awareness to advocacy, pre, during, and post transaction.

For example, German sportswear giant Adidas (among others) has introduced in select locations ad hoc stations where customers can personalize shoes by choosing colours, materials, and certain design elements—enjoying a unique and interactive shopping experience.[5] Another retailer that believes in the power of personalization is the aforementioned Japanese clothing company UNIQLO, which in 2012 in San Francisco introduced the "World's First Magic Mirror" by "linking augmented reality to a Kinnect tracker"; customers trying on one of four different jacket styles in front of the mirror could change the colour of the jacket in the reflection via a touchscreen controller.[6] Although in both cases customers can only choose from a predefined range of options, they still receive personalized treatment and have the potential to combine elements to create one-of-a-kind products.

According to McKinsey & Company, an optichannel personalization strategy, if well executed, can generate an uplift in revenue and retention ranging from 10 to 15%, bring 10 to 30% marketing efficiencies and cost savings, increase customer acquisition of 3 to 5%, and lead to a 5 to 10% jump in customer satisfaction and engagement. However, a mere 15% of marketers report having successfully implemented the full extent of personalization strategies.[7]

Why is that? If customers clearly declare that they expect personalization, and the benefits for businesses are so evident, what is keeping companies from embracing this approach?

The Flip Side

Our consulting experience and the multiple conversations we had with managers all over the world suggest that, although personalization is undoubtedly touted as a crucial aspect of marketing, there are several concerns that need to be considered that might slow down or jeopardize your strategy. In particular, people are willing to trade their personal data only if they receive authentic value in exchange. We often see companies defining and implementing their data strategy prioritizing their interests over that of their customers, which could deteriorate consumer trust over time. To follow are the main challenges professionals should take into consideration:

Privacy concerns: Personalization relies on collecting and analyzing customer data, which can raise privacy concerns. Consumers are becoming more cautious about sharing their personal information, and institutions are introducing new legislation to protect people from abuses. Businesses must navigate the delicate balance between personalization and respecting privacy rights.

Implementation challenges: Achieving comprehensive optichannel personalization can be resource-intensive since it requires skilled personnel, robust technology infrastructure, data integration, and sophisticated analytics capabilities. Small or resource-constrained businesses may struggle to implement and maintain effective personalization strategies, which would limit their ability to compete with better equipped players.

Diminished human touch: Excessive reliance on data, analytics, and technology might reduce human interaction and personal touch in customer experiences. Depending on the nature of the business, the phase in the journey, and the specific touchpoint, there are situations where customers value human interactions, and may feel disconnected or alienated when interactions become overly automated or impersonal.

Risk of overwhelming customers: Personalization attempts must be executed thoughtfully—otherwise, it can bombard customers, which is especially annoying when the messages or product suggestions are irrelevant. Too much personalization can create a boomerang effect, resulting in customer fatigue, and potentially driving them away from the brand. Think, for example, of when you become so exasperated that you unsubscribe from a newsletter.

Homogenization of Experiences: If potential customers are pitched generic products, services, and perspectives, they may miss out on discovering new products or alternative options that could enrich their experiences and unlock unforeseen business opportunities for companies. This leads to a lack of serendipity, and thus a homogenization of experiences.

Bias and stereotyping: Personalization algorithms are not immune to biases and stereotypes, since they are programmed by humans and built on existing patterns. If not carefully monitored and adjusted, personalization efforts can perpetuate discriminatory practices or reinforce existing biases, leading to negative consequences for both businesses and customers.

Businesses must carefully navigate these issues to strike the right balance and foster meaningful customer connections. The promise of technology is to improve to the point that it will mitigate or even resolve all these concerns thanks to machine learning, and deliver mass personalization in a way that could paradoxically be perceived as more human rather than less human, since in the near future people will interact with all devices using their bodies and voices rather than keyboards and screens. We will discuss this aspect in detail in Chapter 16, "Be Human."

In an era where customer journeys span multiple disconnected touchpoints rather than following a linear path, effectively reaching people requires interdisciplinary collaboration. "Be personal" is a guiding principle that seeks to inspire business leaders to find the optimal balance between customization and personalization, as well as between leveraging marketing automation and maintaining a personal touch. We firmly believe that wise professionals should acquire a deep understanding of the intricate nuances that shape the potential for delivering a personalized optichannel onlife customer experience. This understanding is crucial for determining the right strategy and defining the appropriate steps to take—since we take for granted that the need for personalization is here to stay.

This mindset applies to any company, no matter the size, sector, or geography—although it's also true that most challenger brands lack the capacity, resources, and technical expertise to rival industry giants like Adidas, Nike, UNIQLO, Walmart, Walgreens, or Starbucks. In which case, the optimal strategy is to create a data and technology roadmap that outlines very specific, customer-centric use cases with detailed requirements. (For instance, identifying the customer data elements needed to determine the necessary system integrations to offer relevant value-added services—like sending information about renting a car at a specific airport after a customer books a flight.) This approach enables challenger brands to leverage data and technology effectively, even without having the scale or resources of their larger counterparts.

Having reached this point in the book, you've likely realized that there is no one-size-fits-all roadmap that would work for every business. The complexity of the post-digital world, combined with the substantial differences and peculiarities of each company, require business leaders to proceed with accurate case-by-case analysis. But we can offer you the key findings that we distilled from our conversations with retail and consumer brand executives. Once potential structural implementation challenges—skills, capabilities, processes, technology, budget, and so on—have been addressed, we strongly recommend keeping the following in mind:

- Remember that people are willing to trade their data only if they receive authentic value in exchange.
- Reflect on what should be customized versus personalized, consider the necessary investments, and allocate resources accordingly.
- Assess all touchpoints and define which interactions should be automated and which instead must be

handled with the personal touch of a human being. (See the next chapter for more on this aspect.)

- Ensure that decisions are made after you've found the right balance between big and small data to avoid homogenization and data bias, which could have serious repercussions on your brand reputation.
- Constantly monitor national and global legislation established to protect consumers' privacy so you can avoid legal breaches.
- Evaluate and continuously optimize your personalization efforts based on customer feedback and evolving market trends.

By diligently considering the opportunities and challenges outlined in this chapter, and keeping the above guidelines in mind, retailers and consumer brands are in a good position to successfully implement their onlife optichannel personalization strategy. As we've seen, technology is destined to play a crucial role in enabling scalable personalization. However, to ensure authenticity, there will still be cases where organizations need to rely on the capacity of human beings to forge genuine emotional connections. In the following chapter, we will specifically explore the evolving role of humans in a world predominantly shaped by machines and software.

Reflection Summary Questions

- In which channels do you value being acknowledged and recognized as an individual? In which channels are you more interested in rapidly accomplishing your task?

- How can you strike the right balance between customization and personalization in your customer interactions, ensuring that you allocate resources effectively?
- Is your organization addressing the potential challenges of privacy concerns, information overload, bias, and homogenization of experiences in your personalization efforts?
- Are you continuously evaluating and optimizing your personalization efforts based on customer feedback and evolving market trends?

16

Be Human

The Connaught Bar, located in Mayfair, London, has been bestowed with the prestigious title of best bar in the world for both 2020 and 2021. We discussed the secret behind the bar's allure—and its renown for impeccable service and ceremonious presentation of martinis—with Agostino Perrone, the director of mixology, and his first assistant, Giorgio Bargiani. Without hesitation they revealed: "Anyone can create a good cocktail; it ultimately boils down to having the right ingredients and knowing the recipe. What sets the best bartenders apart is the skill to combine the perfect drink with the artistry of crafting a unique ceremony that surpasses expectations and creates an exceptional customer experience."[1] This point emphasizes how effective human creativity and ingenuity can be—which is clearly even truer when one's competition is machines. On the other hand, standardization can provide great efficiency and scale, whether or not enabled by digital technology.

In Chapter 8, "High Tech + High Touch," we discussed the great value that human personnel can bring to the customer journey—as well as the importance of finding the right mix of channels when planning an onlife optichannel strategy. In this chapter we'll discuss the balance between humans and machines when it comes to crafting the best customer experience. This topic is particularly current considering the debate around the role of generative AI in reshaping work. According to the professional services network PwC, 52% of the CEOs they interviewed in a "Workforce of the future" survey are currently exploring the benefits of humans and machines working together, and 58% are already addressing the implications of automation on stakeholder trust.[2]

In *The Wall Street Journal* in August 2011, Marc Andreessen—an American entrepreneur, venture capital investor, and software engineer—likened the fact that more and more businesses across all industries were progressively being "run on software and delivered as online services" to be the equivalent of "software eating the world." Back then there were "only" 2 billion people who could access broadband internet versus 5.18 billion in April 2023. Since 2011, the software industry has experienced astounding growth, with traditional companies increasingly recognizing the need to adopt a software-centric mindset to compete and thrive in the post-digital era. The most emblematic examples of this transition are the debacle of Kodak in the photography industry, the demise of the brick-and-mortar retailer Blockbuster after the rise of the software-based Netflix, and of course the case of Amazon versus traditional booksellers and other retailers. Established players were left no choice but to rapidly adapt or die. Some of them reacted with acquisitions, such as when the "incumbent" Disney bought the "insurgent" software company Pixar so as to remain relevant in the animated-film industry. Other incumbents managed to transition from a traditional model to a more software-infused one. As noted earlier, Walmart very successfully rode the online marketplace wave, remaining the top world retailer despite the rise of digitally native aggressive competitors. Of course, there are industries relatively less impacted by this revolution—including construction, mining, and oil and gas—but it's clear that Andreessen's prediction proved to be absolutely true.[3]

Earlier in the book we discussed the shift toward digitalization and its impact on retailers and consumer brands, referring to it as Retail 4.0. As we move into the post-digital era of Retail 5.0, it becomes crucial for business leaders to understand and address the specific implications of this world to their own organizations. As we stated in the introduction, Retail 5.0 is the time when expectations converge with reality, necessitating strategic decisions and concrete actions about the integration of digital innovation and specific human expertise. For example, consider the following questions: How can organizations strike a balance between leveraging automation and preserving the human touch in customer interactions? What are the unique skills and capabilities that human employees bring to the table, and how can they be effectively harnessed in a technology-driven landscape? In what ways can human employees collaborate with AI and robotics to enhance productivity and innovation? What measures can be taken to reskill and upskill employees to adapt to the changing demands of the digital age? How can businesses foster a culture that values and nurtures human creativity, critical thinking, and emotional intelligence alongside technological advancements? These pressing questions encapsulate the essence of the post-digital world and demand immediate attention from all business leaders who hope to successfully transition to Retail 5.0.

In 2018 [Giuseppe Stigliano speaking here] I had the pleasure of visiting the headquarters of the Italian luxury fashion brand Brunello Cucinelli, a company that has always put humans at the centre of their business philosophy. During the visit, Brunello Cucinelli showed me an area of the large open space where several professionals proficient in multiple languages were dedicatedly handwriting thank-you letters that would later be inserted into the boxes destined for e-commerce clients—each letter crafted in the client's native language. This exemplary policy demonstrates how a sizable organization—operating across three continents with a turnover exceeding $1 billion[4]—has chosen to prioritize the human touch in a specific aspect of the customer journey. The company founder's intention with this practice is to express gratitude for the client's purchase and enhance the experience of receiving the package, aiming to evoke some of the enchantment typically experienced at their physical boutiques. This thoughtful gesture showcases the company's commitment to infusing a sense of warmth and personal connection into the customer experience, even within the realm of e-commerce.

While we acknowledge that implementing a practice like this wouldn't be suitable for every company, our point is that all businesses aspiring to thrive in Retail 5.0 must strategically determine their own optimal optichannel balance, in this case with specific regard to "being human." It's crucial for organizations to carefully select specific touchpoints where they intentionally emphasize the human touch. We'll go so far as to say this alchemy will determine companies' success or failure in Retail 5.0—every element in this alchemy will be instrumental to harnessing the operational efficiencies facilitated by digital technology and, at the same time, nurturing their unique value proposition. Naturally, each company must tailor its approach to strike the right balance and align with their overall business objectives in the evolving retail landscape.

Take the beauty sector for example. Vasiliki Petrou—the group CEO of Unilever Prestige, an umbrella brand that includes various world-class premium beauty brands including Tatcha, Dermalogica, Kate Somerville, Garancia, Murad, Paula's Choice, Ren, Hourglass, and Living Proof[5]—told us: "In the foreseeable future, people are unlikely to prefer machines touching their face and skin over human touch." She explained that "for many customers, the human connection between a professional expert and the client is what truly enhances the overall experience. Having said that, automating the initial assessment of the face and body diagnostics and offering quick tips based on data to predict and recommend a bespoke regime is perfectly acceptable. However, especially for products closely related to one's body, I believe that customers will still desire to interact with a human."[6]

At Canada Goose, the Canadian holding company of winter clothing manufacturers, they too attend to this balance. Chief marketing and experience officer Penny Brook told us: "In the post-COVID world, we've come to understand the heightened importance of establishing emotional connections with our customers. As a result, we have dedicated increased attention and investment in enhancing the way people interact with customers in our stores. From the warm welcome moment to the product presentations and all the accompanying experiences, we strive to create meaningful and memorable interactions. This approach generates positive word-of-mouth both online and offline."[7] This sentiment is echoed by Federico Turconi, CEO of the Americas at Gucci, who told us: "While technology plays a crucial role before and after the store visit, we believe in fostering a pure human-to-human interaction during the in-store experience. This human touch is what truly resonates with our customers, making their time in our stores more meaningful and fostering stronger connections that endure beyond their visit."[8]

Unity Is Strength

The principle "be human" recognizes that true power lies in harnessing the strengths of both machines and humans.

By integrating machine-driven insights and automation with human creativity, empathy, ingenuity, and strategic thinking, organizations can achieve unparalleled marketing excellence in the ever-evolving business landscape. Looking forward, this integration will determine the very value proposition of companies. Some companies will build their positioning around a high degree of machine-powered automation; others will emphasize the human factor in specific stages of the customer journey. The key for success will be dictated by the ability to adapt and continuously refine the strategy in order to maximize both the efficiencies led by machines and the warm touch of people. In fact, although there are situations where one unquestionably performs better than the other, the choice will be also driven by the desire to create differentiation—to offer something that no one else does.

To better reflect on this aspect, let's next consider the strengths and weaknesses of machines and humans. Machines tend to outperform humans in the following domains:

Data analysis and pattern recognition: Machines possess unparalleled computational power, enabling them to swiftly analyze vast amounts of data and identify intricate patterns that would elude human perception. From customer segmentation to predictive analytics, machines excel in extracting actionable insights from complex data sets.

Personalization at scale: As we highlighted in the previous chapter, machines can enable highly personalized experiences across multiple touchpoints because they can effortlessly process immense volumes of customer data.

Through advanced algorithms and machine-learning processes, machines can deliver tailored content, customized offerings, and individualized recommendations to a vast customer base.

Performance-driven real-time optimization: Machines are adept at continuously monitoring and adjusting marketing campaigns in real-time. With their ability to process and respond to data instantaneously, machines can autonomously optimize advertising targeting, bidding strategies, and content delivery to efficiently maximize engagement and conversion rate.

Automated customer support: Machines excel in handling routine customer queries and providing prompt responses. Think of AI-powered chatbots and virtual assistants, for example. Their availability 24/7 ensures immediate assistance for standard queries, reduces customer wait times, and frees up human agents to focus on more complex and value-added interactions.

Measurement, attribution, and prediction: Machines can precisely track and attribute marketing activities to specific outcomes, enabling data-driven decision-making and fairly accurate predictions. Through advanced analytics and attribution models, machines provide valuable insights into the effectiveness and ROI of various marketing channels and campaigns, increasing the efficiency and effectiveness of future campaigns.

As we highlighted in Chapter 8, an interesting example of the growing influence of machines is represented by partially or fully automated stores and robots "employed" as sales associates or servers. When deciding whether or not to take that route, companies should consider different factors, including increasing efficiency, experimenting with new technologies, tapping into emerging customer preferences, and wanting to be perceived as innovators.

To follow are just some of the many ways humans excel over machines:

Creativity and innovation: Human imagination, intuition, ingenuity, lateral thinking, and emotional intelligence foster creativity and innovation in every domain, including of course marketing. Humans possess the ability to think beyond data and algorithms, envision new strategies, and craft compelling narratives that resonate with audiences on a deeper level.

Emotional connection and empathy: Humans possess an innate capacity to empathize and connect emotionally with each other. Skilled human marketers and sales representatives can understand all the nuances of customer motivations, aspirations, and pain points; with this data they can foster genuine emotional connections, build long-lasting relationships, and nurture brand loyalty. The ability to establish trust, engage in meaningful dialogue, and cultivate partnerships remains a uniquely human trait, and it's instrumental even in customer-facing activities such as influencer marketing, in-store promotions, product demonstrations, direct selling, and so on.

Complex problem-solving: Humans excel in tackling intricate and ambiguous challenges that require critical thinking, strategic planning, and adaptability. They can navigate nuanced situations, consider multiple and sometime conflicting perspectives, and develop creative solutions that transcend the constraints of a data-driven approach.

Ethical and value-based decision making: Humans possess moral judgment and ethical reasoning, allowing them to make value-based decisions that align with both an organization's purpose and societal expectations. Human marketers can navigate ethical dilemmas and ensure responsible marketing practices.

Business leaders will need to gain a deep understanding of the strengths and weaknesses of both worlds, analyze the journey of the customer personas that they serve, assess the characteristics of their organizations and the resources at their disposal, and eventually combine all the "ingredients" to create the perfect "cocktail." There will be situations in which a company may favour automated customer support, perhaps because the majority of inquiries from clients are to verify basic information—and others in which the warm touch of a human operator will be preferred. There will be tasks for which a company will double down on performance-based algorithms and others in which gut feeling and human intuition will unlock the power of creative problem-solving. At the other end of the spectrum, customers will choose the value proposition that better suits their preferences and budget.

We discussed this aspect with Martin Lindstrom, a Danish author, consultant, and keynote speaker who has been defined as a modern-day Sherlock Holmes for his ability to harness the power of what he has defined as "small data." He provided us with an interesting perspective on how brands should consider the equilibrium between the power of technology to process data and automate actions and the role of authentic human emotions. Over the years Lindstrom has visited thousands of homes, across almost a hundred different countries, in order to understand what it takes to create cultural transformations that impact both business and society. He asserts that, while Big Data is valuable for analyzing the past, it lacks the ability to predict the future, making it a valuable yet incomplete solution. From his viewpoint, "Big data excels at uncovering correlations in vast data sets, but small data is the key to revealing causation—the 'why' behind consumer behaviour. We require both. However, it's crucial to acknowledge that Big Data alone may not evoke emotions or provide profound insights into the underlying reasons for customer behaviour. Often, the most effective approach to discovering unmet desires, identifying gaps in offerings, and personalizing customer relationships lies in the small, subtle clues." Lindstrom offers companies a complementary perspective that leverages technology's data-processing capabilities while emphasizing that emotions are challenging to describe solely through data. Without a deep understanding of emotions, companies struggle to form genuine connections with their customers.

We are convinced that this ability to establish an emotional connection will be even more crucial in a world progressively more dominated by technology, artificial intelligence, and automation. Therefore, companies should carefully discern the channels where they want to delegate tasks to machines and those where humans are still the killer app. As we have stated in Chapter 8, "High Tech + High Touch," when personalization is informed by technology but performed by a person, its full potential is unleashed.

It's important to acknowledge that applying the Be Human principle to business isn't limited to the business-to-consumer (B2C) realm. Similar to the concept of business-to-people (BTP) and the broader idea of human-to-human (H2H) marketing (which we discussed in another book, *H2H*

Marketing: The Genesis of Human-to-Human Marketing) we advocate for a general paradigm shift to a more human-centred approach in marketing and business. Applying this guiding principle to business-to-business (B2B) contexts involves recognizing the importance of human interactions and values—even within procurement and purchase departments, and among industrial buyers and suppliers. Despite the professional nature of these relationships, it is crucial to understand the role of human beings in these interactions, since all individuals, regardless of their business roles, are driven by the pursuit of value and guided by their own set of values.

In conclusion, the complex problem-solving of the post-digital world requires strategic thinking and adaptability. Humans can navigate ambiguity and uncertainty, incorporating real-time market dynamics and evolving customer expectations into their decision-making process. They can adjust strategies as needed, taking into account unforeseen challenges and opportunities that may arise during the implementation phase. In this scenario, relying solely on machines and data-driven approaches would be insufficient. While machines can provide valuable insights and support decision-making processes by analyzing vast amounts of data, they lack the human ability to think critically, adapt to changing circumstances, and develop innovative solutions that go beyond predefined patterns. Therefore, in a complex post-digital world that includes intricate challenges, human involvement is essential for leveraging critical thinking, strategic planning, and adaptability to drive effective and sustainable solutions. As we write, generative AI is showing astonishing abilities. In the next few years, it will be our responsibility to ensure that unity becomes strength.

Reflection Summary Questions

- What are the unique skills and capabilities that humans bring to the table, and how can they be effectively harnessed in a technology-driven landscape?
- How can businesses foster a culture that values and nurtures human creativity, critical thinking, and emotional intelligence alongside technological advancements?
- In what ways can human employees collaborate with AI and robotics to enhance productivity and innovation?
- What measures can be taken to reskill and upskill employees to adapt to the changing demands of the digital age?
- How can organizations strike a balance between leveraging automation and preserving the human touch in customer interactions?

17

Be a Destination

In 1974 in the *Journal of Retailing*, I [Philip Kotler speaking here] argued that "one of the most important recent advances in business thinking is the recognition that people, in their purchase decision-making, respond to more than simply the tangible product or service being offered. The tangible product—a pair of shoes, a refrigerator, a haircut, or a meal—is only a small part of the total consumption package. Buyers respond to the total product. It includes the services, warranties, packaging, advertising, financing, pleasantries, images, and other features that accompany the product." And I used the concept of atmospherics to define the way stores can be conceived to stimulate customers. "We shall use the term 'atmospherics' to describe the conscious designing of space to create certain effects in buyers. More specifically, atmospherics is the effort to design buying environments to produce specific emotional effects in [buyers] that enhance [their] purchase probability."[1] Indeed, atmospherics is a marketing tool.

By carefully designing and managing the environment in which products or services are presented, businesses can create memorable and emotionally resonant atmospheres that influence consumer perceptions, attitudes, and purchasing decisions. These atmospheres aim to engage customers on a deeper level, fostering brand loyalty and differentiation in a highly competitive market. At the time of the article—in the mid-1970s—the main drivers were colour, brightness, size, shape, volume, scent, temperature, and so on. In a post-digital world, the concept of atmospherics can also be applied to digital or virtual "spaces" as they too represent buying environments and must be designed to produce specific effects aimed at enhancing purchase probability.

"Be a destination" represents an evolution of the concept of "atmospherics as a marketing tool," as it applies to all touchpoints that constitute a three-dimensional customer journey. The ultimate goal is to establish captivating destinations that offer visitors a compelling reason to be there. These destinations can cater to various purposes—such as purely transactional, educational, entertaining, recreational, or immersive experiences—aiming to create places that people genuinely want to visit and engage with. What matters is that every destination lives in harmony with all others in a way that amplifies the overall result along a three-dimensional customer journey. In this case too, the whole is greater than the sum of its parts. We could say that an optichannel strategy is based on a harmonic sequence of carefully designed and seamlessly integrated destinations. Needless to say, this poses challenges that need to be addressed in terms of the coordination, marginal contribution, and skills required to manage the process.

Being a destination means acknowledging the fluidity of the onlife three-dimensional customer journey and the importance of creating want-to-go-to places that lure in customers and are consistent with the broader brand ecosystem. These spaces can be permanent or temporary. For example, at the end of 2022 BMW created the exhibition *The Italians' Touch* in Milan both to pay tribute to the many Italian talents who have contributed to the success of the BMW Group worldwide and to inspire the management of the Italian branch. The exhibition was housed in an innovative space that blends high-tech with high-touch—purpose-built in the centre of Milan—known as the House of BMW. The company's idea was to create a space to establish an emotional connection with the Italian audience.

There are also situations when these destinations are not part of the ecosystem of the brand but are third-party e-commerce intermediaries all over the world that have established themselves as go-to places for millions of people. Think of the likes of Alibaba, Amazon, Americanas, eBay, Farfetch, JD.com, Mercado Libre, Pinduoduo, Rakuten, YNaP, and Zalando. Whether these platforms are used in the "upper funnel" stage, when consumers are researching a future purchase, or down in the "lower funnel" when they become customers, these platforms are unmissable destinations. According to Jungle Scout's Consumer Trends Report, in the US alone, when starting the journey online, 61% of shoppers begin their product hunt on Amazon and 49% on a search engine (respondents could select multiple options). And 77% of respondents overall said they specifically look for reviews; this number is even higher for Gen Z (87%) and millennials (81%). Interestingly, even 11% discover products on TikTok. (And let us not forget, worldwide, retail e-commerce sales are forecasted to surpass $8 trillion by 2026.)[2]

These are very relevant data points, since social media are de facto one of the most reliable and effective sources of inspiration to find new products, services, and experiences—even though the platforms aren't owned by any brands, per se. And this is especially true for younger generations who tend to spend more time online and are less attached to physical stores, at least from a transactional standpoint. Social media destinations attract—daily—almost 5 billion people worldwide, with an average daily usage of 144 minutes.[3] And they go well beyond the discovery/awareness phase; in many cases people buy (and sell) directly within these platforms. This means that users can quickly go from awareness to action in a matter of seconds without leaving the app. (We describe the five A's—Awareness, Appeal, Ask, Act, and Advocacy—in a sidebar in Chapter 14.) Globally, social commerce revenue amounted to around $728 billion in 2022, and forecasts project a remarkable compound annual growth rate (CAGR) of 31.6% from 2023 to 2030, propelling revenues in this segment to reach an estimated $6.2 trillion by 2030.[4]

These digital destinations represent safe environments that people visit on a regular basis, attracted by a familiar user experience, an efficient user interface, secure transactions, effective customer support, the possibility to interact with peers, and the option to discover (and buy) products, services, and experiences away from branded touchpoints, which are inevitably less objective. In other cases, the digital touchpoint to be transformed into a destination is a brand-controlled touchpoint. This happens, for example, with a company's website or a branded content platform, which are typically the best means to collect first-party data about users and therefore represent great value for retailers and brands. In fact, this granular user data is not accessible through third parties such as e-commerce platforms or social media.

We observe a similar dynamic even in relation to the most recent dimension of the customer journey, the virtual. As we saw in Chapter 14, "Be Onlife," players of *Assassin's Creed* can enjoy tours in various countries and travel in time, and players of *Fortnite* can buy NFTs of branded jackets without leaving their favourite platform. And in the next few years the number of virtual worlds in which people will spend part of their life for various reasons—including discovering and purchasing products, education, training, and work—will likely increase. The global metaverse market size, for example, was estimated at $234.04 billion in 2022, and is projected to grow from $416.02 billion in 2023 to $3,409.29 billion by 2027, exhibiting a CAGR of 69.2% during the forecast period.[5] Digital and virtual touchpoints represent in their own right destinations that people will prefer more and more whenever they're not inclined to head to a physical store.

Redefining Brick-and-Mortar Stores

While "being a destination," as a guiding principle of Retail 5.0, holds true for all touchpoints, it's particularly relevant for brick-and-mortar stores for two reasons. First, because the majority of transactions continue to occur in brick-and-mortar stores; and second because, as we've discussed, their relevancy is challenged by a plethora of more recent and potentially more engaging touchpoints. For this reason, retailers and brands need to rethink their value proposition in the light of a three-dimensional onlife customer journey and a post-digital world. Physical stores possess unique qualities that allow them to play a vital role in the overall customer journey. However, to remain relevant, they must establish a compelling reason for their existence.

In a complex landscape where people can do virtually everything with digital and virtual devices, brick-and-mortar stores must build on their peculiarities and double down on very specific features. Retail managers might decide to invest in robots, jumping on the bandwagon of "avatarizing service people," to quote Germany-based software developers Humanizing Technologies. For example, consider the hamburger-cooking robot Flippy, designed to lower the operational costs of restaurants and surprise customers with an innovative experience. Other retailers, such as in fashion, shoes, and accessories, might decide to push in the opposite direction, leveraging the hitherto unique possibility to try on garments—building a ceremony that emphasizes the characteristics of their products while evoking specific emotions, moods, or experiences to influence consumer behaviour. In this case the product tends to become the souvenir of the overall experience[6] and the store a sought-after destination.

Some brands are using the physical space to create an experiential flagship venue. In Paris, the luxury brand Dior has revealed its meticulously renovated flagship store now transformed into a versatile multi-purpose venue. Spanning nearly 108,000 square feet (approximately 10,000 square meters), the grand building boasts a plethora of offerings, including an expansive permanent exhibition space, two exquisite restaurants, three enchanting gardens, and even a lavish private guest suite. As Pietro Beccari, the chairman and CEO of Christian Dior Couture, describes it: "It's not just a flagship—it's a universe that we present." Also in Paris, Galeries Lafayette, the iconic department store on Boulevard Haussmann in the 9th arrondissement, in 2022 unveiled a 3,200 square feet (3,000 square meter) Wellness Galerie—its entire ground floor—intending to be *the* destination for the well-being sphere.[7]

Other retail spaces will dedicate a portion to the community of customers, allowing them to rent the space for private events. For example, the British luxury retailer Selfridges offers nontraditional wedding ceremonies in its iconic, historical Oxford Street site. They offer an array of distinct packages, including an intimate option catering to just six guests. Couples are treated to personalized fashion advice from the store's skilled stylists and can have their hair and makeup expertly done in-store before the ceremony. Additional options include access to a private cinema, exquisite fine-dining experiences, or a four-hour DJ set to enhance the celebration.[8]

Some retailers are targeting families. The United Arab Emirates' Dubai Mall, one of the largest shopping malls in the world, offers various family-oriented attractions, including KidZania (a scaled city where every child is given the freedom to be whoever they want), an indoor ice rink, a VR Park, an aquarium, and a fountain show.

When we discussed this aspect with Lucia Marcuzzo, senior vice president and managing director North Europe at Levi Strauss & Co., she shared with us the company's view: "We understand that in a post-digital world the role of each touchpoint must be distinctive and strategically planned. In our view, our e-commerce website is 'the flagship of all flagships' and must represent our full assortment, with all personalization options available in addition to exclusives that spark deeper engagement. While when it comes to brick-and-mortar stores, we have designed the entire experience to attract, engage and serve a younger audience."[9] And Carlo Colpo, Lavazza's group marketing communication director and brand home director, confirmed this approach aimed at avoiding overlaps and conflicts between different channels. According to Colpo:

> *It is crucial to assign specific objectives to each touchpoint, capitalizing on their individual strengths, regardless of whether the interaction occurs on Lavazza's owned platforms*

> *or third-party channels. In fact, there is no need to compete against players with significant scale and expertise in specific domains. Instead, Lavazza seeks to collaborate in a win-win manner, finding complementary ways to work together. On the other hand, the brand aims to offer customers who engage with Lavazza's proprietary channels unique and exclusive products, services, and experiences. This approach ensures that customers have compelling reasons to choose Lavazza's owned platforms, where they can access unparalleled offerings and engage in distinctive interactions.*[10]

Given the numerous experiments that retailers and brands are conducting worldwide, constantly transforming their physical spaces to adapt to constantly evolving customer expectations, it's clear that the possibilities are endless. In some cases, the lines between the three dimensions of physical, digital, and virtual blend seamlessly.

The telecommunications company Ericsson states that consumers expect hybrid mall experiences to be common by 2030 and predicts the emergence of hybrid connectivity-enabled physical spaces, where AR glasses, waterproof VR glasses, haptic body suits, and tactile gloves could all be part of consumers' gear when visiting malls. A common service will be what they call Meta Tailor, where customers can cocreate bespoke garments to be worn in real life and as avatars, as people will increasingly desire to look as good in both dimensions.[11] This is part of the so-called Crypto-and-Mortar trend described by The Future Laboratory, where brands sell digital assets (NFTs) through traditional stores, in an effort to respond to the growing demand for virtual assets that are more or less aligned with their human owners' style. As reported in their research: "Sportswear brand Adidas and luxury label Prada collaborated on a crowdsourced Crypto-and-Mortar project, launched in January 2022. The brands collated 3,000 consumer-submitted photographs, selected by raffle, to be minted into NFTs for free—while giving the original creator the option to own or sell their NFT. All images were then combined and displayed as a large-scale installation in Prada and Adidas flagship stores."[12]

The concept of stores as social gathering spaces for specific communities is not new, but it's an even more powerful one in a post-digital world. And it's a great way to emphasize the peculiar trait of this touchpoint of providing people with a reason and a place to physically meet. Apple stores, among others, are known for hosting many community events, free workshops, and events on photography, coding, music, and more. These events attract people of all ages and skill levels, turning Apple stores into community learning centres and fostering the bond with the brand. REI, the US speciality outdoor retailer, organizes outdoor classes, workshops, and hiking excursions, encouraging customers to embrace an active lifestyle and connect with like-minded individuals. Isetan, a Japanese department store with branches throughout Japan and South East Asia, often features themed pop-up shops, art installations, and food festivals, turning shopping into a multi-sensory experience and attracting both locals and tourists. Decathlon—a French sporting goods retailer with over 2,080 stores in 56 countries and regions in Europe (2023)—in an effort to promote an active lifestyle and encourage customers to try new sports, offers sports-related workshops and activities such as yoga classes, cycling tours, and climbing sessions. And Eataly, the largest Italian food market and restaurant concept, with over 40 locations worldwide, offers cooking classes, wine tastings, and other educational activities related to the food-and-beverage domain.[13]

The quintessential examples of this concept are represented by the creation of branded hotels and members' clubs, which typically target a high-end audience. Luxury fashion houses such as Armani, Bulgari, Fendi, Louis Vuitton, Missoni, and Versace have all ventured into the hospitality industry and created their own hotel-destinations, offering travelers unique and luxurious experiences that reflect their respective brand identities and provide an additional touchpoint to create a holistic journey. Francesca Bellettini, former CEO of the luxury fashion house Yves Saint Laurent and currently at the helm of Gucci, confirmed to us that "what remains key is to continue to ensure the highest level of customer service through unique desirable experiences. Above all, we will always strive to create desirability, without which luxury becomes a commodity."[14]

In 2023 Harrods, the historic retailer currently owned by the Qatar Investment Authority, launched its first private members' club in Shanghai, China, in a protected building spanning over 5,620 square feet (522 square meters). Members can partake of Gordon Ramsay's first dining experience in Shanghai as well as the lounge, private dining rooms, terraces, tearoom, and piano bar. Michael Ward, the managing director of Harrods, described the space to us as "a home away from home to serve a curated community of discerning members. This is a new format for Harrods and also a unique proposition in Shanghai. Our members will not only enjoy world-class dining and spirits with a like-minded community, but also benefit from exclusive Harrods international lifestyle and concierge services to create an unparalleled customer experience."[15] Private clubs offer brands an exclusive and personalized environment for their customers, aimed at creating a sense of exclusivity and privilege. This more intimate setting facilitates relationship-building and enables retailers to better understand their customers' preferences and needs—knowledge they can use to offer more tailored products and services. Plus, members may be enticed by exclusive events, limited-edition products, or personalized offers, which then can lead to increased sales and revenue for the luxury retailer.

Needless to say, in this context the role of sales people must vary. First and foremost, they need to develop technological capabilities and embrace a more holistic approach. Also, they need to reinterpret their role for a world in which, in many cases, people will expect everything *but* buying products from a store. They need to become savvy curators, hosts, facilitators, advisors—and even anthropologists, sociologists, and psychologists.

Common Traits

In a world where abundance reigns and choices overwhelm, the essence of a successful business destination—whether on land or online—lies in its ability to curate go-to places for customers. These destinations serve as safe harbours where people can confidently navigate the vast sea of options to meet their needs and desires. Drawing from our experience, successful physical, digital, and virtual destinations often exhibit shared characteristics:

Compelling value proposition: Successful destinations have a clear and compelling value proposition that acts in synergy with all touchpoints and resonates with the target audience. The objective is always to fulfill specific needs or desires, either by providing a functional response or by creating captivating atmospherics that capture the attention and interest of visitors, leaving a lasting impression. It's no longer viable to build a competitive advantage on just nuanced differences.

Strong brand identity: Successful destinations have a well-defined brand identity that conveys its values, mission, and unique personality. This consistency builds brand loyalty, trust, and credibility among visitors.

Human-friendly design: Human-friendliness is crucial for digital and virtual destinations. Navigating the platform should be intuitive and straightforward, ensuring a seamless and enjoyable experience for users. Since this is also true in the physical world, a lot of attention must be paid when deploying advances in in-store technologies such as robots and automated interfaces.

Community and social interaction: Successful destinations often foster a sense of community and social interaction. They encourage communication, networking, and the exchange of ideas among visitors, customers, and sales associates. And though this is relevant in most circumstances, it's less true for touchpoints that maximize efficiency.

Responsive customer support: Responsive customer support across all touchpoints is essential to cultivate genuine customer relationships. Providing quick and helpful assistance to resolve issues promptly is a key ingredient in a complex onlife world.

By designing appealing atmospheres (destinations) in physical stores, online platforms, or virtual spaces, businesses can enhance brand perception and customer engagement, and ultimately drive sales by shaping the overall consumer experience. And for those brands that mostly sell through intermediaries, these spaces represent a particularly vital opportunity to build a direct relationship with consumers and potentially collect their precious data without any intermediation (as we have discussed in Chapter 3, referring to the opportunities for manufacturers to operate in a direct-to-consumer mode).

There will also be more extreme scenarios where the main purpose of brick-and-mortar stores is confined to the role of fulfillment centres for online and virtual customer journeys—or perhaps hybrid situations that call for hacking infrastructure and operations to serve multiple functions (e.g., maintaining the current layout and devoting part of the surface to the pickup of online orders by end users or express couriers that manage last-mile delivery). For example, in response to the pandemic the major electronics retailer Best Buy dedicated part of its stores to fulfillment centres, facilitating quick local delivery. Whole Foods and Amazon Fresh stores are adept at delivering online orders directly from their physical locations; they do this care of "dark stores" exclusively dedicated to the task of fulfilling orders.[16]

Whether retailers and brands opt for an ambitious but potentially rewarding push in the direction of a compelling brand experience, or they pivot toward more functional destinations, the bottom line is that in the post-digital realm, destinations must serve a very specific purpose. As we have seen, in an optichannel approach there is no room for everything-for-everyone value propositions. In order to be a destination, retailers and brands would be wise to focus on each touchpoint to ensure relevance and optimization.

In Retail 5.0, all players need to take a comprehensive view of their physical, digital, and virtual presence. These channels shouldn't be seen as substitutes or competitors. Instead, each company will need to find its unique configuration, and optimize all touchpoints/destinations to obtain the highest complementarity.

Reflection Summary Questions

- In a post-digital world, how can brick-and-mortar stores redefine their value proposition to remain relevant and compelling to customers who have access to a plethora of online and virtual shopping options?
- How can businesses effectively create emotionally resonant destinations in both physical and digital spaces to influence consumer perceptions and purchasing decisions?
- How can your company effectively transform touchpoints into destinations?
- What strategies should your company employ to turn brick-and-mortar stores into social gathering spaces that foster community engagement and strengthen the bond with the brand?
- How can retailers and brands equip salespeople with the necessary skills to become savvy curators, hosts, facilitators, and advisors in a post-digital world?

18

Be Exponential

This name of this guiding principle is inspired by the 2014 book *Exponential Organizations: Why New Organizations Are Ten Times Better, Faster, and Cheaper Than Yours (and What to Do About It)* by Salim Ismail with Michael S. Malone and Yuri van Geest.[1] This type of organization leverages exponential technologies and strategies to achieve rapid growth and outperform traditional linear competitors. Exponential organizations are often structured in a decentralized way, relying on networks, platforms, and ecosystems. They leverage external resources to extend their capabilities and access a wide range of expertise.

The "be exponential" principle encourages retailers and brands to embrace an open and flexible approach to innovation. We firmly believe that in today's rapidly evolving world, where industry lines are blending and customer expectations are morphing quickly, relying solely on internal resources for innovation would prove counterproductive. The true path to success lies in collaboration, co-creation, and the seamless integration of diverse ideas and perspectives. Therefore, embracing this principle for an organization calls for accepting its limits, assessing its potential areas of growth, and genuinely exploring all options so as to determine which approach is preferable: trying to develop an internal solution, or looking for one or more partners to codevelop or even manage the development—thus building a strategic alliance. This collaboration can manifest in various forms. Some form tactical partnerships with other brands aimed at launching products that appeal to each other's current or prospective audiences. Or multiple brands might come together for a joint venture to introduce a new service, capitalizing on their respective strengths and capabilities.

Cristiano Fagnani of Reebok told us how they have built their exponential collaboration with their key partners:

> *At Reebok, the direct-to-consumer team manages the relationship and the business with key e-commerce platforms such as Zalando or Farfetch. We are currently developing a "partner programme" that aims to fully transition these clients from wholesale to an integrated digital partnership, based on strategic alignment on the Go To Market and access to a shared inventory. When consumers go online looking/searching for Reebok we want to make sure we can engage and service them at best from all different available access points. We support our digital partners and value their proficiency in establishing direct consumer engagement, complementing the brand efforts on owned channels. Therefore, a more strategic approach is to foster collaboration under the Be Exponential philosophy that you have described, ensuring seamless alignment in communication, access to our complete inventory (beyond agreed-upon stock), and streamlined logistics (eliminating the need for our partners to stock products).*[2]

Although there are many different approaches, the true essence of this principle reaches its pinnacle within an ecosystem, where each participant has the opportunity to experience exponential growth by leveraging the collective strengths of the entire network. We define a business ecosystem as a specific configuration where companies collaborate to combine their specific capabilities to create, deliver, and capture value. This mutually beneficial configuration has the potential to generate greater value, thereby increasing benefits for all stakeholders involved. The ambition is to join forces to create value proposition that meets customers' demand in a "new" way and enables a more efficient modus operandi for all involved. If all works well, it's the proverbial win-win scenario. Of course, this strategy's success depends on both its execution and how effectively the parties can work together. Ecosystems involve various players—suppliers, customers, partners, competitors—working together in a complex, interdependent manner.

Michael G. Jacobides,[3] a professor of strategy and entrepreneurship at London Business School (LBS), is globally recognized as an authority on this topic. He explained to us:

> *Ecosystems are both enabled by and a result of the exponential change of what you describe as a post-digital world. Their rise has been closely intertwined with the dominance of Big Tech such as Google, Apple, Facebook, Microsoft, Amazon, Tencent, and Alibaba, who have based their success on building ecosystems around their platforms. Ecosystems now regard everyone, whether they like it or not, for two reasons: first, digitization enables all firms, including the most traditional ones, to interconnect and reconfigure their activities in unprecedented ways, reconfiguring sectors old and new; and second, deregulation has blurred the boundaries between sectors, leading to a very different approach to production and consumption than what we had until recently.*

Different Types of Business Ecosystems

These ecosystems can be quite articulated. They often involve various players, upstream and downstream. Suppliers, customers, partners, and even competitors work together in a complex, interdependent manner. As we've seen, ecosystems can be intrinsically digital, technology platforms, e-commerce marketplaces, social media, app stores, Internet of Things (IoT)—or they can be enabled by digitization in more mature sectors. (For more on the distinction between "platforms" and "ecosystems," see the following note.)[4] Here are some examples of companies or industries that for the purpose of this chapter we can consider business ecosystems:

Technology platforms: Companies like Google, Apple, and Microsoft can be seen as business ecosystems. They provide platforms that attract developers, app creators, content providers, advertisers, and customers, creating a network effect that benefits all participants. Other examples of tech platforms in the mobility sector include Uber, Lyft, and Didi, which connect drivers, passengers, and additional services through their platforms. Food-delivery platforms such as Deliveroo, DoorDash, Just Eat, Swiggy, and Uber Eats interconnect restaurants, dark kitchens, riders, and customers.

E-commerce: Online marketplaces such as Alibaba, Amazon, Farfetch, Flipkart, JD.com, YNaP, Rakuten, or Zalando facilitate interactions among buyers, sellers, and logistics providers, forming a robust e-commerce ecosystem.

Social media: Platforms such as Facebook, Instagram, LinkedIn, TikTok, and X form business ecosystems where users, advertisers, content creators, and third-party developers interact and contribute to the overall ecosystem's growth.

App stores: Apple App Store and Google Play Store serve as ecosystems for app developers, users, and even other businesses creating complementary apps and services.

Internet of Things: IoT ecosystems involve companies that create and connect smart devices, data analytics services, and software platforms to deliver smart solutions and services.

Beside mobility and food delivery, there are other traditional industries that have been interested by this dynamic, including:

Health care: The health care industry can be viewed as a complex ecosystem involving hospitals, medical practitioners, pharmaceutical companies, insurance providers, medical device manufacturers, and patients. For example, Philips, a health care technology company, has developed the HealthSuite ecosystem, an open, cloud-based platform that collects, compiles, and analyzes clinical and other data from a wide range of devices and sources including medical devices, electronic health records, and health apps to provide personalized health insights for patients and health care providers.[5]

Financial services: The financial sector includes banks, credit card companies, payment processors, fintech start-ups, and other financial institutions, forming an interconnected ecosystem to provide various financial services. For example, Alipay, operated by Ant Group, is a digital payment ecosystem that offers mobile payments, peer-to-peer transfers, wealth management services, and credit facilities. It has transformed the way people conduct financial transactions in China.[6]

Energy: Renewable energy providers, smart grid technologies, energy storage companies, and electric vehicle infrastructure have come together to create more sustainable and efficient energy solutions. For example, the energy company Enel X has developed an e-mobility ecosystem that includes an electric vehicle charging infrastructure, smart charging solutions, and partnerships with automakers and mobility service providers.[7]

These examples are just a few illustrations of the numerous business ecosystems that exist across different industries. The defining characteristic is that they involve multiple interconnected participants collaborating to create, deliver, and capture value.

McKinsey projects that by 2025, the current landscape of over 100 industries and value chains will consolidate into approximately a dozen colossal ecosystems, generating an estimated $60 trillion in revenues. Additionally, a study by BCG revealed that the usage of the term "ecosystem" in the annual reports of major companies increased 13 times from 2012 to 2022. Furthermore, they report that companies that actively embraced and acted on this concept experienced significantly higher growth rates compared to those that did not.[8]

As Jacobides highlights in a paper on the topic, from a commercial perspective "a multi-actor ecosystem denotes an alternative to the conventional make-or-buy decision."[9] In an ecosystem, all involved parties have the unique opportunity to collaboratively build something greater than the sum of its individual parts. This crucial aspect is particularly vital in today's world, where companies are expected to explore new possibilities and efficiently exploit existing resources. By doing so, the ecosystem enables and accelerates the innovation process for all participants, as they jointly shoulder the financial and operational burdens while concentrating on their respective core strengths.

In some cases, established organizations try to be exponential by collaborating with start-ups. This can lead either to collaboration with external venture incubators and accelerators or to the creation of internal corporate accelerators or entrepreneur-in-residence programmes. For example, in 2015 the American retail corporation Target joined forces with Techstars, one of the largest pre-seed investors in the world, to launch a retail-focused start-up accelerator that can fulfill the retailer's innovation needs. And although the accelerator includes a small equity stake, the start-ups are not limited to working with Target. Techstars had formerly partnered with Disney to create an accelerator focused on media and entertainment, and also with Barclays to accelerate and incubate financial tech start-ups.[10] This example illustrates how in a volatile and turbulent market companies may explore innovation in new ways. One of these players is Walmart, which opted to build an internal innovation arm called Store N°8 to incubate and accelerate start-ups "to help leapfrog where the customer and market will go . . . to enrich the lives of Walmart customers and associates."[11]

But Target and Walmart aren't the only industry players exploring how to be exponential. According to Stefano Portu, founder and CEO at ShopFully:

> *Retail is one of the largest industries in the world and its transformation can't be delayed any longer. Today retailers face a multifaceted technological disruption, including very diverse dimensions like e-commerce, drive-to-store, [and] supply and retail media, just to mention a few of the hot-*

test items on our retail partners' tables. Even the largest groups have realized that this is not doable with just an internal effort. On the contrary, it's crucial to combine a few core activities developed inside with a network of specialized partners. Our goal at ShopFully is exactly to offer retailers an easy way to plug in with their audience, data, and promotions into a new digital drive-to-store and retail media ecosystems.

Companies like ShopFully—a leading drive-to-store marketing platform that offers a reach of almost 200 million shoppers to major retailers and brands across 25 countries—position themselves as both a strategic partner on a specific activity (drive-to-store in this case) and the enabler to co-build a cutting-edge ecosystem, bridging online and offline data.[12]

The most relevant example of an ecosystem built by an established retailer brings us once again to Walmart. Over time, their expansion spanned various sectors, allowing them to compete with other retail and e-commerce giants like Amazon.[13] Walmart's ecosystem includes an online marketplace, groceries, health and wellness services, automotive and tyres, pet supplies, electronics, fashion, and more. The retail behemoth built its extensive ecosystem through a combination of internal development and strategic acquisitions, including Jet.com (acquired in 2016 for approximately $3.3 billion to bolster their online presence and discontinued in 2020); Flipkart (a 77% stake in India's leading e-commerce platform was acquired in 2018 for $16 billion); Moosejaw (an outdoor recreation and apparel retailer acquired in 2017 for $51 million and sold to Dick's Sporting Goods in 2023); ModCloth (an online women's fashion retailer acquired in 2017 for an undisclosed sum between $50 and $75 million to expand their fashion offerings and appealing to a broader customer base, sold two years later); Bonobos (a men's clothing brand known for its e-commerce and brick-and-mortar "guideshop" concept acquired for $310 million in 2017 and sold in 2023 to Express, WHP Global); and PhonePe (an Indian digital payments and financial services start-up in which Walmart owns the majority which was worth $12 billion in 2023).[14]

Although some of these acquisitions didn't deliver the expected outcomes and resulted in a net loss, they were part of the intense process of building the articulated ecosystem that allowed Walmart to survive and thrive amidst the rise of digitally native competitors like Amazon. And even when they weren't successful from a pure M&A perspective, they infused the retailer with a wealth of knowledge that enabled the management to reduce the learning curve and contain start-up costs in each specific area. The result is an impressive network of products, services, and experiences obtained through internal development, strategic partnerships, and acquisitions aimed to cater the onlife optichannel customer journey of its customers.[15]

The company strongly believes that this strategy is the best way to nurture their leading position. In the 2022 annual report the management stated: "As we execute on our [ecosystem] strategy, our flywheel is accelerating through offerings such as our Walmart Connect advertising business, Walmart Fulfillment Services, our health and wellness business, including Walmart Health, and our financial services business. These offerings represent mutually reinforcing pieces of our flywheel centred around our customers around the world who are increasingly seeking convenience."[16]

We discussed this with Federico Marchetti, an Italian businessman who in 2000 founded and, until July 2021, was chairman and CEO of YOOX Group (since 2015 named YOOX Net-a-Porter Group after the merger between the two companies), an internet retailer and e-commerce services company. The idea behind YOOX stemmed from Marchetti's observation that the luxury fashion sector was relatively slow to adopt the emerging opportunities presented by the Internet. He saw great potential in building an ecosystem that could bring luxury brands and fashion enthusiasts together in the online realm. YOOX quickly gained popularity and became one of the pioneering companies in the luxury e-commerce space, eventually expanding its offerings and collaborating with various luxury brands worldwide. As Marchetti explained: "I founded the company with the belief that a powerful collaboration between traditional fashion houses and a digitally native partner like us could yield exponential results for both parties. We used a formula to describe this philosophy: C2C + O2O = EC^2 (Content-to-commerce + Online-to-Offline = E-commerce squared)." He further elaborated, "Compelling and relevant content plays a vital role in engaging users and driving commerce alongside the seamless integration of the online shopping experience with physical retail spaces. The combined effect of these elements leads to exponential results."[17] Marchetti's recipe proved highly successful, serving as compelling evidence of the exponential power of collaboration. Without YOOX's support, fashion houses would have lacked the ability and readiness to seize the opportunities presented by nascent e-commerce.

Nor would they have gained access to such a vast audience, digital infrastructure, operational efficiencies, logistic capabilities, and the capacity to leverage content for commerce across various channels.

Unity Is Strength

We encourage retailers and brands to explore the benefits of being exponential, as it allows companies to offer customers a value proposition that is far greater than what they could actually afford if they relied on only their internal resources. It also allows companies to explore adjacent sectors without absorbing all the risks typically connected to innovation processes, including financial exposure, operational implications, talent acquisition, and so on. This idea is very much aligned with the concept of "open innovation", which encourages organizations to not just rely on "their own internal knowledge, sources, and resources (such as their own staff or R&D, for example) for innovation (of products, services, business models, processes, etc.) but [to also use] multiple external sources (such as customer feedback, published patents, competitors, external agencies, the public, etc.) to drive innovation."[18] As we have seen, this exploration can be conducted "outside-in," when an organization constantly scans the market to source ideas, and to partner with or perhaps to acquire external players; or "inside-out," when an organization develops a new product or service internally to maximize the network effect, potentially natively integrating the new solution with a pre-existing one. Outside-in innovation has been used by Lego, the Danish toy company, when it developed an open innovation platform called Lego Ideas to allow fans and enthusiasts to submit their unique designs for new sets. Users can then vote on their favourite submissions, and the company considers the most popular ones for potential production. This platform has resulted in the creation of many successful new sets based on fan suggestions, and has led to the creation of an interesting ecosystem that in this case includes customers. This particular approach to being exponential is defined as "co-creation" and implies an active involvement of customers—but potentially also suppliers and other business partners—in the creative process that leads to the launch of new products, services, and experiences.

In its essence, being exponential translates into finding clever ways to leverage one's capabilities in collaboration with one or more partners with complementary capabilities. As we stated at the beginning of this chapter, although ecosystems represent the zenith of an exponential strategy, the principle is aimed at inspiring leaders and managers to welcome any kind of collaboration—even if it leads to only a temporary alliance with one or other players—in the name of open innovation. This approach is often implemented to enter new sectors or markets. In 2023 the American luxury jewellery house Tiffany and the sport behemoth Nike surprised the world by launching the Nike-Tiffany Air Force 1 1837, sneakers crafted in premium black suede with a Tiffany blue swoosh and the Tiffany logo on the tongue. And though this was not the first time Tiffany forged an unexpected partnership aimed at increasing its cultural relevance on a broader audience, this was the first case in which "the Fifth Avenue jeweler lent its name, hue, or hardware to a shoe."[19]

Another case is the collaboration of Nestlé, a global leader in the food and beverage industry, and L'Oréal, a major player in the cosmetics industry. In 2014 they entered into a 50-50 joint venture called Galderma that focused on research, development, and marketing of dermatological products. By combining their knowledge in different areas, they were able to create a successful venture in the skincare market.[20] Another relevant case is the strategic alliance signed in 2018 between Apple and Best Buy. Best Buy was facing tough competition from online retailers and needed to revamp its stores to provide better customer experiences, and Apple was looking to expand its retail presence and reach more potential customers. So they created Apple sections offering a wide range of Apple products and services within Best Buy stores. Through this alliance, Best Buy gained the advantage of having highly sought Apple products in its stores, and Apple significantly expanded its retail footprint, reaching more locations through Best Buy's extensive network of stores—which provided Apple with a competitive edge against other electronics brands by ensuring a high level of visibility and accessibility.[21] This concept of a store-within-a-store or a shop-in-shop, where one retailer creates a dedicated section or space inside another retailer's store, is an exciting opportunity for exponential growth. It's especially appealing to smaller brands or those seeking to explore new concepts, as it allows them to showcase their products and services to an existing captive audience. Put simply, this approach to the guiding principle of "be exponential" pushes the boundaries of collaboration to achieve results that are exponentially bigger than what an organization could achieve on its own.

Another interesting application of this is the so-called "coopetition"—cooperation with competitors—to achieve mutual benefits. For example, in 2018 Toyota and Mazda, traditional competitors in the automotive market, established a joint venture assembly plant in the United States. This strategic collaboration aimed to capitalize on their combined manufacturing resources, leading to reduced production costs for both companies. Remarkably, they managed to maintain their competitive positions while fostering mutual growth through this innovative partnership.[22] Another example involves long-standing rivals South Korean electronics giant Samsung and Japanese electronics company Sony. They engaged in coopetition by collaborating on the development of the S-LCD Corporation, a joint venture to manufacture and supply LCD panels to both companies, allowing them to reduce production costs and compete more effectively against other display manufacturers. Or consider the online streaming platform Hulu; it is able to offer a wide range of TV shows and movies because it is a joint venture between the Walt Disney Company, Comcast's NBCUniversal, and Warner Media (formerly Time Warner).[23] Though these media giants are competitors in various entertainment sectors, they came together to create Hulu as a response to the changing landscape of media consumption.

Given the rapid pace of technological advancement—not to mention increasing adoption rate and ever-rising experiential benchmarks—numerous traditional players across diverse sectors are seizing the opportunity to collaborate with technology partners for the development of their digital interfaces. By doing so, they not only accelerate the R&D process required for launching innovations, but also offer their customers access to existing ecosystems. A compelling example of this is how the historic German luxury and commercial vehicle automotive brand Mercedes teamed up with Google to integrate Maps and YouTube into its vehicles—rather than "reinventing the wheel" with proprietary technology. Similarly, German automotive giant BMW has partnered with Meta to explore the integration of augmented and virtual reality technologies in their vehicles.[24]

Make, Buy, or Ally

In conclusion, let's recap the key factors that organizations should carefully consider when deciding how to embrace the "be exponential" guiding principle—especially given the fact that understanding whether to develop a solution internally or through collaboration with third parties, including setting up or joining an ecosystem, is such a crucial business decision.

Core competencies, resources, and expertise: Organizations must assess whether the solution aligns with their core competencies and evaluate their internal resources and expertise. If the solution requires capabilities beyond the company's core strengths, a partnership may be more suitable.

Market access: Collaborations can provide access to adjacent markets or customer segments, or even allow a company to launch a new venture completely separate from its core business, as seen in some of the examples mentioned earlier. In some cases, the barriers to entry—particularly the big scale of the market leaders—are such that it may be challenging for a single company to enter alone.

Time to market: Collaboration offers accelerated access to opportunities, and in certain cases speed to market is critical. If a partnership allows the company to access the solution faster, more efficiently, and more effectively than it could do from internal development, collaboration becomes a very favourable option.

Cost considerations: Developing a solution from scratch can be costly compared to partnering with someone whose core strengths complement the organization's competencies, making an alliance a more cost-effective solution in some instances.

Risks and liabilities: Collaborations can help mitigate risks and liabilities, which can be cumbersome in an ever-changing and unpredictable landscape. Sharing these burdens with a partner can be preferable, particularly with complex projects.

Innovation and creativity: Over time, organizations may lose their ability to innovate. Collaborating with external partners can bring fresh perspectives, innovative ideas, and creativity—not only to the collaborative project itself but potentially to the entire organization as well.

Competitive landscape: Analyzing the competitive landscape is crucial. If competitors are forming successful partnerships, it may be a signal to consider a similar approach even if it's only to a way to build a defence against the competitors. However, a first-mover advantage needs to be taken into consideration, as the market opportunity may already be saturated.

By carefully weighing these factors, organizations can make informed decisions and leverage the power of collaboration to drive innovation, growth, and success in a rapidly evolving business environment. More traditional companies can benefit from being exponential, since that can provide the budget, people, time, and risk tolerance to move autonomously. However, there are also some potential downsides to be considered. Based on our experience, the main concerns that arise are the following:

Cultural clash: Organizations have distinct leadership styles, cultures, processes, work ethics, and communication styles. If these differences are not managed carefully, they can hinder effective collaboration and cause friction among team members. For example, this aspect is very delicate when an established organization interacts with a start-up—whether just for a partnership or an M&A process—since the cultural gap tends to be huge.

Loss of control: When partnering with others, an organization might have to share decision-making authority, which can lead to a loss of control over certain aspects of the collaboration. For example, there might be a misalignment in the goals or in the allocation of resources due to conflicting priorities, or there might be an excessive dependency on the partner or on the orchestrator of an ecosystem. Another typical example of loss of control is the risk exposure associated to the other company (or companies) involved—if someone you are associated with engages in unethical practices or faces a public relations crisis, your company's image may also be negatively impacted.

Disagreements and conflicts in decision-making can arise and jeopardize the entire deal.

Intellectual property concerns: Collaborating with other companies may require sharing proprietary information and intellectual property, which are in some cases the main source of competitive advantage of a company. In a partnership, and even more in an ecosystem, protecting sensitive data and ensuring its proper use can be a challenge. This aspect is particularly relevant, considering the different legislation concerning privacy and data management.

Opportunity cost: While collaborating with one partner, you might miss out on opportunities to work with other potential partners or pursue independent ventures that could have been more beneficial for your organization. And given the contractual obligations associated with these agreements, disengaging can be quite complicated. Also, in some cases there is an opportunity cost related to the investments required to engage in a certain collaboration, which may drastically reduce the ability of the company to invest in other activities.

Even considering these concerns, we would still advocate for being exponential. In our experience, thorough assessment of the business opportunity, proper due diligence of all parties involved, clear communication, and a well-defined agreement can not only help mitigate these potential downsides but can also lead to exponentially bigger results. A key ingredient that needs to be constantly nurtured in collaborative strategies is trust, between business partners and with customers. In fact, a lack of trust can destroy a perfectly balanced deal and undermine an otherwise impeccable customer experience.

Drawing from his extensive experience as both a professor and consultant, Jacobides of LBS shared with us a final warning about the risks that firms face when implementing a collaborative strategy. "Assuming there's a validated business opportunity that a company aims to pursue through collaboration, the crucial step is understanding the type of relationship the organization wants to establish. Will it be a tactical partnership, a proper joint venture, or a comprehensive ecosystem? Who will take on the roles of orchestrator, partner, and complementor? What will be the rules governing engagement and collaboration? Why would other players be interested in joining the partnership?" He further elaborated, "The issue we've observed in many of the firms we studied is that they become too fixated on their own objectives, and this leads them to create an *ego*-system instead of an ecosystem."[25]

Reflection Summary Questions

- How can "be exponential" principles inspire retailers and brands to embrace a more open and flexible approach to innovation in today's rapidly evolving market?
- What are the key factors that organizations should consider when deciding whether to develop a solution internally or pursue collaboration with third parties?
- What are the key advantages and the main factors to be considered when engaging in collaboration, co-creation, or coopetition?

- In what ways does the concept of a business ecosystem help organizations effectively navigate the post-digital world and offer a unique value proposition to both companies and customers, compared to traditional business setups?
- What are the potential downsides and risks associated with partnering with other companies, and how can organizations effectively mitigate these concerns?

19

Be Invisible

In the introduction we discussed how, in a post-digital world, retail is entering its fifth wave and technology is becoming less visible but more present. Everywhere, tiny sensors will gather and analyze data about people with increasing accuracy in real time. This will revolutionize the way individuals interact with each other and how brands and retailers communicate and sell. Those communications will be contextually relevant and fully personalized for each customer. Surprisingly, this mass personalization will feel even more human—since people will be engaging with technology through their bodies and communicating with their voice—instead of using keyboards and screens. We also argued that in the post-digital era digital and virtual will feel (nearly) just as real as physical experiences do.

One of the reasons why people expect technology to be invisible is its ubiquity. In Chapter 4, "Experiential Benchmarks," we explored how the widespread adoption of technology is breaking down barriers in various industries and retail sectors. This trend has posed challenges for established brands and retailers, as it has opened up new opportunities for smaller, innovative players to compete head-on. The accessibility of once prohibitively expensive technologies has fueled this virtuous cycle, empowering digitally native companies to experiment and introduce cutting-edge products and services without the constraints of legacy systems. As a result, customer expectations have evolved, setting new experiential benchmarks and compelling established businesses to adapt quickly or risk becoming obsolete.

"Being invisible" is a guiding principle designed to inspire businesses to consider that in Retail 5.0 shoppers and buyers expect technology to be present and persistent—because we have all grown accustomed to its role as the engine of our world. However, with this expectation comes the desire for tech to be seamlessly and effortlessly integrated into their onlife three-dimensional customer journey. In other words, technology should never draw attention to itself or complicate our lives by forcing us to understand how it works. Tech should never be a barrier or a distraction, but rather a tool that enhances our experiences and simplifies our interactions with the world. All combined, technology should be completely invisible, operating behind the scenes, allowing us to enjoy its benefits without experiencing any complexity related to its deployment or maintenance. An "invisible" technology is intuitive, user-friendly, and requires minimal cognitive load to operate. It fades into the background, allowing us to focus on the experience we're engaging in rather than on the technology itself. For example, when using a smartphone, the focus should be on the content, communication, or activities it enables, rather than the device itself. Consider the frustration we experience when one of our devices freezes or doesn't perform the task that it's supposed to; that demonstrates just how much we rely on the benefits technology offers us.

The check-out-free retail experience implemented by Amazon Fresh and Hema is a great example of how technology should interact naturally and effortlessly with its users. The more technology is invisible, the more it becomes accessible to a wider range of people, regardless of their technical expertise. And in turn, this widens the audience of brands and retailers, who can ideally deliver tangible value while creating a harmonious relationship where technology enhances the customer journey without being obtrusive or distracting.

There are many examples of how transformative technologies are seamlessly integrating into our daily lives, making interactions in every touchpoint less obtrusive and more intuitive. Think, for example, of wearable devices like smartwatches (an industry set to reach 456.89 million units by 2028, up from 134.12 million units in 2023, with the Asia-Pacific region leading the adoption rate).[1] The fact that smartwatches are always connected to the Internet and are able to process the data of the surroundings allows users to enjoy seamless experiences such as receiving contextual offers or suggestions about relevant experiences that the user can enjoy in the area. The goal of any invisible technology is always to enhance convenience, efficiency, and the overall user experience, without causing disruption or requiring active user intervention.

An effective rule of thumb for brands and retailers aiming to be invisible is taking advantage of the technologies that consumers are already using, since this enables companies to build on a familiar user experience. For example, as Stephen J. Andriole shares in *MIT Sloane Management Review*:

> *Consider the manner in which Uber Technologies Inc. and Airbnb Inc. have, by degrees, supplanted taxis and hotels, respectively. While emerging technologies have abetted Uber and Airbnb's rises to prominence, their most significant gains have come from leveraging the mainstream networking technologies already in consumers' hands: mobile phones, apps, and websites optimized for quick transactions and location tracking. It's often easier to achieve impact with technologies already in widespread use than it is with emerging technologies.*[2]

The same is true with those business that leverage widespread apps. For example, the popular Spanish fashion retailer Zara has integrated WhatsApp as a customer service channel. Customers can use the app to enquire about product availability, sizes, and styles. The service also allows customers to place orders, receive order updates, and even track their deliveries through the app.[3] And the French beauty and cosmetics retailer Sephora offers a WhatsApp-based beauty assistant. Customers can interact with the assistant to get personalized beauty recommendations, makeup tips, and product information. This type of conversational commerce has been adopted also by Mall of Emirate, the aforementioned shopping mall located in Dubai. They've introduced a concierge service integrated with a popular mobile app that enables customers to engage in real-time conversations with representatives and explore a wide selection of international and local brands available for purchase—the items delivered within a few hours at no extra charge.

The concept of being invisible by leveraging mainstream networking technologies is pushed to the extreme in China, where millions of customers use the so-called super apps (multifunctional digital platforms) for a wide range of services, from messaging and social networking to conversational commerce, e-commerce, financial services, and more. For example, many retailers have integrated the WeChat payment system into their stores, allowing customers to make purchases using the app. Additionally, retailers use WeChat Official Accounts to engage with customers, offer promotions, and provide customer support.[4] And using the all-in-one app Meituan, the self-described "tech-driven retail company," users can order food, flowers, and medicine, book movie tickets, and access various other services.[5]

Five Significant Benefits of Invisible Technologies

As these initiatives show, invisible transformative technologies are redefining customer experience everywhere in the world. Considering the significant impact these ongoing changes will have on business, we've identified five crucial areas that brands and retailers should devote special attention to:

Smart Payments: All over the world businesses are implementing mobile payment technologies to simplify the shopping experience. Apple Pay, GCash, Google Pay, KakaoPay, LINE Pay, OVO, PayPal One Touch, RuPay, Samsung Pay, WeChat Pay—the list goes on. All enable users to make transactions without physically using their credit cards. Some players are already experimenting with similar technologies to integrate biometric systems (fingerprint, palm, or facial recognition) to make the checkout process even more seamless and "human."

Several retailers have developed their own proprietary smart-payment systems to leverage first-party data to enhance the customer experience. With Starbucks' "Mobile Order & Pay," for example, customers of the American multinational chain can use the company's app to order and pay for their drinks ahead of time, reducing wait times in stores. Similarly, McDonald's—the world's largest fast food restaurant chain, with more than 40,000 outlets and $21 billion in sales—has a "Mobile Order & Pay" feature in its app,[6] which allows customers to order and pay for their meals in advance and pick them up at the restaurant. Costa Coffee, a UK-based coffee chain wholly owned by Coca-Cola, offers the Costa Coffee Club app, allowing customers to earn points and rewards for their purchases.[7] Even Falabella, a large retail company based in Chile, has developed a proprietary mobile payment system called CMR Puntos, which allows customers who are part of the CMR loyalty programme to use the mobile app to earn and redeem loyalty points and make payments. And Mercado Libre, one of the largest e-commerce companies in Latin America, offers its own digital wallet called "Mercado Pago," which enables customers to make payments, send money, and access credit services for online and offline transactions. Finally, Lotte Mart, a major retail chain in South Korea, introduced its mobile payment service called L.pay, which customers can use to make payments at Lotte Mart stores and earn rewards points for their purchases.

Cloud Computing: Cloud-based services dematerialize technology and enable users to access and store data, files, and applications across various devices seamlessly. This technology allows for easy collaboration and synchronization without users needing to worry about physical storage or manual backups. Retailers and brands can leverage this technology to collect and analyze vast amounts of customer data from multiple sources—such as online interactions, purchase history, and social media activity. By using this data, retailers can optimize the customer journey, creating personalized recommendations, offers, and promotions tailored to each customer's preferences and needs. Retailers can also leverage cloud computing to enhance their inventory management systems in order to have real-time visibility into their stock levels across all locations. This ensures that customers can access accurate information about product availability and delivery times, reducing the risk of running out of stock and thus improving customer satisfaction.

Internet of Things: IoT devices are designed to be invisible. They seamlessly connect and communicate with each other, often without requiring user intervention. Smart home devices, such as smart thermostats, smart locks, and smart appliances, operate in the background to optimize energy usage and provide a more comfortable living environment. Of course, as people get used to the benefits of this technology, their experiential benchmarks will rise even higher, and retailers and brands will have to cope with those expectations across all touchpoints. IoT technology can be used by retailers to gather data about customer behaviour and preferences while the consumers are within the store, and to consequently offer contextually relevant personalized recommendations and promotions to customers as they shop. The data collected can also be used to predict customer behaviour and manage the inventory more efficiently.

Another implementation concerns smart shelves, which can dynamically adjust product information and promotions based on factors such as demand, inventory levels, and, potentially, individual customer preferences. Smart shelves offer a much more cost-effective approach to updating prices, which in some cases can be very costly indeed. In 2014 and 2022, the US supermarket chain Safeway and Target, respectively, paid million-dollar settlements in California for "pricing inaccuracies," which can result in part when electronic price updates—such as from fluctuations in commodity pricing—don't match the prices on the shelf labels. (Additional chains affected include Walmart and Walgreens.) Two of the biggest reasons for this oversight are high-tech and high-touch: stores lacking the software to check up-to-the-minute prices, and stores lacking the staff to physically change the shelf labels[8] (a problem only exacerbated by the Great Resignation, which gathered steam following the COVID pandemic). So then consider the vast improvement of smart shelves, which seamlessly (and invisibly) integrate online and in-store channels while monitoring engagement metrics. These "intelligent" shelves feature electronic displays that showcase product details like nutritional information and facilitate effortless product comparisons. Equipped with sensors, they also track inventory levels and promptly detect out-of-stock items, often in conjunction with cameras and RFID (Radio Frequency Identification) technologies, as seen in Amazon and Hema's cashier-less stores.

Major retailers such as Walmart, Kroger, and Walgreens have embraced Electronic Shelf Labels (ESLs), sensors, RFID tags, and readers in their stores across the US and Canada. A similar trend is unfolding in APAC (Asia Pacific) and EMEA (Europe, the Middle East, and Africa) regions where the smart shelves market is predicted to experience significant growth, with an estimated threefold increase by 2027.

Globally, the market size is expected to grow from an estimated value of US$3 billion in 2022 to $8.3 billion by 2027, at a CAGR of 22.4% from 2022 to 2027.[9]

IoT, combined with other technologies described here, is driving the so-called retail media—an approach that capitalizes on the retailer's customer base, data insights, and the seamless integration of their sales and communication platforms (even with third parties in some cases) to create a new revenue stream for retailers while providing brands with opportunities to increase business intelligence, visibility, sales, and customer engagement. Retail media is expected to be a $61 billion business by 2024 according to the consultancy Bain & Company.[10]

Artificial Intelligence (AI) and Machine Learning (ML): AI-powered technologies will become increasingly invisible as they are integrated into various applications and services. Chatbots and virtual assistants can engage with customers in real-time, providing instant support and assistance. These AI systems can handle common customer queries, offer product information, and guide customers through the buying process, enhancing customer service before, during, and after the shopping expedition. AI-powered visual search will change the way customers discover and find products by uploading images from the web or using their smartphone cameras to take pictures of products they like and would like to buy. This feature helps customers find products that match their preferences even when they can't describe them in words. Retailers and brands will have to develop technologies able to communicate effectively with this software to enable the seamless dialogue that can bring customers from the upper funnel (Awareness, Appeal, Ask) to the Action (buy the product). (Again, see the "Five A's—Awareness, Appeal, Ask, Act, and Advocacy" sidebar in Chapter 14.)

Blockchain: Blockchain is a decentralized and secure digital ledger that records transactions and information across multiple computers, ensuring transparency, immutability, and trust in the data. It can also be used to create a transparent and traceable supply chain, providing customers with real-time information about the origin and authenticity of products. This builds trust and helps customers make more informed purchasing decisions. For example, Walmart partnered with IBM and Hyperledger to implement a "blockchain-based food traceability system" that enables them to track the origin of dozens of products from various suppliers. In fact, in 2018, following the latest disruption from E. coli, it requested that its leafy greens suppliers "trace their products all the way back to the farm" through their system. Luxury brands are using this invisible technology to combat counterfeiting and assure customers of the authenticity of their products. In 2021 LVMH, Prada Group, and Cartier launched the Aura Blockchain Consortium with the aim of enabling customers to verify the authenticity of their luxury goods through a digital certificate stored on the blockchain.[11] With blockchain, retailers and brands can also give customers more control over their personal data and privacy. Indeed, customers can choose which data to share and with whom, reducing concerns about data breaches and unauthorized use, and can have full control over their loyalty points, transferring them across different business, and even exchange them for cryptocurrencies.

These examples demonstrate how invisible transformative technologies have become—and how they'll become increasingly natural in our daily lives. As technology continues to advance, the trend toward invisible integration is likely to persist, further enhancing the overall customer experience, reaching all the touchpoints of a three-dimensional customer journey, and simplifying the way we interact with the world around us. This is why we strongly advocate that retailers and brands embrace the "be invisible" guiding principle.

Or: Not So Fast

However, there will be circumstances in which some retailers and brands will prefer to more slowly transition toward being invisible—and retaining more visible technologies in their physical spaces. This calculation will depend on a number of variables, including the digital literacy of the target audience, the availability of fast internet connections, the characteristics of the products and services, the strategic positioning of the business vis-à-vis competitors, and the business objectives of the company. It's fair to say that emerging technologies are, by definition, not yet conventional enough to be embraced by a large audience, and this might be an issue for mass retailers. Moreover, in certain retail environments, showcasing cutting-edge technology can be an integral part of the brand experience. Some retailers position themselves as pioneers or innovators in their industry, and by presenting technology in a prominent and visible manner, they can demonstrate their dedication to staying at the forefront of technological developments and offering customers the latest solutions. Customers may be drawn to such stores to experience the latest advancements. For example, Xiaomi, a Chinese electronics company, has gained popularity for its retail stores that display a wide range of devices and gadgets—from smartphones and smartwatches to smart home appliances and wearables—that consumers can interact with in-store, doing their own test runs before purchasing. Similarly, the Samsung 837 store in Manhattan is both the flagship of the South Korean electronics giant and "an interactive playground filled with next-gen gaming stations."[12]

Another case when visible technology is preferable is when AR or VR displays can allow customers to select specific colours, sizes, or design elements that are not available in a brick-and-mortar store—or to visualize products in different settings, or to try out virtual experiences. These displays can also demonstrate features and functionalities in ways that helps customers make more informed decisions about their purchases. For example, the Swedish ready-to-assemble furniture behemoth IKEA has embraced augmented reality in its mobile app, allowing customers to virtually place furniture in exact spots in their homes before making a purchase.

In some retail environments visible technologies can help build trust and transparency. For instance, clearly visible security cameras in shopping malls can demonstrate transparency and strengthen customer confidence.

* * *

Ultimately, the decision to make technology visible or invisible depends on the retailer's overall brand strategy and target audience, as well as the type of shopping experience they aim to deliver. However, the decision to invest in *visible* technologies must be deliberate and strategically planned—not just as the result of a lack of innovation. There is no doubt that the world is heading in the direction of a seamless integration of all available technologies, across the plethora of channels and touchpoints, so neglecting this reality could lead retailers and brands to a dangerous disconnect with their audience. It is essential to thoroughly balance visible technology with invisible seamless integration to ensure that the customer experience is enhanced rather than hindered. People expect companies to create win-win scenarios that simplify their lives.

Reflection Summary Questions

- In the post-digital era, technology is becoming less visible but more present. How can retailers and brands ensure that they seamlessly integrate transformative technologies into their three-dimensional customer journey without causing disruption or complexity?
- How can your company leverage widely used apps like WhatsApp or WeChat to create a seamless and familiar customer experience? How can organizations leverage Cloud Computing, IoT, AI, and Blockchain, to offer a personalized customer experience without being obtrusive?
- How can your company unlock the opportunities of retail media?
- In which circumstances may visible technology be preferred by retailers and brands?

20

Be Loyal

You're at your favourite restaurant, where you and your close friends dine regularly. Amid laughter and chatter, one of your friends announces that a childhood friend from Italy—Gaia—has just moved into town. As your friend regales you with tales of their growing up together, you discover that Gaia and you share a number of interests: visiting museums, hitting the gym—she's even taken a whiskey-tasting course! Given your own deep love for the amber nectar, you're eager to learn more about this likely kindred spirit, so you ask your friend to tell you more about her. When, later that evening, you check Gaia's social media profiles, you're convinced you want to meet her in person—so you ask your friend to invite Gaia for the next dinner. When you finally meet her, you feel an immediate connection, as though you've known each other for years. From there on you see each other regularly. As your friendship grows stronger, Gaia becomes a vital part of your world, and you'll speak glowingly of her to anyone who will listen. However, as with any relationship, challenges emerge. You start seeing sides of Gaia that alienate you, and this friction casts a shadow on your once harmonious connection. You feel a bit betrayed, and you're not sure if you can continue your friendship as it was before. And since you're so sad about the situation, you share your feelings with your friends.

Surely, many of you have experienced similar scenarios. Whenever we, as human beings, connect with others, a familiar journey unfolds. Sometimes when we come to know someone we get the feeling we might like them. Intrigued, we'll seek more information. If that information reinforces our instinct, we're eager to pursue knowing them.

If all goes well, we can develop a strong relationship and progressively open up to the other person, sharing more about ourselves—we even become advocates, introducing them to our circle of friends. However, if discord arises, we can feel disillusioned or let down. If this pattern continues, the relationship can fade—or even fall apart. This journey is strikingly similar to the one we embark upon as customers when building relationships with brands—the journey through the five A's: Awareness, Appeal, Ask, Act, and Advocacy (as a reminder, a fuller description can be found in Chapter 14).

Why are the personal and the customer journies so similar? Because humans are social creatures, and we only know one way to relate with each other. And brands, exactly like people, build and cultivate relationships with an audience. Think of the people you care for the most—those who have also cared for you, supported you, shared experiences with you, or even taught you something unforgettable. This mutually beneficial relationship—this exchange of value—is at the core of the very concept of loyalty, and it can't be limited to transactional aspects. If you are loyal to the people you care about only because of what you can obtain in exchange, you are not moved by a genuine deep emotion; it's purely transactional. And the risk that you will one day barter that relationship for another—from which you can extract *more* value—is very high. This is how we as humans behave; this is what moves us. Therefore, understanding the way people behave in relation to other people—from psychological, sociological, and anthropological standpoints—can teach us a great deal about how people behave as customers.

Of course there are nuances to this analogy, since most relationships aren't transactional. We can be much more forgiving of our loved ones than we are of brands we're loyal to. But a good rule of thumb for creating a loyalty strategy as a brand is to ensure that the value you receive from a loyal customer is commensurate with the value you offer the customer in return—and we're not talking about tangible details like the products or services offered and the funds received in exchange. This is about much more nuanced aspects of relationship.

For example, ask yourself questions like the following:

- Do we share the same values with our customers?
- Are we behaving consistently?
- Are we present in the events that matter to them?
- Are we trading value in the right proportion?
- Are we reciprocating their trust in a meaningful way (beyond transactions)?
- Are we transparently providing the information they need to be reassured and move from Ask to Act?
- Are we incentivizing our happy customers to recommend us to their peers?
- How can we avoid frictions that might lead our customers to consider interrupting the relationship?

If the answers to all these questions are in the affirmative, then you're likely building a strong, long-term relationship with your customer base. If so, that's fantastic news, because this bond is paramount in a post-digital world dominated by volatility, where supply exceeds demand by far, and where alternative options arise every day.

Stakeholders' Loyalty

Being loyal means, first of all, acknowledging that (as of today) 100% of your customers are people—and people have specific needs and desires, and they typically follow certain steps when they build relationships. Being loyal also means understanding that people value consistency, and they pay a lot of attention to if and how others, especially businesses, walk their talk. Hence, customers are increasingly likely to care that the product or service they enjoy didn't come to them at the expense of another—from fair-trade coffee beans to cruelty-free beauty creams to how retail staff are treated by management. In other words, the concept of brand loyalty needs to evolve from basic KPIs—such as customer retention and repurchase rate, the typical "earn-and-burn" loyalty scheme, and so on—to become a consistent exchange of value between the company and all the stakeholders involved in its operations, including of course its customers. (We say more about "earn and burn" later on.)

The Body Shop is an interesting case of stakeholder loyalty because it has demonstrated a strong commitment to prioritizing the needs and interests of various stakeholders beyond a traditional profit-centric model. The company's approach to business focuses on building meaningful and long-term relationships with all the groups that interact with the brand, and they walk their talk from every direction. They have a deep commitment to ethical sourcing and sustainability; they don't just sell only cruelty-free products—they also advocate against animal testing for cosmetics; they invest in employees' welfare and development, including initiatives to empower women and provide fair employment opportunities; they actively engage in social and environmental initiatives to support human rights, environmental conservation, and community empowerment; they've developed a customer loyalty programme that offers various benefits and rewards to repeat customers, and they constantly engage the customer base through community events, campaigns, and social media, encouraging them to become advocates for the causes the brand stands for; and they commit to transparency about their business practices. In other words, The Body Shop's emphasis on stakeholder loyalty has been instrumental in creating a strong brand identity that resonates with individuals who prioritize ethical and sustainable practices.

Talking specifically about customers, a lot of attention needs to be paid to the entire customer journey. That's because brand loyalty is the result of the overall customer experience which in turn is the sum of all the interactions that a customer has with a brand across *all* touchpoints of their onlife three-dimensional customer journey. Every touchpoint counts, and every interaction can nurture or undermine brand awareness, reputation, consideration, repurchase, and advocacy. This is another reason why it's so important to shift from an omnichannel strategy to an optichannel one; otherwise, it'd be virtually impossible to dedicate the same attention to the customer experience in each touchpoint, and brand loyalty would be constantly threatened. Business executives must constantly assess the customer journey of their customer personas to ensure that the trust people give to the company is not only repaid but is also constantly cultivated, in every interaction. Indeed, in a world of ever-higher experiential benchmarks, inconsistencies and frictions can lead to disengagement and potentially bad publicity—or worse. Indeed, in today's world, customers are increasingly observant of what happens behind the scenes, and extend their interest beyond the mere business relationship they share with the brand.

This is why being loyal means for retailers and brands establishing, nurturing, and maintaining a relationship of reciprocal loyalty with all stakeholders who come in contact with your business. In other words, it means that leaders and managers should prioritize and act in the best interests of all those who have a vested interest in the success of the organization. Stakeholders typically include shareholders, employees, customers, suppliers, and the broader community in which the company operates. Each of these groups contributes to the company in various ways and relies on it for certain benefits. Loyalty to stakeholders means that the company should consider the needs, rights, and expectations of these groups when making decisions and taking actions—exactly as it does with its customers.

This is not an easy task for those at the helm of the organization, since different stakeholders can have different priorities, and ensuring consistency while pursuing long-term success could get tricky. Being loyal to shareholders entails acting in a manner that maximizes their long-term value and returns on investment. This includes making strategic decisions that promote growth and profitability while adhering to ethical business practices. Being loyal to employees involves treating them fairly, providing a safe and inclusive work environment, offering opportunities for growth and development, and recognizing their contributions to the company's success. Being loyal to suppliers involves fair and transparent dealings, timely payments, and maintaining mutually beneficial relationships. And finally, being loyal to the broader community means being a good corporate citizen and engaging in socially responsible practices.

Decoding Customer Loyalty and Churn

People offer their loyalty, in both personal and commercial relationships, when they feel that they're in a mutually beneficial relationship, where there is a genuine exchange of value, and where consistency is the norm. Thus, loyalty must be earned through consistently delivering value and meeting customer expectations. Let's analyze some of the main factors that lead to customer loyalty.

Connection: Sharing values is the basis of every genuine relationship. Customers who feel a sense of identification with a brand's values and aesthetics, and who feel a sense of community with other like-minded customers, tend to develop a sense of loyalty (exactly as they do when they relate to other people). This emotional bond can lead to long-term loyalty and advocacy.

Trust: Loyalty derives from trust and a positive reputation. A brand that consistently delivers on its promises, prioritizes customer satisfaction, and maintains ethical practices earns the trust of all its stakeholders. Loyal customers are confident that the brand will act in their best interest and will be willing to trade their personal information in exchange for value. This aspect is especially important in times of uncertainty and change. (Out of 13,000 consumers across 29 countries surveyed in 2023 by Salesforce, an American cloud-based software company, 88% state "trust becomes more important in times of change."[1])

Personalization: As we discussed in Chapter 15, "Be Personal," people like to be treated as individuals—hence, they value personalized customer experiences. Technology can facilitate and enhance this aspect, allowing brands to leverage data to offer tailored recommendations, contextually relevant offers, or access to sought-after events. Personalization can trigger loyalty because it makes customers feel valued and understood.

Quality: Customers are prone to choosing brands that deliver high-quality products or services and a consistent customer experience across all touchpoints. If they have confidence that their expectations will be met or exceeded, this fosters a sense of belonging and reliability, which leads to loyalty. Needless to say, when referring to quality, we must consider both the intrinsic quality of the product itself and the perceived quality, which is generally a result of a plethora of factors, including brand reputation, previous interactions, packaging, customer service, and the overall customer experience.

Familiarity: People tend to go to the same restaurant and buy from the same store or brand because they value familiarity and like being in a comfort zone. Customers become accustomed to a brand's offerings, user interface, and customer service, all of which can make interactions with the brand effortless and intuitive. This familiarity creates a sense of ease and reduces churn, since it simplifies decision-making and shortens transaction time.

Incentives: Many brands make successful use of the effective "earn and burn" loyalty scheme. Loyalty programmes usually allow customers to accumulate points, miles, or other rewards—that can then be redeemed for various benefits, such as discounts, free products or services, exclusive offers, or even cash back. These incentives encourage repeat purchases and reinforce loyalty by providing tangible value for continued engagement with the brand.

In a post-digital world, where touchpoints proliferate and the three dimensions of the onlife customer journey require constant optimization, understanding the reasons for customer churn is crucial for helping businesses identify areas for improvement and build long-term customer loyalty. Salesforce research confirms that "71% of consumers switched brands at least once" over the course of one year (2021).[2] For a closer analysis of some of the main factors that lead to attrition and customer churn, see the accompanying sidebar.

Three Effective Ways to Lose Customers

Poor or unengaging customer experience: Customers are more likely to churn if they don't have positive experiences with a company. Very often this involves issues with product selection or availability, product quality, customer service, delivery and return options, inefficient processes, or friction when switching from one touchpoint to the other. Or, if a customer makes a complaint that isn't promptly responded to and, ultimately, effectively resolved, that customer likely won't return. Frustrated customers may seek alternatives that offer a better overall experience—or, worse, they may vent their frustration, leading to negative word of mouth.

But churn doesn't just result from negative experiences; it can result from a lack of positive experience. For example, [Giuseppe Stigliano speaking here] I love playing tennis. But since my racquets last a few years, I don't really develop a relationship with the retailer who sold my last racket or recommended the brand that I chose—and by the time I need a new racket, I might get a different brand from a different retailer. But what if that tennis-speciality store maintained a mailing list via which it raffled free tickets for tennis matches, or created watching parties during Wimbledon tournaments, or offered discounts on books about tennis, and so on. That regular communication would enhance my customer experience, keep the store top of mind and most likely earn my loyalty.

According to the fifth edition of the Salesforce *State of the Connected Customer* report, 88% of consumers confirm that the experience a company provides matters as much as the products or services that company sells. Salesforce also found out that, among the reasons why people switch brands, 66% of the participants rank "better deals" as the main driver, followed by "product quality" (58%), "customer service" (48%), "product availability" (46%) and "product selection" (40%). This is confirmed by a 2023 Harvard Business Review Analytical Services research report stating that 58% of global executives declared that customer experience is the number one business priority facing their businesses.[3]

Lack of personalization: Customers today expect personalized experiences and offerings. If a company fails to tailor its products, services, and communications to individual preferences and needs, customers may feel dissatisfied or undervalued and seek alternatives that better meet their expectations. For example, frequent fliers often have personal profiles that include details such as dietary requirements or which seat they prefer. So, if a loyal customer trying to book a flight is asked, "window or aisle seat?" they're not likely to be pleased. Whereas, if a grocery store site asks if you'd like to purchase again the items you bought last time, that feature could save you both time and effort. And since the site already has your address and payment method, all you'd have to do is select BUY NOW.

In the previous chapter we saw how invisible technologies such as AI and IoT can be used by brands and retailers to gather data about customer behaviour and preferences, and to consequently offer contextually relevant personalized recommendations and promotions to customers as they shop—online, offline, and soon in virtual worlds. Data collected can also be leveraged in terms of predictive analytics to anticipate individual customer behaviour and personalize the customer experience. The bar of expectations is very high: 66% of global customers expect brands to understand their unique needs and expectations (personalization), 68% expect brands to demonstrate empathy (understanding), 76% expect consistent interactions across departments (integration); and 65% will remain loyal to companies if they offer a more personalized experience. According to Brian Solis writing in *Forbes*, brands should develop "digital empathy," which is "the ability to humanize customer behaviours, preferences, and aspirations through the connection between human-centred data, insights, and the meaningful customer engagement powered by those insights." This point is masterfully synthesized by Seth Godin, who said: "No one wants anything to be personalized, they want it to be personal, and those are two totally different things."[4]

Scarce value for money: If customers perceive that a product, a service, or an experience is overpriced or does not provide sufficient value compared to competitors, they may soon look for a better provider. Consider the frustration you feel when your home internet connection malfunctions, or when you pay for expedited delivery but still don't receive your order on time. For companies, the cost of this customer's frustration is very high, because the investment needed to acquire new customers is generally much higher than the investment required to appease an existing one. Loyal customers are also the most profitable. And as the loyalty life cycle unfolds, loyal customers become business builders, since they tend to increase their purchases, are more prone to pay premium prices, and are likely to advocate through word of mouth and positive reviews. That's why most loyalty programmes aim to create a lock-in with clients by offering a range of benefits and incentives—such as the different ways you can redeem your airline miles or the points earned on your credit card. This strategy increases the likelihood of satisfying customers while minimizing the risk of upsetting them due to a single negative interaction.

AGGRESSIVE COMPETITION: Customers appreciate companies that continuously innovate and offer new and improved products, services, or features. If a company fails to innovate and adapt to changing customer needs and preferences, customers may seek more innovative options elsewhere—especially if they're already aware that a competitor provides an appealing alternative. This is the competitive pressure that many established players suffer when nimble start-ups launch competitive products and services. There are also some cases in which an aggressive competitor with an equivalent or even lower offering can induce customers to churn through an aggressive promotional strategy. If faced with such a scenario, instead of engaging in a pricing war brands should double down on other attributes to defend their market share. Lucia Marcuzzo, senior vice president managing director North Europe at Levi Strauss & Co., told us: "Each time we provide a product, service, or experience, and whenever we surpass customer expectations in any touchpoint, we are effectively investing in building brand loyalty. Brand loyalty, in my view, serves as the culmination of all the positive interactions customers have with our brand. It is a natural outcome. Instead of expecting customers to be loyal to the brand, we believe the brand should be loyal to its customers, should be earning that loyalty at every turn by putting its customers firmly at the centre of every decision."[5]

DISRUPTED CONTEXT: Customer churn can also occur due to changes in personal circumstances, such as relocation, lifestyle changes, or financial constraints. These changes may make a product or service less relevant or affordable—particularly during an economic slowdown, since that activates different market dynamics that businesses must take into consideration. For example, during times of inflation, consumers tend to gravitate toward discount stores unless higher-end retailers swiftly adjust their pricing strategies to counterbalance the decline in purchasing power. But it's also true that when the pool of full-price buyers diminishes, remaining relevant for shoppers who are less price-sensitive can significantly impact a store's success.

Loyalty, Habit, and Communities

It's important to acknowledge that people are rarely inclined to strict monogamy when it comes to brand loyalty. This is true in our personal lives as well as in our lives as consumers. Although we do have single preferences in some categories, in many other cases we tend to favour a relatively big basket of brands on the basis of habit and convenience.

Loyal customers are those who have a strong emotional connection and attachment to one or a few brands. They actively choose to repeat their purchases and engage with the brands based on positive experiences, trust, and satisfaction. They are also more likely to recommend the brands to others, and may be willing to pay premium prices for the products or services they love. Their loyalty is driven by a combination of all the factors described above.

On the other hand, habitual customers are those who may repeatedly purchase from a brand, but are driven by convenience or habit (or lack of alternative) rather than by a strong emotional connection. They may not have a deep attachment to the brand, but they continue to purchase since it serves its purpose. This is an aspect of the equation that businesses need to carefully consider when building their loyalty strategy so as to define the most effective KPIs, metrics, and incentives.

An interesting approach to stimulating brand loyalty beyond habit involves member-only stores and communities where customers pay a fee just to join—before making actual purchases. Many brands and retailers all over the world have developed a premium version of their programme in exchange for a fee. A very popular example is

Amazon Prime, which offers members a wide range of benefits and services, including free and fast shipping, easy (and sometimes free) returns, video and music streaming services, cloud photo storage, and more. In China, the leading food-delivery and lifestyle-services platform Meituan offers VIP Program, via which members can access benefits such as discounts on food orders, priority access to restaurant reservations, and special offers on entertainment and travel services. And the US outdoor sporting goods retailer REI (Recreational Equipment, Inc.) has a programme called REI Co-Op that rewards members for their loyalty with store credit toward additional purchases.[6] According to McKinsey & Company: "Paid programmes have a higher burden of proof to acquire customers, but they typically derive higher customer value from those who sign up . . . . When done right, paid loyalty elevates the overall consumer experience, delivering bespoke, high-value rewards and drawing the consumer into an exclusive community oriented around a shared brand promise or offering." Needless to say, the only way to convince customers to pay to become members of a loyalty programme is to deliver great value in exchange.

Continuing with McKinsey & Company research, in order to be viable, paid loyalty programmes must (1) offer more value than the price of admission; (2) keep members engaged; and (3) offer experiential advantages. Regarding the latter, to "avoid losing [members] at renewal, brands must use the membership fees to invest in exclusive offerings with more emotional resonance, such as access to personalized experiences or members-only content . . . . brand affinity and experiential benefits are more important factors in driving subscriber retention than the hard-value benefits that led them to sign up."[7]

Another way to build your customer base, establish an emotional connection, and nurture the relationship—thus creating a relevant value exchange—is to build community, perhaps by leveraging social networks. Since we are social creatures, we're naturally drawn to that which stimulates our sense of belonging; brand communities capitalize on that fact by creating a positive feedback loop. When members share interests and values, they develop deep relationships with their peers—and in turn, increasingly trust the brand. The nature of the relationship tends to be less transactional and more authentic, paving the way for a long-term relationship and potentially a genuine loyal behaviour. As we saw in Chapter 3, "The Direct-to-Consumer (D2C) Revolution," the brand Glossier, which began as a spinoff of a blog, developed into a multibillion-dollar company.

Another brand with similar roots is the Canadian athletic apparel company Lululemon, which originated in 1998 from the community built around the yoga studio of the founder Chip Wilson. As the yoga community around Yoga West grew, Wilson noticed how few options there were for comfortable, functional clothing suitable for yoga practice. (Most athletic wear at the time was designed primarily for traditional sports like running and cycling.) Drawing inspiration from the feedback of the yoga community, Wilson created his own line of high-quality, yoga-inspired athletic wear. Over time, Lululemon expanded beyond the yoga community and became a popular brand among fitness enthusiasts and athleisure wear consumers. In 2011, 13 years after its founding, the company brought in $1 billion in revenue; a little more than a decade later, that figure revenue skyrocketed to $8 billion (2022), with a market cap of over $45 billion.

Lululemon's success can unequivocally be attributed to its commitment to engaging with its community, understanding their needs, and incorporating their feedback into product development. As stated in their website:

> *Our vision for our store was to create more than a place where people could get gear to sweat in; we wanted to create a community hub where people could learn and discuss the physical aspects of healthy living, mindfulness, and living a life of possibility. It was also important for us to create real relationships with our guests and understand what they were passionate about and how they liked to sweat, and [to] help them celebrate their goals. Today, we do this in our stores around the globe.*

Jono Bacon, an expert on community strategy and leadership, draws a parallel between Lululemon and Nike, the leader in their market: "Nike is edging into community-building, but its business is still anchored to a large extent on big marketing campaigns and paid celebrity endorsers. On the other hand, Lululemon has created a much more powerful community through its 1,500-member ambassador programme and its user-generated content."[8] This bottom-up approach is a complete reversal of the consolidated model whereby companies define the product or service and the brand, advertise it to create awareness and consideration, engage in sales, and only afterward build their community.

* * *

In the post-digital age, building strong brand loyalty requires businesses to both understand the dynamics of human relationships and apply them to their customer interactions. Just like in personal relationships, brand loyalty is a two-way street where both the brand and the customer should be loyal to each other. It's not just about transactional benefits; rather, it's about creating a genuine emotional connection with customers based on shared values, trust, personalization, and consistent delivery of value. To foster brand loyalty, businesses must prioritize the customer journey, ensuring that every touchpoint contributes to a positive and seamless experience. This includes being attentive to customer needs, providing personalized recommendations, and consistently meeting or exceeding expectations. Brands should leverage invisible technology to gather customer data and use it to tailor their offerings and communications to individual preferences, creating a sense of familiarity and ease. It goes without saying that this relationship will have to be mutually beneficial and built on trust. Ultimately, people are willing to trade their personal data, and even to pay a subscription, if what they receive in exchange is perceived as real value.

However, building loyalty goes beyond just focusing on customers. Companies must also be loyal to their employees, suppliers, shareholders, and the broader community in which they operate. Being loyal to all stakeholders involves making decisions that prioritize their best interests and contribute to their well-being. While loyalty programmes can be effective in encouraging repeat purchases and incentivizing customers, they should go beyond simple earn-and-burn schemes. Paid loyalty programmes and communities offer unique benefits and exclusive experiences, fostering a deeper sense of belonging and attachment to the brand. Ultimately, brand loyalty is a culmination of positive interactions, trust, shared values, and emotional connection. If businesses understand the factors that drive loyalty, and avoid the common pitfalls that lead to customer churn, they can create lasting bonds with their customers and thrive in the ever-changing landscape of Retail 5.0.

Reflection Summary Questions

- How can we adapt our idea of loyalty from a transactional focus on customers to a more holistic exchange of value with all stakeholders, including employees and suppliers?
- How do we strike the right balance between offering incentives for loyalty and fostering genuine emotional connections with our customers to drive long-term loyalty?
- How can we differentiate between true loyal customers driven by emotional connection and habitual customers who repeat purchases out of convenience or routine?
- What strategies can we employ to create and nurture a brand community, where customers share interests and values, fostering a sense of belonging and loyalty?
- Considering the importance of trust in customer loyalty, how can we consistently deliver on our promises and ensure ethical practices in our business operations?

Conclusion: Embracing the Post-Digital Retail 5.0 Journey

As we conclude our journey in the post-digital world and its impact on retail, we find ourselves at a pivotal moment where change is not only constant but also unprecedented. We've stated that the very concept of retail must be redefined, for two primary reasons: (1) because of the blurring lines between B2B and B2C, which caused an earthquake in the once-clear boundary between the two worlds, and (2) because of the huge pressure exerted by technological disruption.

The convergence of general-purpose technologies, the maturity of key enablers, and the rapid adoption of critical technologies such as AI, IoT, AR, VR, ML, robotics, and blockchain have ushered in a new era of commerce that we call "retail 5.0." In this era, technology will be less visible but far more present, making every interaction effortless, contextually relevant, and personalized to each individual customer. Natural language processing, sensors, and voice interfaces will allow people to engage in seemingly natural interactions with new technologies. We will seamlessly interact with a plethora of "things," and those things will interact with each other seamlessly in the physical, digital, and virtual worlds.

In particular, the surge of generative-AI applications is spurring exciting innovations and pushing both organizational and customer expectations—but it also worries many who are concerned about data privacy. Consumer companies will be attracted by the opportunity to combine traditional AI and machine-learning models with generative AI to deliver personalized messages and offers to customers, as this represents a tempting opportunity to increase operational efficiency, maximize the return of ad spend (ROAS), and minimize staff costs. Other companies will see an opportunity to leverage these technologies to get the most out of their direct-to-consumer effort. In fact, one can create a significant competitive edge bypassing intermediaries in the sales process, gaining direct access to customer's data, and then retargeting the most promising customer personas with the efficiency and effectiveness of software. Other companies will find ways to strengthen customers' connections—by augmenting with AI the capabilities of their sales associates to deliver personalization at scale, including recommending the next best action with a specific client.

The opportunities are endless in virtually every sector. For instance, AI-powered chatbots will progressively be able to interact with customers using natural language, empathizing and learning from experience and recalling previous interactions. Hence, over time they will feel more human: they will be more personal; they will more quickly address customer queries—suggesting suitable products, providing tailored advice, and proactively resolving concerns—all in real-time, 24/7, 365 days a year. This enhanced customer engagement and these bespoke experiences will cultivate a sense of trust between customers and retailers/brands. When harnessed effectively, the synergy of AI, machine learning (ML), and natural language processing (NLP) can significantly strengthen brand loyalty. Another relevant application for retailers is the use of IoT combined with computer vision-based systems to monitor products' turnover and discern in-store consumer behaviour in real time. This will optimize replenishment processes, dwell time (the length of time an individual spends in front of a shelf) and gaze time (the time spent examining an item) propelling the retail media trend to new heights.

However, the essential prerequisite for all these opportunities to materialize is meticulous data management—and this data carried with it a significant responsibility. It necessitates substantial investments to ensure robust cybersecurity measures are in place. In fact, as we progress into the post-digital era, customers will become even more sensitive to the way their personal data is treated, especially considering that these technologies can often mimic human behaviour. Wise organizational leaders will dedicate significant efforts toward crafting a value proposition built on a thorough mix of authentic human intelligence—encompassing empathy, emotions, social skills—seamlessly combined with the vast computational power of computers, in an effort to enhance the lives of their customers.

At the end of this journey in the post-digital world of commerce, one crucial question remains for retailers and brands—will brick-and-mortar stores be able to survive and thrive in the post-digital world? Our view is that, in a world where people are constantly immersed in a dense digital and virtual clutter, face-to-face interactions will always have a role to play. Hence, it is paramount that brands double down on optimizing a three-dimensional customer journey, creating their unique alchemy of physical, digital, and virtual and assigning to each touchpoint a relevant role. In successfully doing so, companies will keep attracting customers, and this in turn will foster an optichannel virtuous cycle thanks to the first-party data and insights that store managers will be able to collect in face-to-face in-store interactions.

* * *

In the first part of the book we discussed the B2Cization or how the old distinction between B2B and B2C has become outdated in a world where (1) experiential benchmarks are contaminating all sectors across the board and (2) the democratization of technology allows everyone to be a retailer. In the next few years we expect this phenomenon to undergo another evolution that may very likely catch retail and consumer brand leaders unprepared. As we delegate growing portions of the shopping journey to artificial intelligent agents that will act as our assistants and autonomously interact with merchants, questions will arise for marketers on how to do what we could define as B2Ai or B2R—where the "R" stands for robots. How could we influence a customer who walks some of the steps of the journey in a virtual world? What is the ideal next-best action for a young customer who has discovered a brand on an online gaming platform or in a metaverse—can we interest them in becoming a client of the brand in the real world as well? Should they be channeled toward a social media channel? And if yes, which one? And, considering the three dimensions of the journey, this will bring about a further multiplication of touchpoints, making embracing optichannel even more vital. But who knows how to optimize a three-dimensional onlife customer journey considering that some of the touchpoints to take into consideration are being created as we speak? These are some of the questions that retail and consumer brand leaders will need to deal with in just the next few years.

Moreover, given the growing manifestation of the damages produced by the toxic cocktail of capitalism, consumerism, overconsumption, and bad marketing on our planet, we predict that the quest for sustainability and purpose-driven initiatives will shape consumer behaviour and strongly influence governments and businesses. Successful post-digital business leaders are those who understand that profitability is essential for the sustainability and growth of their organization—but it is not the sole driving force. Successful post-digital leaders will prioritize creating value for all stakeholders, including customers, employees, suppliers, communities, and the environment. They will be committed to conducting business ethically, transparently, and responsibly, ensuring that their organization contributes positively to the world around them. They will recognize that long-term success is contingent on fostering positive relationships and making a meaningful impact on society. By aligning their business strategies with a clear purpose, they can inspire their teams, attract new talent, and engage customers on a deeper level.

As we consider the potential future evolution of retail and consumer brands, we see a world where businesses must continuously adapt and evolve to meet the changing needs and preferences of consumers. The post-digital era will witness the further integration of advanced technologies into the fabric of commerce. Physical, digital, and virtual worlds will become increasingly real and interconnected, blurring the lines into a three-dimensional onlife customer journey. To navigate the complexity and uncertainty of this post-digital world, we have proposed a strategic framework of ten guiding principles—the 10 BEs of Retail 5.0. These principles encompass overarching mental postures and specific priorities that business leaders and managers would be wise to embrace if they want to thrive in the post-digital landscape. All the principles are designed to inspire more than to dictate, since we are very conscious that, in such complex scenarios, it would be unrealistic to prescribe granular rules to follow. There can't be a one-size-fits-all approach.

The Retail 5.0 journey commands a relentless commitment to innovation, adaptability, and human-centred strategies. It calls for a profound understanding of the dynamic interplay between technology and human nature. Embracing the 10 BEs of Retail 5.0 and adopting a culture of continuous learning and collaboration will enable businesses to chart their course successfully in this transformative era.

As we move forward, it's crucial to recognize that the journey has just begun. In such an ever-evolving landscape, retailers and consumer brand leaders must remain agile and receptive to change—continuously adapting and willing to challenge the status quo—in order to avoid the risk of finding themselves with an obsolete value proposition. The post-digital world offers boundless opportunities for those who can navigate its complexities with vision, purpose, ambition, humility, agility, and a genuine commitment to customer needs.

The path to success lies in embracing the 10 BEs of Retail 5.0. Together, these guiding principles will empower businesses to redefine retail and thrive in a world where change is the only constant. By embarking on this transformative path, retailer and consumer brands executives can create a new era of customer-centric personalized commerce, ushering in a future where innovation, sustainability, and human connection intertwine to shape a better world for all of us—as customers and as human beings.

Per aspera ad astra.

Notes

Introduction

1. This term derives from the work of economists and university professors Warren Bennis and Burt Nanus in their 1985 book *Leaders: The Strategies for Taking Charge* (New York: HarperCollins). Gavin Wright and Ivy Wigmor, "VUCA (Volatility, Uncertainty, Complexity and Ambiguity)," *WhatIS?.com*, TechTarget, last updated in February 2023, www.techtarget.com/whatis/definition/VUCA-volatility-uncertainty-complexity-and-ambiguity.
2. Jamais Cascio, "Facing the Age of Chaos," *Medium*, April 29, 2020, https://medium.com/@cascio/facing-the-age-of-chaos-b00687b1f51d
3. David Shariatmadari, "A Year of 'Permacrisis,'" Word of the Year 2022, *Collins Language Lovers Blog*, November 1, 2022, https://blog.collinsdictionary.com/language-lovers/a-year-of-permacrisis/.
4. Peter F. Drucker, *The Age of Discontinuity: Guidelines to Our Changing Society* (New York: Harper & Row, 1969), p. 34.
5. Azeem Azhar, *The Exponential Age: How Accelerating Technology Is Transforming Business, Politics and Society* (London: Penguin Random House, 2021).
6. Richard G. Lipsey, Kenneth Carlaw, and Clifford Bekar, *Economic Transformations: General Purpose Technologies and Long-Term Economic Growth* (Oxford: Oxford University Press, 2005).
7. Philip Kotler, Hermawan Kartajaya, and Iwan Setiawan, *Marketing 5.0: Technology for Humanity* (Hoboken, NJ: John Wiley & Sons, 2021), p. 91, fig. 6.1.

8. *The Economist*, "Investors Conclude that Tesla Is a Carmaker, Not a Tech Firm," The Economist Group Limited, January 4, 2023, www.economist.com/business/2023/01/04/investors-conclude-that-tesla-is-a-carmaker-not-a-tech-firm.
9. Freek Vermeulen, "What So Many Strategists Get Wrong About Digital Disruption," *Harvard Business Review,* January 3, 2017, https://hbr.org/2017/01/what-so-many-strategists-get-wrong-about-digital-disruption.
10. Stephen J. Andriole, "Five Myths About Digital Transformation," *MIT Sloane Management Review*, February 6, 2017, https://sloanreview.mit.edu/article/five-myths-about-digital-transformation/.
11. Marcello Pace, personal interview with the authors, October 20, 2022.
12. Simon Fox, personal interview with the authors, November 17, 2022.
13. Parag Desai, Ali Potia, and Brian Salsberg, "Retail 4.0: The Future of Retail Grocery in a Digital World," McKinsey & Company, Asia Consumer and Retail Practice, n.d. [2014], accessed April 7, 2023, www.mckinsey.com/~/media/mckinsey/dotcom/client_service/retail/articles/the_future_of_retail_grocery_in_digital_world%20(3).pdf.
14. Peter Holslin, "Your Ultimate Guide to Internet Speed: Everything You Need to Know," HighSpeedInternet.com, November 16, 2022,www.highspeedinternet.com/resources/the-consumers-guide-to-internet-speed.
15. Desai et al., "Retail 4.0."
16. Alasdair Sandford & Euronews with AP, AFP, "Coronavirus: Half of Humanity Now on Lockdown as 90 Countries Call for Confinement," *Euronews*, updated March 4, 2020, www.euronews.com/2020/04/02/coronavirus-in-europe-spain-s-death-toll-hits-10-000-after-record-950-new-deaths-in-24-hou.
17. Catherine Clifford, "From Chatty Employees to $5 Wine: How Trader Joe's Turns Customers into Fanatics," *CNBC Make It*, updated July 20, 2020, 5:41 PM EDT, www.cnbc.com/2020/03/09/psychology-behind-how-trader-joes-became-a-favorite-grocery-

store.html; see also "General FAQs," Trader Joe's, n.d., accessed April 9, 2023, www.traderjoes.com/home/FAQ/general-faqs.

18. Hugh Fletcher, *The Future Shopper Report 2022*, Wunderman Thompson, accessed April 9, 2023, www.wundermanthompson.com/insight/the-future-shopper-2022.

Part I

1. William Gibson on when he first said this: "The idea would have preceded its first recorded public utterance by quite some time . . . . I would assume I thought it, then eventually said it to friends, and that by the time I said it in an interview (the most likely scenario) it had become an idea I took for granted. It wasn't something generated to give a talk, nor was it in some essay or article." From "The Future Has Arrived—It's Just Not Evenly Distributed Yet," *Quote Investigator*, January 24, 2012, https://quoteinvestigator.com/2012/01/24/future-has-arrived/.

Chapter 1

1. James Estrin, "Kodak's First Digital Moment," *New York Times*, August 12, 2015, https://archive.nytimes.com/lens.blogs.nytimes.com/2015/08/12/kodaks-first-digital-moment/.
2. Clayton M. Christensen and Michael Overdorf, "Meeting the Challenge of Disruptive Change," *Harvard Business Review*, March–April2000,https://hbr.org/2000/03/meeting-the-challenge-of-disruptive-change.
3. Freek Vermeulen, "What So Many Strategists Get Wrong About Digital Disruption," *Harvard Business Review*, January 3, 2017, https://hbr.org/2017/01/what-so-many-strategists-get-wrong-about-digital-disruption.
4. Vermeulen, "What So Many Strategists Get Wrong."
5. Christensen and Overdorf, "Meeting the Challenge."

Chapter 2

1. Jonathan Knowles, B. Tom Hunsaker, Hannah Grove, and Alison James, "What Is the Purpose of Your Purpose?," *Harvard Business Review*, March–April 2022, https://hbr.org/2022/03/what-is-the-purpose-of-your-purpose. See also Thomas W. Malnight, Ivy Buche, and Charles Dhanaraj, "Put Purpose at the Core of Your Strategy," *Harvard Business Review*, September–October 2019, https://hbr.org/2019/09/put-purpose-at-the-core-of-your-strategy.
2. Milton Friedman, "A Friedman Doctrine: The Social Responsibility of Business Is to Increase Its Profits," *New York Times*, September 13, 1970, www.nytimes.com/1970/09/13/archives/a-friedman-doctrine-the-social-responsibility-of-business-is-to.html.
3. Tensie Whelan, Ulrich Atz, Tracy Van Holt and Casey Clark, *ESG and Financial Performance: Uncovering the Relationship by Aggregating Evidence from 1,000 Plus Studies Published between 2015–2020*, NYU Stern Center for Sustainable Business and Rockefeller Asset Management, n.d., www.stern.nyu.edu/sites/default/files/assets/documents/NYU-RAM_ESG-Paper_2021%20Rev_0.pdf.
4. Paolo Taticchi, personal interview with the authors, August 10, 2023.
5. "TIME100 Most Influential Companies," *TIME*, June 2023, https://time.com/collection/time100-companies-2023/.
6. Andrea Baldo, Zoom call with the authors, August 14, 2023.
7. Hugh Fletcher, *The Future Shopper Report 2022*, Wunderman Thompson, accessed April 9, 2023, www.wundermanthompson.com/insight/the-future-shopper-2022.
8. Economic Commission for Europe Executive Committee, Centre for Trade Facilitation and Electronic Business, "Enabling Sustainability and Circularity in the Garment and Footwear Sector: Policy Developments and Industry Perspectives on Traceability and Transparency," 28th session, Geneva, October 6, 2022, United Nations Economic and Social Council, https://

unece.org/sites/default/files/2022-10/ECE-TRADE-C-CEFACT-2022-10E.pdf.

9. Michael E. Porter and Mark R. Kramer, "Creating Shared Value," *Harvard Business Review*, January–February 2011, https://hbr.org/2011/01/the-big-idea-creating-shared-value.

Chapter 3

1. Tim Brown, quoted in Cathaleen Chen, "Allbirds CEO on Why DTC Brands Are Going Multichannel," *Business of Fashion*, December 8, 2022, www.businessoffashion.com/articles/direct-to-consumer/the-state-of-fashion-2023-report-dtc-online-stores-multi-channel/. See also https://www.allbirds.com/.
2. Enrico Casati and Jacopo Sebastio, cofounders of Velasca, personal interview with the authors on February 15, 2023.
3. Paolo Taticchi and Giuseppe Stigliano, *Velasca: a Fashion Brand Competing in a Red Ocean*, UCL School of Management, Revision 1, February 2023, www.mgmt.ucl.ac.uk/sites/default/files/upload/pdfs/Velasca%20170223.pdf. (This link is to a partial report; to get the full report, please email Giuseppe Stigliano at info@giuseppestigliano.com.)
4. Elizabeth Segran, "What Happened to Glossier," *Fast Company*, February 16, 2023, www.fastcompany.com/90849720/glossiers-sephora-launch-is-part-of-a-bigger-transformation; V. Kasturi Rangan, Daniel Corsten, Matt Higgins, and Leonard A. Schlesinger, "How Direct-to-Consumer Brands Can Continue to Grow," *Harvard Business Review*, November–December 2021, https://hbr.org/2021/11/how-direct-to-consumer-brands-can-continue-to-grow.
5. Hugh Fletcher, *The Future Shopper Report 2022*, Wunderman Thompson, p. 32, www.wundermanthompson.com/insight/the-future-shopper-2022 (accessed April 9, 2023).
6. V. Kasturi Rangan, Daniel Corsten, Matt Higgins, and Leonard A. Schlesinger, "How Direct-to-Consumer Brands Can Continue to Grow," *Harvard Business Review*, November–December 2021,

https://hbr.org/2021/11/how-direct-to-consumer-brands-can-continue-to-grow.

7. Dianna Dilworth, "Innovator Interviews: AB InBev's Lucas Herscovici," *Brand Innovators*, March 22, 2023, www.brand-innovators.com/news/innovator-interviews-abinbevs-lucas-herscovici; Keith Nunes, "PepsiCo Launches Two Direct-to-Consumer Platforms," *Food Business News*, May 11, 2020, www.foodbusinessnews.net/articles/16005-pepsico-launches-two-direct-to-consumer-platforms; Simon Harvey interviewing Jean-Philippe Nier, "Kraft Heinz Ventures into Direct-to-Consumer," *Just Food Magazine*, Issue 38, August 2020, https://just-food.nridigital.com/just-food_aug20/kraft_heinz_d2c; Heinz to Home, https://heinztohome.co.uk/ (accessed April 19, 2023); Misha Pabari, "What's in Store for Direct-to-Consumer Ecommerce in 2021?," *Pattern Blog*, February 10, 2021, https://pattern.com/blog/whats-in-store-for-direct-to-consumer-ecommerce-in-2021/.
8. Automotive News Europe, "Mercedes, BMW, Stellantis Favor Agency Sales Model, but Others Disagree," July 20, 2022, https://europe.autonews.com/automakers/mercedes-bmw-stellantis-favor-agency-sales-model-others-disagree; Tom Ryan, "The History of Automotive Retail and a Guide to the Dealership of the Future," *Fuse Autotech*, March 31, 2022, https://fuseautotech.com/blog/dealership-business-model-the-future-of-automotive-retail.
9. Segran, "What Happened to Glossier"; Everlane "About" page, www.everlane.com/about (accessed April 20, 2023); "Harry's," Target website, www.target.com/b/harry-s/-/N-o66wk (accessed April 20, 2023).
10. Kasturi Rangan et al., "How Direct-to-Consumer Brands Can Continue to Grow,"; Lola website, https://mylola.com/ (accessed April 13, 2023); Patrycja Malinowska, "Walmart Adds a Digital-Native Period Brand," Path to Purchase Institute, September 13, 2020, https://p2pi.com/walmart-adds-digital-native-period-brand; Tyler Koslow, "Why We Chose to Retail Our Products at CVS," Public Goods website, October 19, 2020, https://blog.publicgoods.com/why-we-chose-to-retail-our-products-at-cvs/.

11. Shoshy Ciment, "Nike Might Need Wholesale Partners More Than It Thought, Analysts Say," *Yahoo Finance*, March 13, 2023, https://finance.yahoo.com/news/nike-might-wholesale-partners-more-162646993.html; Max Greenwood, "Nike's Digital Ecosystem Paved the Way for D2C Transformation," *Brainstation Magazine*, February 23, 2021, https://brainstation.io/magazine/nikes-digital-ecosystem-paved-the-way-for-d2c-transformation; "Total Nike Retail Stores Worldwide from 2009 to 2022," *Statista*, July 2022, www.statista.com/statistics/250287/total-number-of-nike-retail-stores-worldwide/.
12. Tom Ryan, "Nike Says Goodbye to More Longtime Wholesale Partners," *RetailWire*, March 30, 2021, https://retailwire.com/discussion/nike-says-goodbye-to-more-longtime-wholesale-partners/; Juozas Kaziukėnas, "Amazon Is the Default Search Engine," *Marketplace Pulse*, November 9, 2021, www.marketplacepulse.com/articles/amazon-is-the-default-search-engine.
13. Statista, "Nike's Revenue Worldwide from the Fiscal Years of 2016 to 2022, by Sales Channel," July 2022, www.statista.com/statistics/888725/nikes-revenue-by-sales-channel-worldwide/.
14. Shoshy Ciment, "Nike Might Need Wholesale Partners More Than It Thought, Analysts Say," *Yahoo Finance*, March 13, 2023, https://finance.yahoo.com/news/nike-might-wholesale-partners-more-162646993.html.
15. Euronics website, www.euronics.com/pages/the-group; Hans Carpels, email correspondence with Giuseppe Stigliano, May 15–August 16, 2023.
16. Max Greenwood, "Nike's Digital Ecosystem Paved the Way for D2C Transformation," *BrainStation Magazine*, February 23, 2021, https://brainstation.io/magazine/nikes-digital-ecosystem-paved-the-way-for-d2c-transformation.

Chapter 4

1. "Leadership Development as a Competitive Advantage," McKinsey & Company, April 2, 2018, www.mckinsey.com/

capabilities/people-and-organizational-performance/our-insights/leadership-development-as-a-competitive-advantage.

2. Brian Solis, "Innovation Is a Gift Worth Getting: Competing for the Future Starts with Letting Go of the Past," *Brian Solis blog*, October 19, 2016, www.briansolis.com/2016/10/innovation-gift-worth-getting-competing-future-starts-letting-go-past/.
3. Niraj Dawar, "When Marketing Is Strategy," *Harvard Business Review*, December 2013, https://hbr.org/2013/12/when-marketing-is-strategy.
4. Hugh Fletcher, *The Future Shopper Report 2022*, Wunderman Thompson, www.wundermanthompson.com/insight/the-future-shopper-2022 (accessed April 9, 2023).
5. Holger Blecker, email correspondence with the authors, last exchange on August 14, 2023.
6. Gloria Oladipo, "New York City Could Lose 10,000 Airbnb Listings in Short-term Rental Crackdown," *The Guardian*, January 26, 2023, www.theguardian.com/us-news/2023/jan/26/nyc-airbnb-short-term-rental-new-law; Caitlin Moore, "This Italian City Is Banning Airbnbs with Immediate Effect," *HolidayPirates*, September 6, 2023, www.holidaypirates.com/travel-magazine/this-italian-city-is-banning-airbnbs-with-immediate-effect; Julia Buckley, "Venice and Florence Demand a Curb on Airbnb," *CNN*, updated March 25, 2021, https://edition.cnn.com/travel/article/venice-florence-airbnb-restrictions/index.html.
7. Paris Martineau, "Inside Airbnb's 'Guerrilla War' Against Local Governments," *Wired*, March 20, 2019, www.wired.com/story/inside-airbnbs-guerrilla-war-against-local-governments/.
8. In September 2023, New York City implemented stringent new regulations governing the conditions and timing under which residents can offer their homes for rent. See "New York City's Crackdown on Airbnb Is Starting. Here's What to Expect," *New York Times*, September 5, 2023, www.nytimes.com/2023/09/05/nyregion/airbnb-regulations-nyc-housing.html#:~:text=airbnb%20said%20that%20since%20mid,expected%20to%20be%20taken%20down; "The End of Airbnb in New York," *Wired*, September 5, 2023, www.wired.com/story/airbnb-ban-new-york-city/

9. Jaclyn Peiser, "The Age of Free Online Returns Is Ending," *Washington Post*, December 9, 2022, www.washingtonpost.com/business/2022/12/09/free-returns-holiday-shopping/.
10. Emine Saner, "Delivery Disaster: The Hidden Environmental Cost of Your Online Shopping," *The Guardian*, February 17, 2020, www.theguardian.com/news/shortcuts/2020/feb/17/hidden-costs-of-online-delivery-environment.
11. Daniel Kahneman and Amos Tversky, "Prospect Theory: An Analysis of Decision under Risk," *Econometrica* 47, no. 2 (March 1979), pp. 263–92, www.jstor.org/stable/1914185.
12. Sandro Veronesi, personal interview with the authors, January 18, 2023.
13. Tim Heffernan, "How to Shop Online More Sustainably," *New York Times*, April 22, 2021, www.nytimes.com/wirecutter/blog/shop-online-sustainably/.

Chapter 5

1. In late 2011 John V. Willshire began spreading the concept that "Making Things People Want > Making People Want Things," *Medium*, June 9, 2015, https://medium.com/smithery/making-things-451aacaec170.
2. Peter F. Drucker, *Management: Tasks, Responsibilities, Practices* (New York: Truman Talley Books/E.P. Dutton, 1973), p. 49, www.academia.edu/7194379/Management_Tasks_Responsibilitiesit_Peter_Drucker_
3. Jack Trout, "Peter Drucker on Marketing," *Forbes*, July 3, 2006, www.forbes.com/2006/06/30/jack-trout-on-marketing-cx_jt_0703drucker.html; see also Peter F. Drucker, *The Practice of Management* (New York: HarperBusiness, 2006).
4. Niraj Dawar, *Harvard Business Review*, December 2013, https://hbr.org/2013/12/when-marketing-is-strategy.
5. Craig Stedman and Ed Burns, "business intelligence (BI)," *TechTarget Business Analytics*, last updated in February 2023, www.techtarget.com/searchbusinessanalytics/definition/business-intelligence-BI#.

6. Madeline Jacobson, "Data vs Information: What's the Difference?," *Bloomfire Blog*, updated June 2023, https://bloomfire.com/blog/data-vs-information/.
7. Matt Harker, quoted in *2023 Digital Trends: Experience Index*, Econsultancy x Adobe, n.d., p. 15, https://business.adobe.com/content/dam/dx/us/en/resources/digital-trends-2023/adobe-digital-trends-2023-report.pdf.
8. Adobe Communications Team, "2022 Trust Report: Customer Trust Is Earned or Broken with Every Experience," *Adobe Blog*, March 15, 2022, https://blog.adobe.com/en/publish/2022/03/15/2022-trust-report-customer-trust-is-earned-or-broken-with-every-experience; *2022 Adobe Trust* report, p. 11, https://business.adobe.com/resources/reports/adobe-trust-report.html.
9. Frederic Lardinois, "Google Will Disable Third-Party Cookies for 1% of Chrome Users in Q1 2024," *TechCrunch*, May 18, 2023, https://techcrunch.com/2023/05/18/google-will-disable-third-party-cookies-for-1-of-chrome-users-in-q1-2024/.
10. Steve Lohr, "Without Its Master of Design, Apple Will Face Many Challenges," *New York Times*, August 24, 2011, www.nytimes.com/2011/08/25/technology/without-its-master-of-design-apple-will-face-challenges.html.

Chapter 6

1. Cyril Lamblard, quoted in Brian Solis, "Leading Trends in Retail Innovation," December 3, 2019, p. 14, www.slideshare.net/briansolis/leading-trends-in-retail-innovation-by-brian-solis.
2. Darrell Rigby, "The Future of Shopping," *Harvard Business Review*, December 2011, https://hbr.org/2011/12/the-future-of-shopping.
3. Raffaella Bianchi, Michal Cermak, and Ondrej Dusek, "More Than Digital Plus Traditional: A Truly Omnichannel Customer Experience," McKinsey & Company, July 28, 2016, www.mckinsey.com/capabilities/operations/our-insights/more-than-digital-plus-traditional-a-truly-omnichannel-customer.

4. Emma Sopadjieva, Utpal M. Dholakia, and Beth Benjamin, "A Study of 46,000 Shoppers Shows that Omnichannel Retailing Works," *Harvard Business Review*, January 03, 2017, https://hbr.org/2017/01/a-study-of-46000-shoppers-shows-that-omnichannel-retailing-works.
5. Salesforce Research, *State of the Connected Customer*, 5th edition (May 2022), p. 22, www.salesforce.com/resources/research-reports/state-of-the-connected-customer/.
6. Martin Lindstrom, personal interview with the authors, May 5, 2023.
7. *Retail Speaks: Seven Imperatives for the Industry*, Retail Industry Leaders Association (RILA) and McKinsey & Company (April 2021), www.mckinsey.com/~/media/McKinsey/Industries/Retail/Our%20Insights/retail%20speaks%20seven%20imperatives%20for%20the%20industry/retail-speaks-full-report.pdf.

Chapter 7

1. Peter Drucker, *The Practice of Management* (New York: Harper & Row, 1954).
2. Katherine N. Lemon and Peter C. Verhoef, "Understanding Customer Experience Throughout the Customer Journey," *Journal of Marketing* 80, no. 6 (2016), pp. 69–96, https://doi.org/10.1509/jm.15.0420.
3. The stages of the buyer's decision process were first introduced by John Dewey in *How We Think* (Boston and London: D.C. Heath, 1909).
4. Philip Kotler, Hermawan Kartajaya, and Iwan Setiawan, *Marketing 4.0: Moving from Traditional to Digital* (Hoboken, NJ: Wiley, 2016), p. 64, fig. 5.2.
5. Trefor Moss, "Lego Builds on Its Position as World's No. 1 Toy Maker," *Wall Street Journal*, September 28, 2021, www.wsj.com/articles/lego-builds-on-its-position-as-worlds-no-1-toy-maker-11632843755; "The LEGO Group and the LEGO Foundation," UNICEF, last updated November 22, 2021, www.unicef.org/

partnerships/lego; "Early Learning," Lego Education, n.d., https://education.lego.com/en-gb/earlylearning; "Fabulous New LEGO® Queer Eye Set to Celebrate Creative Expression and Promote Positivity," LEGO, n.d., www.lego.com/en-us/sustainability/promoting-positivity.

6. Luciano Floridi, *The Onlife Manifesto: Being Human in a Hyperconnected Era* (Cham, Switzerland: Springer, 2015).
7. Jennifer Faull, "'Our Future Is Physical, Digital and Virtual': L'Oréal's CMO Is Committed to web3," *The Drum*, January 24, 2023, www.thedrum.com/news/2023/01/24/our-future-physical-digital-and-virtual-l-oreal-s-cmo-committed-web3.
8. Steven Melendez, "Walmart's New AR Feature Lets You See How Furniture Purchases Would Look in Your Home," *Fast Company,* June 23, 2022, www.fastcompany.com/90763528/walmarts-new-ar-feature-lets-you-see-how-home-decor-purchases-would-look-in-your-home; "IKEA Launches IKEA Place, a New App That Allows People to Virtually Place Furniture in Their Home," IKEA, September 12, 2017, https://about.ikea.com/en/newsroom/2017/09/12/ikea-launches-ikea-place-a-new-app-that-allows-people-to-virtually-place-furniture-in-their-home; Ingrid Lunden, "IKEA Place, the Retailer's First ARKit App, Creates Lifelike Pictures of Furniture in Your Home," *TechCrunch*, September 12, 2017, https://techcrunch.com/2017/09/12/ikea-place-the-retailers-first-arkit-app-creates-lifelike-pictures-of-furniture-in-your-home/.
9. Darrell Rigby, "The Future of Shopping," *Harvard Business Review*, December 2011, p. 8, https://hbr.org/2011/12/the-future-of-shopping.
10. "Chipotle Introduces New Garlic Guajillo Steak Across the U.S., Canada and the Metaverse," Chipotle Mexican Grill, September 13, 2022, https://newsroom.chipotle.com/2022-09-13-CHIPOTLE-INTRODUCES-NEW-GARLIC-GUAJILLO-STEAK-ACROSS-THE-U-S-,-CANADA-AND-THE-METAVERSE.
11. "Ralph Lauren and Epic Games Debut a Groundbreaking Fortnite Partnership," Ralph Lauren Corporation, October 31, 2022, https://corporate.ralphlauren.com/pr_221101_Fortnite.html.

12. "Livestreaming Ecommerce Sales in China, 2019–2023 (billions, % change, and % of total retail sales)," *Insider Intelligence*, May 28, 2021, www.insiderintelligence.com/chart/247622/livestreaming-ecommerce-sales-china-2019-2023-billions-change-of-total-retail-sales.
13. www.warbyparker.com/app; www.ray-ban.com/uk/c/face-shape-guide; "How Cosmetic Brands Use Virtual Makeovers to Sell Real Makeup," *CNN Business*, February 14, 2019, www.cnn.com/videos/business/2019/02/14/beauty-cosmetic-makeup-augmented-reality-app-sephora-zw-orig.cnn; Madeleine Schulz, "Virtual Try-on Is Being Hit by Class Actions. Should Brands Worry?," *Vogue Business*, March 7, 2023, www.voguebusiness.com/technology/virtual-try-on-is-being-hit-by-class-actions-should-brands-worry.
14. Madeleine Schulz, "What to Expect at the First AI Fashion Week," *Vogue*, April 5, 2023, www.vogue.com/article/what-to-expect-at-the-first-ai-fashion-week.
15. "Customer Personas," Gartner Glossary, n.d., www.gartner.com/en/marketing/glossary/customer-personas/.

Chapter 8

1. Philip Kotler, Hermawan Kartajaya, and Iwan Setiawan, *Marketing 5.0: Technology for Humanity* (Hoboken, NJ: Wiley, 2021).
2. David C. Edelman and Mark Abraham, "Customer Experience in the Age of AI," *Harvard Business Review*, March–April 2022, https://hbr.org/2022/03/customer-experience-in-the-age-of-ai.
3. Billy Brown, "Review: Future," *Wired*, October 14, 2022, www.wired.com/review/future-fitness-app/.
4. This comment from Greg Hoffman plus the one following are from a videocall with the authors, April 4, 2023.
5. Cristiano Fagnani, in-person and WhatsApp communication, July 16, 2023.

6. "Are Western Companies Becoming Less Global?," *The Economist*, March 16, 2023, www.economist.com/business/2023/03/16/are-western-companies-becoming-less-global.
7. Doug McMillon, "CEO Doug McMillon Said at a Morgan Stanley Conference Last Week," *Grocery Dive*, December 12, 2022, www.grocerydive.com/news/how-walmart-is-pursuing-omnichannel-profitability/638265/.
8. Heather Lalley, "Walmart Opens its 2nd In-store Fulfillment Center," *Winsight Grocery Business*, May 23, 2023, www.winsightgrocerybusiness.com/walmart/walmart-opens-its-2nd-store-fulfillment-center.
9. Amazon Staff, "Join Our Team on a Guided Video-tour through a Fulfillment Center," *Amazon News/Operations*, September 24, 2020, www.aboutamazon.com/amazon-fulfillment/our-innovation/what-robots-do-and-dont-do-at-amazon-fulfillment-centers/; "Amazon Fulfillment Center Video Tour," *YouTube video*, 10:03, uploaded August 28, 2020, www.youtube.com/watch?v=e3QgE4Vs5Cs.
10. Ben Forgan, "What Robots Can Do for Retail," *Harvard Business Review*, October 1, 2020, https://hbr.org/2020/10/what-robots-can-do-for-retail; "Kroger Delivery Expands with New Fulfillment Centers," Kroger, October 12, 2021, https://ir.kroger.com/CorporateProfile/press-releases/press-release/2021/Kroger-Delivery-Expands-with-New-Fulfillment-Centers/default.aspx.
11. Michelle Toh, "300 Million Jobs Could Be Affected by Latest Wave of AI, Says Goldman Sachs," *CNN*, March 29, 2023, www.cnn.com/2023/03/29/tech/chatgpt-ai-automation-jobs-impact-intl-hnk/index.html.

Chapter 9

1. Don-Alvin Adegeest, "The Decline of the American Mall Continues," *Fashion United*, October 14, 2022, https://fashionunited.uk/news/retail/the-decline-of-the-american-mall-

continues/2022101465694; "The History of Malls in the U.S.," Sunset Plaza, n.d., https://sunsetplaza.com/the-history-of-malls-in-the-u-s/; Frank Olito, Erin McDowell, and Alex Bitter, "The Oldest Mall in Every State," *Insider*, updated April 12, 2023, www.businessinsider.com/oldest-mall-in-every-state; "Shopping Mall Statistics and Trends in 2023," *Gitnux Blog*, last edited June 5, 2023, https://blog.gitnux.com/shopping-mall-statistics/; Richard A. Feinberg and Jennifer Meoli, "A Brief History of the Mall," in Rebecca H. Holman and Michael R. Solomon, eds., *NA: Advances in Consumer Research*, vol. 18, pp. 426–27 (Provo, UT: Association for Consumer Research, 1991), www.acrwebsite.org/volumes/7196/volumes/v18/NA(-)18%7C.

2. "Changing Shopping Habits are Transforming America's Malls," *The Economist*, June 2, 2022, www.economist.com/united-states/2022/06/02/changing-shopping-habits-are-transforming-americas-malls.
3. "Shopping Center Density: CEE/SEE Cities Clearly Overstored," *RegioData Research*, April 27, 2023, www.regiodata.eu/en/europe-shopping-center-density-cee-see-cities-clearly-overstored/.
4. This quote by Alejandro Camino, plus another that appears later in the chapter, are from a personal interview with Giuseppe Stigliano, Lima, Peru, April 25, 2023.
5. "The Luxury of Asia's Malls Is No Substitute for Genuine Public Spaces," *The Economist*, June 2, 2022, www.economist.com/asia/2022/06/02/the-luxury-of-asias-malls-is-no-substitute-for-genuine-public-spaces.
6. "The Rise, Fall and Rebirth of the Shopping Centre," *Financial Times*, May 15, 2022, www.ft.com/content/1f024fd8-ade5-4468-9cb0-0a73d2a66364.

Chapter 10

1. "Amazon Research and Development Expenses 2010–2023 | AMZN," *Macrotrends*, n.d., www.macrotrends.net/stocks/charts/AMZN/amazon/research-development-expenses.

2. Nassim Nicholas Taleb, *The Black Swan: The Impact of the Highly Improbable* (New York: Penguin, 2008).
3. Abha Bhattarai, "Private Equity's Role in Retail Has Killed 1.3 Million Jobs, Study Says," *Washington Post*, July 24, 2019, www.washingtonpost.com/business/2019/07/24/private-equitys-role-retail-has-decimated-million-jobs-study-says/.
4. Tim Jackson, "FT Business of Luxury 2023," *Stylus*, June 12, 2023, https://stylus.com/consumer-attitudes/ft-business-of-luxury-summit-2023.

Part II

1. IBM's Jane Harper "says that the term was coined by researchers at Bell Labs who were looking to describe the personal attributes of the most effective scientists and engineers." Dave Kinnear, "Leadership: Humbition," DBK Associates (blog), May 7, 2014, https://execleadercoach.com/2014/05/07/humbition/.
2. Charles O'Reilly and Michael Tushman, "Organizational Ambidexterity: Past, Present and Future," *SSRN Electronic Journal* 27, no. 4 (last revised November 13, 2013): http://dx.doi.org/10.2139/ssrn.2285704.
3. Luciano Floridi (ed.), *The Onlife Manifesto: Being Human in a Hyperconnected Era* (Cham, Switzerland: Springer), p. 1. https://doi.org/10.1007/978-3-319-04093-6_1.
4. Salim Ismail, Michael S. Malone, and Yuri van Geest, *Exponential Organizations: Why New Organizations Are Ten Times Better, Faster, and Cheaper Than Yours (And What to Do About It)* (New York: Diversion Books, 2014).

Chapter 11

1. Bill Taylor, "On the 'Battle for Talent' and the Power of 'Humbition,'" *Harvard Business Review*, February 27, 2008, https://hbr.org/2008/02/on-the-battle-for-talent-and-t.

2. Rasmus Hougaard and Jacqueline Carter, "Ego Is the Enemy of Good Leadership," *Harvard Business Review*, November 6, 2018, https://hbr.org/2018/11/ego-is-the-enemy-of-good-leadership.
3. Paolo Gallo, *The Seven Games of Leadership: Navigating the Inner Journey of Leaders* (New York: Bloomsbury Business, 2023), p. 71.
4. From, in part, "Satya Nadella Quotes on Culture, Innovation, and Leadership," JD Meier (blog), n.d., https://jdmeier.com/satya-nadella-quotes/.
5. Sue Shellenbarger, "The Best Bosses Are Humble Bosses," *The Wall Street Journal*, October 9, 2018, www.wsj.com/articles/the-best-bosses-are-humble-bosses-1539092123.
6. Robert Greenleaf, *Servant Leadership: A Journey into the Nature of Legitimate Power and Greatness* (New York: Paulist Press, 1977, 2002, 2008); Vaneet Kashyap and Santosh Rangnekar, "Servant Leadership, Employer Brand Perception, Trust in Leaders and Turnover Intentions: A Sequential Mediation Model," *Review of Managerial Science* 10, no. 3 (July 2016), pp. 437–461, https://doi.org/10.1007/s11846-014-0152-6; Dan Cable, "How Humble Leadership Really Works," *Harvard Business Review*, April 23, 2018, https://hbr.org/2018/04/how-humble-leadership-really-works.
7. Peter Economy, "21 Super Inspiring Quotes for Leaders," *Inc.*, December 26, 2015, www.inc.com/peter-economy/21-inspiring-quotes-for-leaders.html.
8. Mauro Porcini, personal conversation with the authors, April 30, 2023.
9. Michael D. Watkins, "Picking the Right Transition Strategy," *Harvard Business Review*, January 2009, https://hbr.org/2009/01/picking-the-right-transition-strategy; Michael D. Watkins, *The First 90 Days: Proven Strategies for Getting Up to Speed Faster and Smarter, Updated and Expanded* (Boston: Harvard Business Review Press, 2013).

Chapter 12

1. Milton Friedman, "A Friedman Doctrine: The Social Responsibility of Business Is to Increase Its Profits," *New York Times,* September 13, 1970, www.nytimes.com/1970/09/13/archives/a-friedman-doctrine-the-social-responsibility-of-business-is-to.html.
2. Colin Mayer, Leo E. Strine Jr., and Jaap Winter, "50 Years Later, Milton Friedman's Shareholder Doctrine Is Dead," *Fortune,* September 13, 2020, https://fortune.com/2020/09/13/milton-friedman-anniversary-business-purpose/
3. Salesforce Research, *State of the Connected Customer*, 5th edition (May 2022), p. 8, www.salesforce.com/resources/research-reports/state-of-the-connected-customer/.
4. *Retail Speaks: Seven Imperatives for the Industry*, Retail Industry Leaders Association (RILA) and McKinsey & Company (April 2021), p. 7, www.mckinsey.com/~/media/McKinsey/Industries/Retail/Our%20Insights/retail%20speaks%20seven%20imperatives%20for%20the%20industry/retail-speaks-full-report.pdf; Philip Kotler and Nancy R. Lee, *Corporate Social Responsibility: Doing the Most Good for Your Company and Your Cause* (Hoboken, NJ: Wiley, 2004).
5. Tom Schoenwaelder, John Mennel, Amy E. Silverstein, and Shira Beery, *The Purpose Premium: Why a Purpose-Driven Strategy Is Good for Business,* Monitor Deloitte, n.d., p. 4, www2.deloitte.com/content/dam/Deloitte/us/Documents/process-and-operations/purpose-premium-pov.pdf.
6. "Our Core Values," Patagonia.com, 2022, www.patagonia.com/core-values/.
7. David Gelles, "Billionaire No More: Patagonia Founder Gives Away the Company," *New York Times*, September 21, 2022, www.nytimes.com/2022/09/14/climate/patagonia-climate-philanthropy-chouinard.html.
8. Michael Porter and Mark Kramer, "Creating Shared Value: How to Reinvent Capitalism and Unleash a Wave of Innovation and Growth," *Harvard Business Review,* January–February 2011, https://hbr.org/2011/01/the-big-idea-creating-shared-value.

9. "A Broken System Needs Urgent Repairs," *The Economist*, July 21, 2022, www.economist.com/special-report/2022/07/21/a-broken-system-needs-urgent-repairs.
10. "The 17 Goals," United Nations, Department of Economic and Social Affairs Sustainable Development, n.d., https://sdgs.un.org/goals.
11. Michelle Toh, "L'Oréal Buys Aesop in $2.5 Billion Deal, Its Biggest Acquisition Ever," *CNN*, updated April 4, 2023, www.cnn.com/2023/04/04/business/australia-aesop-loreal-natura-deal-intl-hnk.
12. "B CORP," Danone, n.d., www.danone.com/about-danone/sustainable-value-creation/BCorpAmbition.html.
13. Vikram Alexei Kansara, "Uniqlo Boss: 'Without a Soul, a Company Is Nothing,'" *Business of Fashion*, October 17, 2016, www.businessoffashion.com/articles/retail/uniqlo-fast-retailing-ceo-tadashi-yanai-management-principles/.
14. "Results Summary," UNIQLO FY2023 Third Quarter, *Fast Retailing*, last updated July 13, 2023, www.fastretailing.com/eng/ir/financial/summary.html.
15. "RE.UNIQLO STUDIO," n.d., www.uniqlo.com/uk/en/content/reuniqlo-studio.html; https://faq-us.uniqlo.com/articles/en_US/FAQ/UNIQLO-SOHO-Repair-Services/; "A New Life for Uniqlo Clothing," UNIQLO Sustainability, n.d., www.uniqlo.com/jp/en/contents/sustainability/planet/clothes_recycling/re-uniqlo/.
16. Riccardo Stefanelli, personal interviews with the authors, July 31, 2023.
17. Sherry Frey, Jordan Bar Am, Vinit Doshi, Anandi Malik, and Steve Noble, "Consumers Care about Sustainability—and Back it Up with Their Wallets," McKinsey & Company, February 6, 2023, www.mckinsey.com/industries/consumer-packaged-goods/our-insights/consumers-care-about-sustainability-and-back-it-up-with-their-wallets.
18. Frey et al., "Consumers Care about Sustainability."
19. "Adidas Reveals When it Will Sell Leftover Yeezy Shoes from Defunct Kanye West Partnership," *Sky News*, May 20, 2023, https://news.sky.com/story/adidas-reveals-when-it-will-sell-leftover-yeezy-shoes-from-defunct-kanye-west-partnership-12884930.

20. Sarah Butler, Philip Oltermann, and Morwenna Ferrier, "Adidas Cuts Ties with Kanye West over Antisemitic Comments," *The Guardian*, October 25, 2022, www.theguardian.com/music/2022/oct/25/adidas-cuts-ties-with-kanye-west-over-antisemitic-comments; Tim Loh, "Adidas's New CEO Has a $1.3 Billion Pile of Unsold Yeezy Gear," *Bloomberg*, updated February 10, 2023, www.bloomberg.com/news/articles/2023-02-09/adidas-says-losses-may-hit-700-million-this-year-amid-ye-row#xj4y7vzkg.
21. dylanmulvaney, Instagram post, April 1, 2023, www.instagram.com/p/CqgTftujqZc/.
22. Danielle Wiener-Bronner, "Bud Light Wanted to Market to All. Instead, It's Alienating Everyone," *CNN Business*, May 1, 2023, https://edition.cnn.com/2023/05/01/business/bud-light-marketing/; Jennifer Maloney and Lauren Weber, "How Bud Light Handled an Uproar over a Promotion with a Transgender Advocate," *Wall Street Journal*, updated May 22, 2023, www.wsj.com/articles/how-bud-light-handled-an-uproar-over-a-promotion-with-a-transgender-advocate-e457d5c6.
23. Susie Heller, "Here's the Back Story of Everyone Who Appeared in the New Nike 'Dream Crazy' Ad Featuring Colin Kaepernick," *Insider*, September 10, 2018, www.insider.com/all-the-athletes-in-the-nike-dream-crazy-ad-with-colin-kaepernick-2018-9#football-player-shaquem-griffin-is-the-first-one-handed-player-to-be-drafted-into-the-nfl-15; Steve Wyche, "Colin Kaepernick Explains Why He Sat during National Anthem," NFL.com, August 27, 2016, www.nfl.com/news/colin-kaepernick-explains-why-he-sat-during-national-anthem-0ap3000000691077.
24. "Colin Kaepernick Becomes the Face of Nike's Just Do It Campaign," updated September 4, 2018, *The Guardian*, https://www.theguardian.com/sport/2018/sep/03/colin-kaepernick-nike-just-do-it-campaign-nfl; Jeff Beer, "One Year Later, What Did We Learn from Nike's Blockbuster Colin Kaepernick Ad?," *Fast Company*, September 5, 2019, www.fastcompany.com/90399316/one-year-later-what-did-we-learn-from-nikes-blockbuster-colin-kaepernick-ad; "Nike's 'Dream Crazy' Advert Starring Colin Kaepernick Wins Emmy," *The Guardian*, September 19,

2019, www.theguardian.com/sport/2019/sep/16/nikes-dream-crazy-advert-starring-colin-kaepernick-wins-emmy.

25. Selvane Mohandas du Ménil, Zoom interview with the authors, May 31, 2023.

Chapter 13

1. Charles A. O'Reilly and Michael L. Tushman, "Organizational Ambidexterity: Past, Present and Future," *SSRN Electronic Journal* 27, no. 4 (December 2013), http://dx.doi.org/10.2139/ssrn.2285704; Charles A. O'Reilly III and Michael L. Tushman, "The Ambidextrous Organization," *Harvard Business Review*, April 2004, https://hbr.org/2004/04/the-ambidextrous-organization.
2. Chris Kohler, "September 23, 1889: Success Is in the Cards for Nintendo," *Wired*, September 23, 2010, www.wired.com/2010/09/0923nintendo-founded/; Matthew Byrd, "How the GameCube Made Nintendo Cynical," *Den of Geek*, February 27, 2017, www.denofgeek.com/games/how-the-gamecube-made-nintendo-cynical/; Reggie Fils-Aime, "Perspective: Nintendo on the Latest 'Technical Divide,'" Nintendo, May 9, 2007, https://web.archive.org/web/20090806203242/http://news.cnet.com/Nintendo-on-the-latest-technical-divide/2010-1041_3-6180215.html; Howard Wisniowski, "Analog Devices and Nintendo Collaboration Drives Video Game Innovation with iMEMS Motion Signal Processing Technology," *Analog Devices*, May 9, 2006, https://web.archive.org/web/20090625055416/http://www.analog.com/en/press-release/May_09_2006_ADI_Nintendo_Collaboration/press.html; Scott D. Anthony, "Nintendo Wii's Growing Market of 'Nonconsumers,'" *Harvard Business Review*, Apr 30, 2008, https://hbr.org/2008/04/nintendo-wiis-growing-market-o.
3. "Walmart," *Fortune*, last updated August 2, 2023, https://fortune.com/company/walmart/; "Unit Counts and Square Footage," *Walmart Financials*, as of July 31, 2023, https://stock.walmart.com/financials/unit-counts-and-square-footage/default

.aspx; "Unit Counts by Country," Walmart, October 31, 2022, https://s201.q4cdn.com/262069030/files/doc_downloads/2022/FY2023-Q3-Unit-Count-Market-Summary-for-IR.pdf; "1990 Sales Lift Wal-mart into Top Spot," *Dallas Morning News*, February 15, 1991, https://web.archive.org/web/20130904035126/articles.sun-sentinel.com/1991-02-15/business/9101080852_1_wal-mart-stores-supercenter-stores-hypermart-usa-units.

4. "Walmart Agrees to Acquire Jet.com, One of the Fastest Growing e-Commerce Companies in the U.S.," *Walmart newsroom*, August 8, 2016, https://corporate.walmart.com/newsroom/2016/08/08/walmart-agrees-to-acquire-jet-com-one-of-the-fastest-growing-e-commerce-companies-in-the-u-s; IBM, "Walmart, IBM and Tsinghua University Explore the Use of Blockchain to Help Bring Safer Food to Dinner Tables across China," *PR Newswire/Cision*, October 19, 2016, www.prnewswire.com/news-releases/walmart-ibm-and-tsinghua-university-explore-the-use-of-blockchain-to-help-bring-safer-food-to-dinner-tables-across-china-300347302.html; Leslie Picker and Rachel Abrams, "Walmart Rewrites Its E-Commerce Strategy with $3.3 Billion Deal for Jet.com," *New York Times*, August 8, 2016, www.nytimes.com/2016/08/09/business/dealbook/walmart-jet-com.html; Aisha Malik, "Walmart Sells E-Commerce Outdoor Retailer Moosejaw after Acquiring It in 2017," *TechCrunch*, February 23, 2023, https://techcrunch.com/2023/02/23/walmart-sells-e-commerce-outdoor-retailer-moosejaw/; Daphne Howland, "Walmart Is Selling Bonobos to Express, WHP Global for $75M," *Retail Dive*, April 14, 2023, www.retaildive.com/news/walmart-sells-bonobos-express-seventy-five-million/647654/.
5. T. Ozbun, "Online Sales of Walmart Worldwide from Fiscal Year 2019 to 2023, by Division," *Statista*, March 20, 2023, www.statista.com/statistics/1109330/walmart-ecommerce-sales-by-division-worldwide/; David Marcotte, "A Look at the 2022 Top 50 Global Retailers," *Kantar Retail*, March 23, 2022, https://nrf.com/blog/look-2022-top-50-global-retailers.
6. Rita Gunther McGrath, *The End of Competitive Advantage: How to Keep Your Strategy Moving as Fast as Your Business* (Boston: Harvard Business Review Press, 2013).

7. "America's Corporate Giants Are Getting Harder to Topple," *The Economist*, August 21, 2023, www.economist.com/business/2023/08/21/americas-corporate-giants-are-getting-harder-to-topple.
8. Gunther McGrath, *The End of Competitive Advantage*; Clayton M. Christensen, *The Innovator's Dilemma: When New Technologies Cause Great Firms to Fail* (Boston: Harvard Business Review Press, 2016); Eric Ries, *The Lean Startup: How Today's Entrepreneurs Use Continuous Innovation to Create Radically Successful Businesses* (New York: Crown Business, 2011).
9. Stéphane de la Faverie, in-person interview with the authors, April 18, 2023.
10. Joanna Stern, "Jeff Bezos Says *Washington Post* Could Take a Page from Amazon," *ABC News*, September 24, 2013, https://abcnews.go.com/Technology/jeff-bezos-washington-post-page-amazon/story?id=20364644.
11. Charles A. O'Reilly III and Michael L. Tushman, "The Ambidextrous Organization," *Harvard Business Review*, April 2004, https://hbr.org/2004/04/the-ambidextrous-organization.
12. Nicola Zotta, video call with Giuseppe Stigliano, June 12, 2023.
13. Joseph Pistrui and Dimo Dimov, "The Role of a Manager Has to Change in 5 Key Ways," *Harvard Business Review*, October 26, 2018, https://hbr.org/2018/10/the-role-of-a-manager-has-to-change-in-5-key-ways.
14. Sergei Goncharov, "How a Russian Retailer Is Building a Next-Generation Grocery Business," McKinsey & Company, March 24, 2021, www.mckinsey.com/industries/retail/our-insights/how-a-russian-retailer-is-building-a-next-generation-grocery-business.

Chapter 14

1. Todd Thompson, "From Omnichannel to Optichannel, Marketing's Return to Rationality," *ClickZ*, March 3, 2020, www.clickz.com/from-omnichannel-to-optichannel-marketings-return-to-rationality/260551/.

2. Tricia McKinnon, "The Future of Retail: 9 Ways Alibaba Is Redefining Retail Stores," *Indigo9 Digital*, August 2, 2022, www.indigo9digital.com/blog/futureofretailalibaba.
3. Sophie Smith, "Moncler Collaborates with Fortnite to Launch New In-Game Reactive Outfits," *The Industry.fashion*, November 24, 2021, www.theindustry.fashion/moncler-collaborates-with-fortnite-to-launch-new-in-game-reactive-outfits/.
4. Mauro Porcini, Zoom conversation with Giuseppe Stigliano, May 23, 2023.
5. David Droga and Baiju Shah, "Keeping Up with Customers' Increasingly Dynamic Needs," *Harvard Business Review*, September 27, 2022, https://hbr.org/2022/09/keeping-up-with-customers-increasingly-dynamic-needs.
6. Giovanni Valentini, telephone conversation with Giuseppe Stigliano, July 14, 2023.
7. Greg Hoffman, Zoom interview with Giuseppe Stigliano, April 23, 2023.
8. Manuel Arroyo, Zoom interview with Giuseppe Stigliano, June 29, 2023.

Chapter 15

1. Alex Barseghian, "How Nike Is Using Analytics to Personalize Their Customer Experience," *Forbes*, October 7, 2019, www.forbes.com/sites/forbestechcouncil/2019/10/07/how-nike-is-using-analytics-to-personalize-their-customer-experience/.
2. Maghan McDowell, "Google Introduces Virtual Try-On Using Generative AI," *Vogue Business*, June 14, 2023, www.voguebusiness.com/technology/google-introduces-virtual-try-on-using-generative-ai; "The Impact of Textile Production and Waste on the Environment (Infographics)," European Parliament, updated May 6, 2023, www.europarl.europa.eu/news/en/headlines/society/20201208STO93327/the-impact-of-textile-production-and-waste-on-the-environment-infographics.

3. Creative Works, *The Open Creative Project*, Google, n.d. [2023], p. 13, www.thinkwithgoogle.com/_qs/documents/18302/OpenCreative_Final_Reduced.pdf; "Attitude of Consumers Worldwide Toward Personalization and Customer Experience Provided by a Company, 2020 & 2022 (% of respondents)," *Salesforce*, May 13, 2022, www.insiderintelligence.com/chart/256614/Attitude-of-Consumers-Worldwide-Toward-Personalization-Customer-Experience-Provided-by-Company-2020-2022-of-respondents.
4. *2023 Digital Trends Report*, Adobe, n.d., p. 15, https://business.adobe.com/resources/digital-trends-report.html.
5. Patty Seybold, "Adidas Pioneered in Providing Custom Footwear," *Outside Innovation: New Ways to Engage Customers in Co-Designing Your Company's Future* (weblog of book *Outside Innovation*), February 21, 2009, https://outsideinnovation.blogs.com/pseybold/2009/02/adidas-pioneered-in-providing-custom-footwear.html; Hilary Murdock, "Top 4 Customizable Options People Want in an Adidas Shoe Configurator," *Threekit*, July 20, 2021, www.threekit.com/blog/top-4-customizable-options-people-want-in-adidas-shoe-configurator.
6. "Uniqlo: World's First Magic Mirror," *Holition* (2012), https://holition.com/work/uniqlo-world-s-first-magic-mirror; Craig William Smith, "UniQlo's Magic Mirror," *Retail Innovation*, April 1, 2013, https://retail-innovation.com/uniqlos-magic-mirror.
7. *Retail Speaks: Seven Imperatives for the Industry*, Retail Industry Leaders Association (RILA) and McKinsey & Company, n.d., www.mckinsey.com/~/media/McKinsey/Industries/Retail/Our%20Insights/retail%20speaks%20seven%20imperatives%20for%20the%20industry/retail-speaks-full-report.pdf.

Chapter 16

1. Agostino Perrone and Giorgio Bargiani, personal interview with Giuseppe Stigliano, January 23, 2023.

2. PwC, *Workforce of the Future: The Competing Forces Shaping 2030,* n.d., https://pwc.to/2Rfozuq.
3. Marc Andreessen, "Why Software Is Eating the World," *Wall Street Journal*, updated August 20, 2011, www.wsj.com/articles/SB10001424053111903480904576512250915629460; Ani Petrosyan, "Number of Internet and Social Media Users Worldwide as of April 2023," May 22, 2023, www.statista.com/statistics/617136/digital-population-worldwide/#:~:text=Worldwide%20digital%20population%202023&text=As%20of%20April%202023%2C%20there,percent%20of%20the%20global%20population.
4. Financial highlights: "2022 – Summary of Data," Brunello Cucinelli, n.d., http://investor.brunellocucinelli.com/en/financials/financial-highlights.
5. "Nurturing the Soul of a Brand," *Women's Wear Daily*, n.d., https://wwd.com/business-news/business-features/unilever-founders-nurturing-the-soul-of-a-brand-1235407060.
6. Vasiliki Petrou, in-person interview with Giuseppe Stigliano, June 21, 2023.
7. Penny Brook, Zoom interview with Giuseppe Stigliano, June 29, 2023.
8. Federico Turconi, personal interview with Giuseppe Stigliano, April 18, 2023.

Chapter 17

1. Philip Kotler, "Atmospherics as a Marketing Tool," *Journal of Retailing* 49, no. 4 (January 1974), pp. 48–64, www.researchgate.net/publication/239435728_Atmospherics_as_a_Marketing_Tool.
2. Sara Lebow, "Over 60% of US Online Shoppers Start Their Product Search on Amazon," *Insider Intelligence*, August 9, 2022, www.insiderintelligence.com/content/online-shoppers-search-on-amazon; Danny Goodwin, "50% of Product Searches Start on Amazon," *Search Engine Land*, May 16, 2023, https://

searchengineland.com/50-of-product-searches-start-on-amazon-424451; Stephanie Chevalier, "Retail E-Commerce Sales Worldwide from 2014 to 2026," *Statista*, September 21, 2022, www.statista.com/statistics/379046/worldwide-retail-e-commerce-sales/.

3. Dave Chaffey, "Global Social Media Statistics Research Summary 2023," *Smart Insights*, June 7, 2023, www.smartinsights.com/social-media-marketing/social-media-strategy/new-global-social-media-research/.
4. Stephanie Chevalier, "Social Commerce Revenue Worldwide from 2022 to 2030," *Statista*, April 12, 2023, www.statista.com/statistics/1231944/social-commerce-global-market-size/.
5. "Metaverse Market Size, Share & COVID-19 Impact Analysis, by. . . 2023–2027," Report ID: FBI106574, *Fortune Business Insights*, May 2023, www.fortunebusinessinsights.com/metaverse-market-106574.
6. Humanizing Technologies website, https://humanizing.com/en/; Brian Heater, "Flippy, the Hamburger-Cooking Robot, Gets More Capable," *TechCrunch*, November 2, 2021, https://techcrunch.com/2021/11/02/flippy-the-hamburger-cooking-robogets-a-more-capable-successor/; Fiona Noble, a former CMO of Quintessentially, used the expression "the product has become a souvenir for the experience" during the Forbes CMO Summit in 2019.
7. *Retail Futures 2022*, The Future Laboratory, n.d., p. 20, www.thefuturelaboratory.com/reports/2022/retail-futures; Stephanie Hirschmiller, "Galeries Lafayette Wellness Floor Is the Largest in Europe and Has Its Own 14-Strong Concierge Team," *Forbes*, July 30, 2022, www.forbes.com/sites/stephaniehirschmiller/2022/07/30/galeries-lafayette-wellness-floor-is-the-largest-in-europe/?sh=73f16e993ed9.
8. Oliver Barnes, "Selfridges Granted Licence to Host Weddings," *Financial Times*, May 11, 2021, www-ft-com.ezp.lib.cam.ac.uk/content/bdc7d3f7-2367-4c4b-836c-8fc3d5a5f4c2.
9. Lucia Marcuzzo, Zoom call with Giuseppe Stigliano, August 14, 2023.

10. Carlo Colpo, in-person interview with the authors, June 23, 2023.
11. "Ericsson ConsumerLab: Ten Hot Consumer Trends 2030—The Hybrid Mall," December 15, 2021, www.ericsson.com/en/press-releases/2021/12/ericsson-consumerlab-ten-hot-consumer-trends-2030--the-hybrid-mall.
12. *Retail Futures 2022*, The Future Laboratory, n.d., p. 9, www.thefuturelaboratory.com/reports/2022/retail-futures.
13. *#TomorrowStartsToday: Non-Financial Reporting Declaration 2020*, Decathlon, n.d., https://drive.google.com/file/d/1qCmtb2mXP_CBCSAyqYre7RBxazxyyidF/view; "12 Fun Facts about Eataly," Eataly website, n.d. [January 2019], www.eataly.com/us_en/about-eataly/news/fun-facts-about-eataly; "Eataly vede rosso per 25 milioni, Farinetti," *Economia*, July 4, 2023, https://www.targatocn.it/2023/07/04/amp/argomenti/economia-7/articolo/eataly-vede-rosso-per-25-milioni-farinetti-numeri-come-da-previsioni-in-arrivo-200-milioni-per-r.html.
14. Francesca Bellettini, email correspondence with the authors for *Onlife Fashion: 10 Rules for the Future of High-End Fashion*, July 2020.
15. Michael Ward, in-person conversation with the authors at Harrods, April 3, 2023.
16. Matthew Boyle, "Best Buy Tests Smaller Shopping Areas to Focus on E-Commerce," Bloomberg, updated on February 23, 2021, www.bloomberg.com/news/articles/2021-02-23/best-buy-said-to-expand-rollout-of-smaller-store-footprints?in_source=embedded-checkout-banner; Russell Redman, "Whole Foods Opens Online-Only 'Dark Store' in Brooklyn," *Supermarket News*, September 2, 2020, www.supermarketnews.com/online-retail/whole-foods-opens-online-only-dark-store-brooklyn.

Chapter 18

1. Salim Ismail, Michael S. Malone, and Yuri van Geest, *Exponential Organizations: Why New Organizations Are Ten Times Better,*

Faster, and Cheaper Than Yours (and What to Do About It) (New York: Diversion Books, 2014).

2. Cristiano Fagnani, in-person and WhatsApp communication, July 16, 2023.
3. Michael G. Jacobides, conversation with Giuseppe Stigliano, July 2023.
4. Michael G. Jacobides would partially disagree with this list. In fact, he also suggested we consider a distinction between technology platforms (technologically based solutions that allow multiple actors to interact) and proper ecosystems (which are groups of connected products or services and the players that collaborate to produce them). He told us that the best way to summarize this distinction is: "Platforms are made of technology, ecosystems are made of people, products, and organizations." For more details about the "confusion" between the two terms please see Michael G. Jacobides, "How to Compete When Industries Digitize and Collide: An Ecosystem Development Framework," California Management Review 64, no. 3 (2022), pp. 99–123, https://doi.org/10.1177/00081256221083352.
5. "HealthSuite: Powering the Next Generation of Connected Cloud Health Applications," Philips website, n.d., www.usa.philips.com/healthcare/innovation/about-health-suite.
6. "What the Largest Global Fintech Can Teach Us About What's Next in Financial Services," CB Insights, October 4, 2018, www.cbinsights.com/research/ant-financial-alipay-fintech/.
7. Enel X website, https://corporate.enelx.com/en.
8. Venkat Atluri, Miklós Dietz, and Nicolaus Henke, "Competing in a World of Sectors without Borders," McKinsey/Digital: Insights, July 12, 2017, www.mckinsey.com/capabilities/quantumblack/our-insights/competing-in-a-world-of-sectors-without-borders; Ulrich Pidun, Martin Reeves, and Maximilian Schüssler, "Do You Need a Business Ecosystem?" BCG Henderson Institute Publications Online, September 27, 2019, www.bcg.com/publications/2019/do-you-need-business-ecosystem.
9. Jacobides, "How to Compete When Industries Digitize and Collide," p. 103.

10. "Target Teams Up with Techstars for Retail Accelerator in Minneapolis," A Bullseye View, September 16, 2015, https://corporate.target.com/article/2015/09/techstars-announcement; Anthony Ha, "Target Teams Up with Techstars to Create A Retail-Focused Startup Accelerator," TechCrunch, October 18, 2015, https://techcrunch.com/2015/10/18/target-retail-accelerator/.
11. Store No. 8, n.d., www.storeno8.com/.
12. Stefano Portu, email correspondence with Giuseppe Stigliano, July 27, 2023.
13. To delve deeper into this topic, we recommend Nirmalya Kumar's book *Clash: Amazon versus Walmart* (New York: Penguin Random House, 2024).
14. "Walmart Agrees to Acquire Jet.com, One of the Fastest Growing E-Commerce Companies in the U.S.," Walmart, August 8, 2016, https://corporate.walmart.com/newsroom/2016/08/08/walmart-agrees-to-acquire-jet-com-one-of-the-fastest-growing-e-commerce-companies-in-the-u-s; Melissa Repko, "Walmart Winds Down Jet .com Four Years after $3.3 Billion Acquisition of e-Commerce Company," CNBC, updated May 19 2020, www.cnbc.com/2020/05/19/walmart-winds-down-jetcom-four-years-after-3point3-billion-acquisition.html; "Walmart to Invest in Flipkart Group, India's Innovative eCommerce Company," Walmart, May 9, 2018, https://corporate.walmart.com/newsroom/2018/05/09/walmart-to-invest-in-flipkart-group-indias-innovative-ecommerce-company; "Walmart Announces the Acquisition of Moosejaw, a Leading Online Outdoor Retailer," Walmart, February 15, 2017, https://corporate.walmart.com/newsroom/2017/02/15/walmart-announces-the-acquisition-of-moosejaw-a-leading-online-outdoor-retailer; Gabrielle Fonrouge, "Dick's Sporting Goods to Buy E-Commerce Outdoor Retailer Moosejaw from Walmart," CNBC, February 22, 2023, www.cnbc.com/2023/02/22/dicks-sporting-goods-buys-moosejaw-walmart.html; "Walmart Announces the Acquisition of ModCloth, a Leading Online Women's Fashion Retailer," Walmart, March 17, 2017, https://corporate.walmart .com/newsroom/2017/03/17/walmart-announces-the-acquisition-of-modcloth-a-leading-online-womens-fashion-retailer; Zoe Schiffer,

"Walmart Sells ModCloth Just Two Years after Buying It," The Verge, October 4, 2019, www.theverge.com/2019/10/4/20899540/walmart-sells-modcloth-acquisition-compete-amazon; "Walmart to Acquire Bonobos and Appoint Andy Dunn to Oversee Exclusive Consumer Brands Offered Online," Walmart, June 16, 2017, https://corporate.walmart.com/newsroom/2017/06/16/walmart-to-acquire-bonobos-and-appoint-andy-dunn-to-oversee-exclusive-consumer-brands-offered-online; Daphne Howland, "Walmart Is Selling Bonobos to Express, WHP Global for $75M," Retail Dive, April 14, 2023, www.retaildive.com/news/walmart-sells-bonobos-express-seventy-five-million/647654/; Meenakshi Maidas, "Walmart Pumps $200 Million in Indian Fintech PhonePe in Ongoing Fundraise," Reuters, March 18, 2023, www.reuters.com/world/india/walmart-pumps-200-mln-indian-fintech-phonepe-ongoing-fundraise-2023-03-17/.

15. In Walmart's 2019 annual report there is a graphic on page 2 that captures their complex global "ecosystem"; see 2019 Annual Report: Defining the Future of Retail, p. 2, Walmart, https://corporate.walmart.com/media-library/document/walmart-2019-ar/_proxyDocument?id=0000016a-4b37-d6c1-ab7f-6ff7725b0000.
16. 2022 Annual Report: Building Our Flywheel, p. 8, Walmart, https://s201.q4cdn.com/262069030/files/doc_financials/2022/ar/WMT-FY2022-Annual-Report.pdf.
17. Federico Marchetti, discussion with Giuseppe Stigliano during a lecture at UCL School of Management, January 24, 2022.
18. "Open Innovation: Definition and Explanation," Oxford Review Briefings, n.d., https://oxford-review.com/oxford-review-encyclopaedia-terms/encyclopaedia-open-innovation-definition-explanation/. For more on this topic, see Henry Chesbrough's Open Innovation: The New Imperative for Creating and Profiting from Technology (Boston: Harvard Business School Press, 2006).
19. "Nike/Tiffany," Tiffany & Co., n.d., www.tiffany.co.uk/stories/tiffany-and-nike-air-force/; Samuel Hine, "Nike and Tiffany & Co. Made Sneaker Dynamite," GQ, January 31, 2023, www.gq.com/story/nike-tiffany-air-force-1.

20. "Nestlé Acquisition of L'Oréal's 50% Stake in Galderma Completed," Nestlé, July 8, 2014, www.nestle.com/media/pressreleases/allpressreleases/nestle-acquisition-loreal-galderma-complete.
21. "Apple Partners with Best Buy for Expanded Repair Service," Apple Newsroom, June 19, 2019, www.apple.com/newsroom/2019/06/apple-partners-with-best-buy-for-expanded-repair-service/.
22. "Mazda and Toyota Establish Joint-Venture Company: 'Mazda Toyota Manufacturing, U.S.A., Inc.'" Toyota, March 9, 2018, https://global.toyota/en/newsroom/corporate/21408293.html.
23. Peter Clarke, "S-LCD Joint Venture to Be Born of Samsung, Sony Display Deal," EE Times, March 8, 2004, www.eetimes.com/s-lcd-joint-venture-to-be-born-of-samsung-sony-display-deal/; "About Hulu," Hulu Press, n.d., https://press.hulu.com/corporate/.
24. Kirsten Korosec, "Mercedes Partners with Google to Bring Maps and YouTube into Its Vehicles," TechCrunch, February 22, 2023, https://techcrunch.com/2023/02/22/mercedes-google-maps-youtube/; "Meta and BMW: Taking AR and VR Experiences on the Road," Meta website, May 17, 2023, https://about.fb.com/news/2023/05/meta-bmw-ar-vr-experiences/.
25. Michael Jacobides, in-person conversation with the authors, July 2023. For a deeper analysis of the steps to follow when building an ecosystem and an accurate description of the different roles that firms can play, please see Jacobides, "How to Compete When Industries Digitize and Collide," p. 112. On this specific aspect and about ecosystems in general, see also Ulrich Pidun, Martin Reeves, and Maximilian Schüssler, "Do You Need a Business Ecosystem?," Boston Consulting Group, September 27, 2019, www.bcg.com/publications/2022/what-is-your-business-ecosystem-strategy.

Chapter 19

1. "Smartwatch Market Size & Share Analysis: Growth Trends & Forecasts (2023–2028)," *Mordor Intelligence*, n.d., www.mordorintelligence.com/industry-reports/smartwatch-market.

2. Stephen J. Andriole, "Five Myths About Digital Transformation," *MIT Sloane Management Review*, February 6, 2017, https://sloanreview.mit.edu/article/five-myths-about-digital-transformation/.
3. C. Juárez, "Hello, It's Zara: How Fashion Is Entering WhatsApp," *MDS*, May 20, 2019, www.themds.com/companies/zara-on-hows-fashion-is-entering-whatsapp.html.
4. Mark J. Greeven, Katherine Xin, and George S. Yip, "How Chinese Retailers Are Reinventing the Customer Journey," *Harvard Business Review*, September–October 2021, https://hbr.org/2021/09/how-chinese-retailers-are-reinventing-the-customer-journey. "WeChat Pay + Official Account," WeChat Pay website, n.d., https://pay.weixin.qq.com/index.php/public/wechatpay.
5. Meemi O., "Introducing Meituan," *Investor Insights Asia*, January 11, 2023, www.investorinsights.asia/post/introducing-meituan.
6. Brielle Jaekel, "Starbucks' Mobile Order & Pay Drives Sales During Peak Hours," *Retail Dive*, n.d., www.retaildive.com/ex/mobilecommercedaily/elevated-foot-traffic-means-higher-mobile-order-pay-usage-for-starbucks; "Biggest Fast Food Chain in the World," *Statistics and Data*, n.d., https://statisticsanddata.org/data/biggest-fast-food-chain-in-the-world/; "Mobile Order & Pay," McDonald's,n.d.,www.mcdonalds.com/us/en-us/mobile-order-and-pay.html.
7. "Let the Free Times Roll," Costa Coffee, n.d., www.costa.co.uk/costa-club; CMR Puntos website, www.cmrpuntos.cl/; Mercado Pago website, Mercado Libre, www.mercadopago.com.ar/; "L.pay," PaymentWall Docs, n.d., https://docs.paymentwall.com/payment-method/lpay.
8. Kellie Hwang, "Safeway Was Caught Overcharging. How to Find Out if Your Grocery Store Is Doing the Same," *San Francsico Chronicle*, August 20, 2023, www.sfchronicle.com/bayarea/article/grocery-stores-overcharging-18303789.php.
9. The smart shelves market is projected to grow at a CAGR of 27.63% to reach US$4,892.39 in APAC, and at a CAGR of 26.98% to reach US$7,432.90 in EMEA. "The Worldwide Smart Shelves Industry is Expected to Reach $19 Billion by 2027," *Business Wire*, October 19, 2022, www.businesswire.com/news/

home/20221019005813/en/The-Worldwide-Smart-Shelves-Industry-is-Expected-to-Reach-19-Billion-by-2027---ResearchAndMarkets.com; "Global Smart Shelves Market Report 2022: Increased Use of Technologies Like IoT and RFID in Retail Driving Growth," *GlobeNewswire*, September 2, 2022, www.globenewswire.com/en/news-release/2022/09/02/2509214/28124/en/Global-Smart-Shelves-Market-Report-2022-Increased-Use-of-Technologies-Like-IoT-and-RFID-in-Retail-Driving-Growth.html.

10. Nikhil Raj, Christian Fenner, Anastassia Dobrinevskaia, and Stephen Mewborn, "Are You Ready for the Retail Media Revolution?," Bain & Company, n.d., www.bain.com/how-we-help/are-you-ready-for-the-retail-media-revolution/.
11. "How Walmart Brought Unprecedented Transparency to the Food Supply Chain with Hyperledger Fabric," Hyperledger, n.d., Linux Foundation, www.hyperledger.org/learn/publications/walmart-case-study; Matt Smith, "In Wake of Romaine E. coli Scare, Walmart Deploys Blockchain to Track Leafy Greens," *Walmart Communications*, September 24, 2018, https://corporate.walmart.com/newsroom/2018/09/24/in-wake-of-romaine-e-coli-scare-walmart-deploys-blockchain-to-track-leafy-greens; Aura Blockchain Consortium website, n.d., https://auraluxuryblockchain.com/.
12. "Experience a Whole New Samsung 837," Samsung website, n.d., www.samsung.com/us/explore/837/.

Chapter 20

1. Salesforce Research, *State of the Connected Customer*, 5th edition (May 2022), p. 5, www.salesforce.com/resources/research-reports/state-of-the-connected-customer/.
2. Salesforce Research, *State of the Connected Customer*, p. 13.
3. Salesforce Research, *State of the Connected Customer*, pp. 10, 13; *Making Customer Experience the Heart of the Enterprise: How Organizations Are Uniting around the Customer in Order*

to Thrive, Harvard Business Review Analytical Services research report sponsored by Salesforce, July 2, 2021, www.salesforce .com/resources/research-reports/customer-experience-report/; https://hbr.org/sponsored/2021/07/making-customer-experience-the-heart-of-the-enterprise.

4. Salesforce Research, *State of the Connected Customer*, 4th edition (October 27, 2020), https://tlm-business-2.com/salesforce/7158/1/; Brian Solis, "Learn to Speak Your Customers' Love Language Through Digital Empathy," *Forbes*, February 13, 2023, www.forbes.com/sites/briansolis/2023/02/13/think-relationship-advice-is-only-for-your-love-life-learn-the-love-language-of-digital-empathy-to-innovate-your-customer-experience/?sh=32eb013e4760.
5. Lucia Marcuzzo, Zoom call with Giuseppe Stigliano, August 14, 2023.
6. "Amazon Prime," Amazon website, n.d., www.amazon.com/gp/help/customer/display.html?nodeId=G6LDPN7YJHYKH2J6; PZ, "Meituan-Dianping: Amazon of Services," Digital Information and Transformation, Harvard Business School Digital Initiative, March 15, 2020, https://d3.harvard.edu/platform-digit/submission/meituan-dianping-amazon-of-services/; "How the Co-op Member Reward Works," REI Co-op Membership, n.d., www.rei.com/membership/co-op-member-reward.
7. Julien Boudet, Jess Huang, and Ryter von Difloe, "Coping with the Big Switch: How Paid Loyalty Programmes Can Help Bring Consumers Back to Your Brand," McKinsey & Company, October 22, 2020, www.mckinsey.com/capabilities/growth-marketing-and-sales/our-insights/coping-with-the-big-switch-how-paid-loyalty-programs-can-help-bring-consumers-back-to-your-brand.
8. Tricia McKinnon, "Lululemon's Strategy for Success: 5 Things to Emulate," *Indigo9 Digital*, May 17, 2023, www.indigo9digital .com/blog/lululemongrowthstrategy.

Acknowledgments

First and foremost, I gratefully acknowledge my coauthor Philip Kotler for once again being such an exceptional partner in this book, marking our third collaboration since 2018.

We also want to convey our deepest appreciation to our amazing editor, Kirsten Janene-Nelson. Her hard work in editing and researching has played an indispensable role in bringing this book to your hands. We extend a special thanks to Annie Knight, Richard Narramore, and Susan Cerra from the Wiley team for their unwavering belief in this project and their flexibility throughout the process.

This book stands upon the foundation of the global success achieved by *Retail 4.0*, our previous collaborative work on this subject. Since the release of that book, we have delivered more than 300 talks and lectures on this topic, enabling us to refine the original concepts, recognize the most relevant ideas, and identify actionable guiding principles. The world has evolved significantly since then, and so the majority of what you've read here was not covered in the previous book.

The concepts that we have explored have been distilled from countless meetings, projects, and discussions with business executives worldwide. While it's not feasible to individually list each contributor here—though we do credit everyone in citations—we express our sincere appreciation to all for their significant input in shaping the content of this book and serving as inspiration for our 10 BEs of Retail 5.0 (outlined in Part II).

Numerous individuals have participated in the final review of the content, and their insights have been invaluable. Therefore, we express our sincere thanks to Daniele Cazzani for his peer review, and to Nicola Di Francesco for his inputs on brand purpose. We are grateful to Sir Rocco Forte and Aldo Melpignano for their perspectives on hospitality; Salvatore Calabrese, Agostino Perrone, and Giorgio Bargiani for their insights into the world's top bars; and Marco Marlia for his insights on the automotive sector. We also want to express our appreciation to Jacopo Sebastio and Enrico Casati for their view on the shoe business, and to Andrea Dorigo for his invaluable insights into the dynamics of integrating brick-and-mortar stores and e-commerce.

We also extend appreciation to Paolo De Cesare, Luigi Di Gregorio, Peter Falks, Lucio Lamberti, Paolo Mascio, Giuseppe Mayer, Giuliano Noci, Firdaus Nagree, Roberto Olivi, Frank Pagano, Stefano Potortì, Nick Rosa, Stefano Sala, Nicola Spagnuolo, Walter Susini, Max Volpe, and the Spring Studios team for their thought-provoking insights and for unlocking numerous opportunities.

Our gratitude goes to Luciano Floridi for inspiring the guiding principle "Be Onlife" and for the invaluable insights shared over the years. We are thankful to Sandro, Maria, Michele, and the entire Adeo family for inspiring thoughts on Optichannel and Customer Experience. To Eva, Andrea, Ilaria, and the Adobe team; Katia and the Seminarium Peru team; Valerio, Benedetta, and The European House Ambrosetti team; and to the Retail Institute team—we are grateful for the numerous opportunities to share our views on marketing innovation.

At the initial stage when the strategic framework described in this book was taking shape, we had the privilege of sharing it with the students of Professor Thomaï Serdari in the Fashion & Luxury Digital Solutions master programme at NYU Stern during fall 2022. Their feedback proved instrumental in fine-tuning some of the ideas presented in the final version. Our heartfelt thanks go out to Manuel "Manolo" Arroyo, Andrea Baldo, Holger Blecker, Francesca Bellettini, Penny Brook, Alejandro Camino, Hans Carpels, Carlo Colpo, Cristiano Fagnani, Stéphane de La Faverie, Simon Fox, Paolo Gallo, Greg Hoffman, Michael G. Jacobides, Nikos Koumettis, Martin Lindsdrom, Federico Marchetti, Lucia Marcuzzo, Selvane Mohandas du Ménil, Vasiliki Petrou, Mauro Porcini, Stefano Portu, Riccardo Stefanelli, Federico Turconi, Giovanni Valentini, Sandro Veronesi, Michael Ward, and Nicola Zotta.

Finally, our profound appreciation goes to our families, whose patience, understanding, and support have been crucial to realizing such an ambitious project. Nancy and Gaia—your support has fueled the creation of this book. Ginevra and Carlo, may you one day come across this manuscript and generously forgive your dad for borrowing precious hours from our weekends together. . .

Index